PENGUIN BOOKS
The Species that Changed Itself

Edwin Gale studied English Literature at Cambridge before switching to a career in medicine. He worked in Cambridge, Nottingham, Copenhagen, and as a professor at St Bartholomew's Hospital, London. Research into the rise of diabetes stimulated his interest in our changing phenotype. He moved with his team to the University of Bristol in 1997, and retired in 2011.

EDWIN GALE

The Species that Changed Itself

How Prosperity Reshaped Humanity

PENGUIN BOOKS

PENGUIN BOOKS

UK | USA | Canada | Ireland | Australia
India | New Zealand | South Africa

Penguin Books is part of the Penguin Random House group of companies
whose addresses can be found at global.penguinrandomhouse.com.

First published in the United States of America by Allen Lane 2020
Published in Penguin Books 2021
001

Typeset by Jouve (UK), Milton Keynes.
Printed and bound in Great Britain by Clays Ltd, Elcograf S.p.A.

The authorized representative in the EEA is Penguin Random House Ireland,
Morrison Chambers, 32 Nassau Street, Dublin D02 YH68

A CIP catalogue record for this book is available from the British Library

ISBN: 978-0-141-98498-8

www.greenpenguin.co.uk

Contents

PART 1
The Great Escape

PART 2
Plasticity

CONTENTS

PART 3
Life's Journey

PART 4
Changing Our Minds

PART 5
Living Together

List of Illustrations

Every effort has been made to contact all copyright holders. The publishers will be pleased to amend in future editions any errors or omissions brought to their attention.

Acknowledgements

It started with a chance meeting with Frances Ashcroft over a hotel breakfast four years ago. I asked how her writing was going and mentioned that I was working on an idea for a book. She asked me to write it down, forwarded it to her agent Felicity Bryan, and I had a publisher four weeks later. It's not always that easy, as I have since discovered. Felicity, a legend in her own lifetime, died during preparation of this book, but I will always be grateful for the help that she and Frances gave me.

Like most people, I thought I knew how to write a book and – like most people – I was wrong. Unstinted thanks therefore to Laura Stickney, Holly Hunter and Rowan Cope for their coaching, to Cecilia Mackay for the pictures and to David Watson and the production team for showing me what professionalism is.

The central theme of this book has been revolving in my head for many years, and it would be impossible to thank everyone who helped me along the way. Warm thanks to Bernard Keegan-Fischer and Peter and Vicky Balabanski for being honest. Peter Dunn, Mike Lean, Ashley Moffett and Gordon Wilcock read selected chapters. Lukas Stalpers, known only by email, has been a loyal reader, supporter and critic; and so too has John Kershaw.

At a more personal level, this has been a two-cat book, and Tom Socks and Sophie have slumbered peacefully in a desk drawer throughout its gestation. Emily, Rebecca and John viewed the whole enterprise with healthy scepticism and useful insights and have made it all feel worthwhile. It has been said 'show me a man with an obsession, and I will show you a happy man'. When I mentioned this to my wife, she responded with 'and I'll show you an unhappy woman!' Thank you for reassuring me that this has not been your experience, Judith, and this book is yours.

Author's Note

The coronavirus epidemic struck while this book was in proof, and it changed the ground rules of life in the twenty-first century. My book describes (among other things) the way in which we have distanced ourselves from traditional causes of infectious disease, but I did not foresee the extent to which this might also increase our vulnerability to a shape-shifting virus. Our attempts to contain this have – to date – managed to limit its spread, but they threaten to precipitate an economic recession that could cost more lives than the virus itself.

Enforced isolation has caused untold misery to many, but I was fortunate enough to be stranded by a river in one of the most beautiful parts of Wales. Contrails and pollution vanished from the sky, and an uncanny silence filled with birdsong settled upon us. Life shifted down a gear, and it was an unimagined opportunity to revisit the world we have lost.

The enforced global shutdown was a once-in-a-lifetime opportunity for reflection. To borrow John Cage's phrase, it gave us all an interval of time that was free from intention. More important, it finally shattered our collective illusion of control. It was a reminder that our lives are shaped by the world we made, and that this will be our legacy – poisoned or otherwise – to the next edition of humanity.

Prologue

The prophet Isaiah saw the New Jerusalem in a vision. 'Never again', he said, 'will there be in it an infant who lives but a few days, or an old man who does not live out his years: he who dies at a hundred will be thought a mere youth: he who fails to reach a hundred will be accursed.'[1] Isaiah could not have imagined that we might reach this happy state by our own unaided efforts, yet we are getting close. Death has for the most part been banished into old age and we are, in material terms, the most fortunate generation ever to have lived.

If you release rabbits on an island without predators, feed them well and free them from major infections, their numbers will increase exponentially. They will have escaped the constraints of natural selection, just as we have done. Our own escape began some 200 years ago, when people from Western Europe tapped into fossil energy and hit upon a recipe for generating wealth and knowledge in ever-increasing amounts. Earth scientists refer to this as the Anthropocene – the man-made era.

In theory, Rabbit Island should result in population overgrowth followed by population collapse. This has not happened to us – as yet – because we have been able to limit population growth and to expand our food supply. In doing so, we changed the world – but we also changed ourselves. A typical European is nearly 20 cm taller than two centuries ago, and young adult Americans have gained 12 kg over the past 100 years. Our skeletal proportions have altered, as have our skulls and faces. We reach sexual maturity three to four years earlier, live forty years longer and die of once-rare diseases. Our experience of life has altered, and we think differently. All this took place within a few generations. I call it the phenotypic transition, and this book is about what happened and why.

THE KINGDOM OF COCKAIGNE

A medieval legend tells of an imaginary land in which food is present in inexhaustible quantities. Italians knew it as the *Paese di Chucagna* – the land of cake – and the French celebrated it in a thirteenth-century ballad called the *Recueil des Fabliaux et Contes de Cocaigne*. In Cocaigne (known to the English as the Kingdom of Cockaigne) there are six Sundays to every month and four Easters each year. Lent comes round every twenty years, and fasting is optional. Germans knew it as *Schlaraffenland*, the Glutton's Paradise,[2] and the Dutch as *Luilekkerland*, roughly translated as 'sweet and happy land'. Pieter Breughel the Elder's depiction shows a soldier, a clerk and a peasant – representatives of the three orders of society – sleeping with distended bellies in a world where 'roasted pigs wander about with knives in

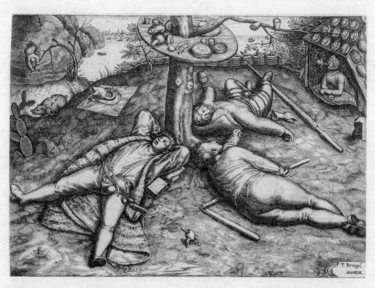

Figure 1: *Luilekkerland*. Engraving after Pieter Breughel the Elder (1567).

their backs to make carving easy, where grilled geese fly directly into one's mouth, where cooked fish jump out of the water and land at one's feet. The weather is always mild, the wine flows freely, sex is readily available, and all people enjoy eternal youth.'[3]

We live in a world that our ancestors could only dream about, and we reached it in three stages. The first was largely complete when people with genes like ours left Africa. The second stage, driven by our own activities, committed us to ever-accelerating technical development. The third came when we reached escape velocity from the tug of natural selection and began to hurtle towards an unknown future, self-domesticated animals in a world tailored to our convenience.

Our genes express themselves differently in different environments. Each form of gene expression is known as the *phenotype*, a term proposed by the Danish botanist Wilhelm Johannsen in 1911. He showed that genetically identical beans grow differently in varied conditions of soil and light – no surprise there – but that their descendants revert to the same size and shape when planted side by side. Geneticists of the time believed that characteristics acquired by parents would be inherited by their children, but Johannsen had confirmed Mendel's belief that the units of inheritance travel in sealed packages, unaffected by the parental environment. These mysterious units still lacked a name, and Johannsen opted to call them *genes*. Collectively they formed the 'gene type' or *genotype*, and he called the expression of that genotype in a given environment the 'phenomenon type' or *phenotype*.[4]

Like beans, like people. Koreans were traditionally short; in the nineteenth century men averaged 161 cm and women 149 cm. The war of 1950–53 had the effect of dividing them between a free enterprise economy and a repressive totalitarian regime. Those born before 1950 grew to much the same size on either side of the 38th Parallel, but a United Nations survey in 2002 showed that pre-school children in North Korea were 13 cm shorter and 7 kg lighter than in the South. The height of adult North Koreans was unchanged, whereas South Korean women had set an international growth record of 20.2 cm and enjoyed the fourth-longest life expectancy in the world.[5] A line on the map had translated into a difference in biology.

People talk about genes with remarkable confidence, given that the experts still argue about what exactly a gene is or how many we have. The concept that your environment is reflected in your phenotype is less familiar, which might explain why we have been slow to appreciate that our phenotype is changing. So, what exactly is a phenotype? Johannsen said it was anything about an organism that you can see or measure. There is not much to see or measure in a bean, but people are endlessly variable.

A dating site is a good place to begin. You will be looking for someone of a certain age and have certain preferences as to background and appearance. You will probably want to know if they smoke and consider themselves to have a sense of humour. Weeks later, you meet up with the phenotype of interest in a restaurant. Your first glance takes in outward appearance – middle height, reddish hair, trim shape, a pleasant face, a hint of laughter lines around the eyes. Before long, you are deep in conversation, for you grew up in similar circumstances, you laugh at the same things, your temperaments match, and so too do your interests. Above all, your date seems kind, considerate, a possible future friend and companion.

What then is a phenotype? The short answer is that it represents everything about the person you just met. It is the expression of their genes, filtered through their environment and moulded by their journey through life. Some aspects of a phenotype – eye colour for example – are wired into you. These are *simple traits*, and you can't change them. You will not dwell on the colour of your date's eyes, however, unless you happen to be falling in love. You will be more interested in such things as charm, personality and intelligence. These are *complex traits* – complex because they arise from the interaction of many genes, and because the outcome of that interaction will vary from one person to the next. Simple traits are *categorical*; you either have blue eyes or you do not. Complex traits are of the 'more-or-less' variety and imply a comparison between people: they are *dimensional*.

The dialogue between genes and environment begins when a fertilized egg – a zygote – implants in the lining of a mother's womb, and it ends with our final breath. The journey in between has its own unique history. Things happened in one way and not in another; some paths were taken, others were not, and the combination of genes and happenstance finally converged upon the person holding this book. Time is the true medium of our existence, and a phenotype is the narrative of a journey through time.

THE WAR OF THE EGG

When Lemuel Gulliver visited the world of Lilliput, he found its tiny inhabitants at war with their neighbours concerning an important point of doctrine. The Lilliputians insisted that an egg should be eaten from the small end, and their enemies claimed that you should eat it from the big end. The debate as to whether nature or nurture, genes or environment, are 'more important' is of comparable significance.

The answer, as so often happens, will depend upon the way you ask the question. If you raise laboratory rats in the same cage, for example, any difference between them will largely be due to their genes. The same will apply to people who share the same environment. But what happens when people with the same genes inhabit different environments? Korea is a striking example, another being a classic study from the 1930s which showed that second- and third-generation Japanese immigrants to Hawaii were physically very different from people in the villages they left behind.[6]

Genes largely determine differences *within* a population, whereas the environment determines differences *between* populations. You might picture this in terms of boats at anchor in a tidal basin. The relative height of their masts will vary according to design ('genes'), but all boats will rise together when the tide comes in. Those who argue for the importance of genes are comparing boats, and those who argue for the environment are comparing tides.

Reports of identical twins separated at birth are routinely quoted to emphasize the paramount importance of genes, and remarkable coincidences have been reported. Confirmation bias apart, we should remember that these twins shared the same uterus and grew up in the same society. But suppose that they had been separated following conception and implanted in different surrogate mothers? One twin might grow up in North Korea, for example, and the other in the South. Or – since the imagination knows no limits – one might develop in Cro-Magnon times and the other in modern New York.

What then? Our twins will have the same face, but they will differ in other important respects, and this difference is what we will be interested in. Charles Darwin said that 'it is not the strongest of the species that survive, nor the most intelligent, but the one most responsive to change'. Our genes can be the agents of change. The flexibility this confers is known as *phenotypic plasticity*, and natural selection operates on the phenotype rather than the gene.

A SHORT HISTORY OF
THE PHENOTYPE

Our journey through time has been driven by the quest for food: a quest that took us all the way from vegetarian primates to the adult baby food that lines the shelves of our supermarkets. Food is reflected in our growth and development, and each major transition in food production has generated its own characteristic phenotype.

Homo sapiens lived in small mobile groups for 95 per cent of its existence as a species, and twentieth-century hunter-gatherers who followed the same way of life were often as lean and fit as marathon runners. I call this archetypal pattern the *Palaeolithic* phenotype. Things changed 10,000 or so years ago – a blink of an eye in evolutionary terms – as the cultivation and consumption of grain came to shape our bodies and our societies. The bony remains of people who lived by subsistence agriculture testify to lives of toil, disease and recurrent famine, and they varied remarkably little between the foundation of Jericho and modern times. I call this the *agrarian* phenotype. Subsistence farmers left us no record, for history was made and written by those who lived on their labour. These, the elite members of past societies, were better housed, better fed and taller – people looked up to them. Theirs was the *privileged* phenotype and, to some extent, it anticipated our own.

Plagues and famines swept through agrarian populations, generating a fluctuating equilibrium between birth and death which economists refer to as the 'Malthusian trap'.[7] The escape from this trap began in Europe. In England, for example, the years leading up to AD 1300 were years of prosperity, and its population increased rapidly, only to be halved by plague and famine in the disastrous fourteenth century. The respite from population pressure created space for innovations in food production, thus creating a 'Malthusian holiday'. England's population took four centuries to recover to the level of AD 1300, but the country produced 50 per cent more milk and wheat and twice as much beef in 1700 – and with fewer acres under cultivation.[8]

Increasing prosperity brought more food, better living conditions and better health to nineteenth-century Europe. Its population rocketed, but it avoided a Rabbit Island scenario by importing food and exporting its surplus population. Even so, famine threatened when the frontiers of global cultivation were reached towards the end of the century, and was only averted by the subsequent revolution in agriculture. The whole world could now enjoy a Malthusian holiday.

All this lay in the future at the start of the twentieth century. Prosperity was largely restricted to the western nations, and numbers had expanded so rapidly that one in three of the global population could claim European ancestry by 1930. This was set to change, however, for the European birth rate had gone into sharp decline, and contemporary demographers saw the 'population problem' as one of falling numbers. A declining birth rate heralded what became known as the demographic transition.

The global economy entered a new phase after 1950. Europe and Asia had been devastated by war, but the demands of wartime production had generated massive investment, a central command economy and mobilization of scientific and technical know-how in the United States, thus jerking it out of stagnation. Food was cheap, energy was cheap, and automation brought a new dimension to productivity, increasingly tailored to desire rather than to need. The new model spread rapidly, and the triumph of capitalism marked the emergence of the *consumer* phenotype. A worldwide population boom followed in the second half of the twentieth century, but food production kept pace. Famines still occurred, but for preventable reasons such as political breakdown. Food abundance, freedom from infectious disease and a sedentary lifestyle spread around the world, and the consumer phenotype went global.

THE PHENOTYPIC TRANSITION

People of European descent towered over most other populations at the start of the twentieth century, for the combination of rising affluence and a declining birth rate was reflected in the accelerated growth of their children. Increasing height and longevity became a feature of many western populations from around 1870, as did many other changes in our phenotype.

Life begins with a mother, and the interaction of genes with environment begins with conception. High fecundity was an essential feature of our species when only one child in two or three survived to reproduce, but became a handicap when survival into adult life was the norm. Management of reproductive life was a precondition of the phenotypic transition, and the possibilities of womanhood were transformed in the process.

A mother's quality of life is reflected in her child, and birth weight has risen progressively over several generations. This is partly because mothers are healthier and better fed, partly because taller women have bigger babies, and partly because bigger babies turn into taller adults. The long bones of our arms and legs have increased in length, changing our physical proportions. Our skulls are taller and narrower and our jaws are lighter, crowding teeth together and making more work for dentists. Bigger bodies combined with an increased capacity to pile on muscle changed the face of power-to-weight sports. Athletic records have tumbled even as those who prefer a sedentary lifestyle have acquired smaller muscles and more fat.

We are not alone in our journey through life, and multitudinous unseen life-forms live in and on our bodies. The Palaeolithic phenotype favoured long-lived parasites and infections that were transmitted vertically from one generation to the next. The transition to agrarian life crowded people into permanent communities, thus allowing a range of new infections to take root in the human population. Some gave rise to the epidemic diseases that feature in our history books. Our co-existence with invisible life-forms changed once again in recent times. Age-old partners have been lost, the terms of engagement are different, and there have been far-reaching consequences for our health and well-being. All this is reflected in the development of our immune phenotype.

A phenotype is a journey through time, and the average lifespan has virtually doubled in the course of a century, not just because of better living conditions and medical care – although these are important – but also because we are ageing more slowly. The combination of increasing longevity and overconsumption has placed increasing stress upon the internal economy of our bodies, as shown for example in the 'metabolic syndrome', a characteristic phenotype in which accumulating obesity predisposes to progressive failure of regulatory systems controlling blood pressure, sugars and fat. We view the so-called 'degenerative' disorders of later life as diseases, but they might equally be seen as natural responses of an ageing phenotype.

The phenotypic transition has produced many detectable changes in our physical lives, but what about the changes we cannot see? Are we the same, or are we different? Some passages from Homer speak to our understanding in a way that makes time stand still, but the past really was another country. Premature death and bereavement have become rare events, and the death of a child is experienced as a dreadful tragedy rather than as a routine occurrence. 'Had five, buried two' was a standard response to the usual medical question in the first half of the last century. Parents grieved for their children then as now, but recurrent bereavement might explain the curiously flat emotional affect of parents in the early modern period.[9] Their ability to shrug off the death of a child – or to inflict violence upon the living – appears at times to border on the pathological. In *Pilgrim's Progress*, an allegory of the Christian journey through life, John Bunyan's protagonist abandons his wife and children to their fate in order to seek his own salvation, a decision that we would scarcely consider praiseworthy.

How can we be so different, and yet the same? Our phenotype, broadly defined, encompasses the way our brains and bodies work, our emotional repertoire, the way we interact and our social identity. If these things change, so too must we. I was born into a world of landline telephones with operators, wireless sets with valves and typewriters with ribbons, yet I walk around with a hand-held device that allows me to talk to people anywhere on the planet and to access almost any piece of information. And yet – it is an age-old paradox – my younger self is somehow embedded within an older man with different physical capabilities, desires, expectations, knowledge and experience. He is contained in me, but I am not contained in him. As with the individual, so it is with the collective. Our predecessors are embedded in our experience. We have some insight into their lives, but what would they make of us?

Literary critics write of something called sensibility, an elusive concept that describes the way in which novelists or writers of diaries experience the world around them. The way in which this is expressed, and therefore presumably felt, has changed over the past three centuries. The psychologist Steven Pinker argues in *The Better Angels of Our Nature* that (despite many horrific instances to the contrary) people have developed a much greater capacity for empathy. One simple fact stands out: we are far more literate. UNESCO estimated that around 10 per cent of the world's population could read 200 years ago, as against 90 per cent in 2017.[10] This probably had greater impact upon the way in which people think and feel about themselves than any other feature of the phenotypic transition.

It is challenging enough to understand our own thought processes, let alone those of others, especially people who come from a radically different culture. How, then, is it possible to measure our minds against those of previous generations? Intelligence tests offer one objective measure, since they purport to measure raw intellectual ability, unaffected by training effects or cultural background, and independent of time, place or circumstance. The IQ test is adjusted to the mean of the population tested, which is arbitrarily set at 100. The psychologist James Flynn noticed in 1984 that IQ testing centres were obliged to adjust the mean upwards on a regular basis.[11] His analysis suggested that test scores were increasing at a rate of three to five points per decade. Are we becoming more intelligent – unlikely – or do we just use our minds differently?

PHENOTYPES AND SOCIETY

We created Rabbit Island, but other creatures share it with us. No wild species has ever changed as we have done, but our domestic animals have changed even faster. They too grow bigger and mature earlier; they too breed in and out of season; and they too live longer and get fat. Like us, they have lighter bones and skulls with more crowded teeth. They too accept hierarchy and live in crowded conditions without undue resort to violence. The parallels are obvious. Are we a self-domesticated species? The answers, as Tom Sawyer might have said, are 'tough but interesting'.

Domesticated or not, we are social animals. In pre-industrial times the age structure of the population was pyramid-shaped, and children greatly outnumbered old people. Rapid growth, earlier sexual maturity, compulsory education and a minimum age limit for employment created the phenomenon of adolescence, and a distinctive youth culture emerged when young people entered the workforce with increased spending power and fewer responsibilities. More recently, a declining industrial base has produced a free-floating population of underemployed young people in western countries, and an explosive surplus elsewhere in the world. Meanwhile, older people accumulate at the other end of the age spectrum. Their prolonged survival hinders the transfer of wealth, property and responsibility from one generation to the next, high-tech medical interventions have made the business of dying more expensive, and wealth is siphoned off by care for the elderly instead of moving between generations. Even the most prosperous nations are beginning to stagger under this burden.

Other consequences of a longer lifespan are less obvious. Marriages last as long today as they did 200 years ago, but terminate in divorce rather than death. Kurt Vonnegut describes the union of two perfectly matched but immortal humans in one of his novels and concludes that no marriage could survive eternity. Another consequence of increased security is the pursuit of safety, now an obsession among the safest people who ever lived. No surprise in this, for people with a lifespan of 200 years might well take extra care when crossing the road.

A changing phenotype has altered the face of society, and a changing society has taken on much greater responsibility for the phenotype of its citizens. My ancestor John Gale featured in the census of 1801, only six generations ago, but he knew nothing of central government, and government knew only his name. States became more organized as the century went on and made increasing use of information (appropriately known as 'statistics') concerning their citizens. Intrepid Victorians discovered a heart of darkness in the slums of their cities, hard-headed employers sought workers with educational skills, generals needed healthy soldiers, and the British dreamed of a new imperial race. Nation-states took more interest in the lives of those they governed, even as the economic clout of the industrial masses resulted in political trade-offs which acknowledged their importance. National insurance schemes came into being, states assumed greater responsibility for the lives of those insured, and political parties quarrelled about the extent of that responsibility.

APOLOGIA

I reached this book by a roundabout route. As a research physician, I was puzzled by the fact that both major varieties of diabetes were increasing so rapidly. Why should a disease change? The answer, when it came, seemed obvious enough: *diabetes isn't changing, we are.* The more I looked, the more obvious it became that we are a species in transition, yet this rather obvious fact scarcely rates a mention in many accounts of human biology. Since genes don't change within a generation or two, it seemed equally obvious that this transformation must have something to do with the way genes function. Genes make us what we are, but they do not execute an unchanging blueprint. Instead, they operate a growth programme which is responsive to cues from the environment. Flexibility is built into our genome.

The history of biology tells us that each generation underestimates its ignorance. We are no different. An understanding of our plasticity is beginning to emerge, notably from the study of epigenetics, but there is still a long way to go. My task, therefore, is merely to offer a brief history of the phenotype, and to describe what others will need to explain.

I begin by showing how the pursuit of food has shaped both our long-term evolution and our changing phenotype. In time, we managed to free ourselves, if only in part, from the major agents of natural selection. Overpopulation and famine should have followed, as in the fable of Rabbit Island, but food production increased faster than population in more fortunate parts of the world and promoted the emergence of the consumer phenotype. I then go on to describe the phenotypic transition in more detail, starting with our bodies and our experience of old age and disease, and moving on to our changing minds. We will then look at the way in which our changing phenotype has affected society, and at how society shapes our phenotype. I conclude with the inevitable question: is it possible to change so much – and yet remain the same?

PART I

The Great Escape

I

The Promethean Moment

Imagine yourself on the African veldt, watching the rise of a huge red sun. It is 100,000 years ago, and vast herds are roaming in the distance. You are naked: no clothes, no tools, no power objects. Your skin is defenceless against biting insects, and your hands and feet are too soft to be useful. If you could find something to eat – a tuber, perhaps – you would be unable to chew or digest it. That noble organ, your brain, is not much help. Who might imagine that people like you would inherit the earth?

We are, to all appearances, the most helpless of species. Plato's version of the Prometheus legend relates that the gods set out to create mortal creatures, got bored and left the job unfinished. Roughly shaped figures lay inert in the clay, awaiting the summons to life. Prometheus and his brother Epimetheus (two titans whose names mean forethought and afterthought) were asked to finish the job, and Epimetheus volunteered for the task. Conscious that creatures need to survive in the wild, he equipped them with an eye to the balance of nature. A hunting animal should not starve, for instance, but neither should it exterminate its prey. Predators should be rare, and the hunted should be fertile. He allocated coverings of fur, hide or feather, and handed out hooves and claws. So absorbed in this task was he that every single gift and attribute had been handed out by the time he reached the human race. Prometheus returned to find that that other animals were 'well off for everything, but man [was] naked, unshod, unbedded, and unarmed: and already the appointed day had come, when man too was to emerge from within the earth into the daylight'.[1] Naked and helpless, we were about to be massacred. Prometheus felt such pity for us that he stole fire from heaven, concealed within a giant stalk of fennel, and taught people the arts of civilization. His one omission was the art of politics, which gave Plato the starting point for his dialogue between Socrates and Protagoras. The punishment for his transgression was to be chained to a mountain in the Caucasus while an eagle tore endlessly at his liver.

It is easy enough to see that Plato got the story back to front. We are helpless without fire precisely because we evolved to depend upon it. The German-American anthropologist Franz Boas pointed out in 1911 that we are a cooking species. 'The art of cookery', he said, 'is universal. By its means the character of the food and with it the demands made upon the digestive organs are materially changed.'[2] Cooking means fire, and *Homo erectus* may have made use of fire 1.8 million years ago,[3] quite enough time for evolution to reorganize our digestive apparatus and other features of our anatomy. Let us see what happened.

THE FOOD LADDER

The pursuit of food shaped our evolution and continues to shape our phenotype. On 1 January 1700, the Royal Society of London published an exchange of letters between an elderly physician called John Wallis and the anatomist Edward Tyson, famous for dissecting *Homo sylvestris*, better known to us as the chimpanzee.[4] Wallis's question was this: were we intended to eat meat? He began in theological mode by pointing out that Adam and Eve must have been vegetarian, for God told Adam 'I have given you every herb bearing seed, and every ... fruit of a tree-yielding seed, to you it shall be for meat [i.e. food].' This remit was extended when Noah was told (presumably after the animals had quit the Ark) that 'every moving thing that liveth, shall be meat for you'. Consumption of meat, said Wallis, is a degenerate characteristic which post-dates the Fall of Man. We are lapsed vegetarians. He admits one difficulty with this argument, which is that plant-eating animals have a very big large intestine, whereas humans resemble carnivores in having a small one. The difference between our primate relatives and us is striking in this respect (see figure 2).

Plants invest the energy from sunlight in fruit, fuel and structural

Relative Gut Volume (%)

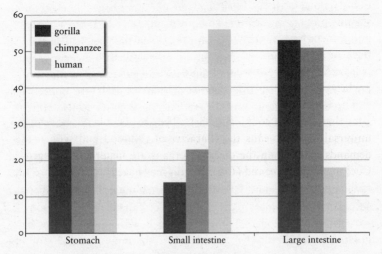

Figure 2: The proportions of the large and small intestines are reversed in humans and our closest primate relatives.[5]

material. Fruit is energy-dense and designed to be eaten: so much so that people with a plentiful supply – from the lotus-eaters encountered by Odysseus to the Kalahari Bushman who could see no point in cultivation when mongongo nuts were so plentiful[6] – are not motivated to change their ways. Energy is stored as starch and oils, and we cultivate plants that produce them in abundant quantities. Plants invest the rest of their energy in structural carbohydrates such as cellulose, a dense polymer woven from glucose molecules held together by chemical bonds that we and other animals are unable to digest because we don't have the necessary enzymes. We are locked out of the most abundant source of food energy on the planet, and plant-eaters must therefore team up with symbiotic bacteria (which do have the enzymes) in order to access it. Animals that chew the cud keep these bacteria in a special accessory stomach, and other herbivores house them in a capacious large intestine. Since this arrangement is highly inefficient, vegetarian primates spend an estimated 48 per cent of their waking lives eating, as against 4.7 per cent of ours.[7]

Carnivores are much less reliant on intestinal bacteria than herbivores and, as Wallis pointed out, our intestines resemble those of a carnivore. Why are we then able to digest large quantities of vegetable matter? Because cooking breaks down the chemical bonds in food, reducing our reliance on bacteria. We still need our gut bacteria – about 10 per cent of our food energy reaches us this way – but a raw food diet is so inefficient that its users are obliged to consume large amounts of vegetation. Since cooking also softens what we eat, previous anatomical arrangements for crushing plant food became redundant; our upper jaws receded and our lower jaws became smaller but more prominent. Flatter faces allowed our facial muscles to convey a complex emotional repertoire, and speech and song entered the world. Social skills became the key to reproductive success, driving evolution of what has been called the social brain.

Anatomically modern humans equipped with these features originated in northern Africa, with a last common ancestor around 200,000 years ago. From the neck down there is little to distinguish us from *Homo erectus*, although modern humans are taller and lighter, and the two sexes are closer in size. The difference is above the neck, for we have bigger brains (1,350 vs 700–900 ml), and our cerebral cortex has mushroomed upwards to give our skulls their characteristic rounded appearance. The brain is our most highly evolved organ, but the energy cost of maintaining an electrical charge across nerve membranes is high – some 20–25 per cent of all the energy required by a resting body. Cooking made supersized brains possible.[8]

THE PALAEOLITHIC PHENOTYPE

Homo sapiens left Africa some 80,000 years ago, possibly earlier. We may visit the unspoilt world our ancestors encountered in our dreams, but we should not forget to wrap up warmly, for global temperatures were 6–8°C below present levels. Mountains of ice covered the Northern Hemisphere, blocking access to North America and opening the sea route to Australia. *Homo erectus* and *Homo neanderthalis* were already widely dispersed in Asia and Europe and co-existed with us for a long time before vanishing from the face of the earth. Why did we prevail? It would be nice to imagine that our ancestors showed early signs of superior ability, but these are lacking in the archaeological record. Evidence of so-called behavioural modernity – technical innovation, artistic expression, care for the infirm and respect for the dead – first appeared some 40–50,000 years ago. This was when our ancestors invented bows and arrows, learned how to fish, carved bone and stone, clothed and adorned themselves and left glorious cave paintings. In the words of the anthropologist Richard Klein, 'the behavioral transformation that occurred 50 thousand years ago represents the most dramatic behavioral shift that archeologists will ever detect, and it demands explanation'.[9]

The Brain Change has puzzled evolutionary thinkers. Darwin's rival Alfred Russel Wallace argued that evolution should have stopped when it had crafted a brain that was smart enough to outperform other animals. 'Natural selection', he said, 'could only have endowed savage man with a brain a few degrees superior to that of an ape, whereas he actually possesses one very little inferior to that of a philosopher.' He concluded from this that the ability to compose music and build cathedrals must have arisen by some sort of spiritual infusion.[10] Arthur C. Clarke's novel *2001*, in which extra-terrestrial beings provide the necessary stimulus to an ape's brain, was a secular version of the same idea.

How did we come into possession of a brain so far in excess of our immediate requirements? One explanation is *exaptation*, a term used by evolutionary thinkers for a trait which evolved for one purpose and proved useful for another. Feathers evolved for warmth but made flight possible. Our tongues discovered a new function when we learned to speak. The exaptation hypothesis suggests that the quantum leap associated with the Brain Change came about because we had already acquired sufficient computing power to make it possible. The likely explanation for this was social interaction and competition within our own species. But there is general agreement that, for whatever reason, a radical change in our behaviour made itself apparent some 50,000 years ago and set us on the road to the present.

The Palaeolithic or 'Old Stone' Age is conventionally divided into an early phase, which runs from 50,000 to 20,000 years ago, and a later phase, from 20,000 to 10,000 years ago. These were separated by the end of the last ice age, otherwise known as the last glacial maximum. The world warmed slowly from around 20,000 years ago, and pollen traces show that dense forests followed the retreating ice. Life moved northwards, and *Homo sapiens*, the last remaining human, moved with it. Hunting requires a high level of physical fitness, but the work of a forager is more sustained than that of a hunter and just as exhausting. Observation of the !Kung San of the Kalahari showed that a mother carried each child for something like 7,800 km during the first four years of its life, and gathered 7–10 kg of plant food in the course of a typical day. Hunter-gatherers ate less fat and more protein than we do, and consumed more vegetable fibre but a lot less salt. People raised in this way are lithe and physically fit; their bodies contain as little fat as modern marathon runners, averaging around 15–20 per cent in men and 20–25 per cent in women. Their exercise capacity (estimated by oxygen consumption) was typically 30 per cent greater than that of age-matched westerners. Some were capable of running an antelope to exhaustion. Unlike us, they did not gain weight as they aged, their blood pressure did not rise, and diabetes and vascular disease were almost unknown.[11]

Reconstructing people from a few fragments of bone is tricky, and early archaeologists conjured up early ancestors 2 metres in height. More sober estimates followed, but some of our predecessors were relatively tall: In Europe, men averaged 174 cm 20,000 years ago, as against 162 cm for women.

Another 'modern' feature was the length of their legs relative to their overall height (figure 3). This was particularly marked in skeletal remains found in Italy and former Yugoslavia amid bones of mammoth, rhinoceros and reindeer. The Gravettians lived 20–30,000 years ago, and many were more than 183 cm tall. Studies of the Y haplotype (which marks male descent) show that many modern Europeans are descended from them.

Figure 3: Gravettian skeleton from Grottes des Enfants 4, Grimaldi, Italy.

Genes determine relative height, as we saw earlier, but the absolute height of a population depends upon its environment. This being the case, the interest lies in the fact that Europeans were taller in the Ice Age and did not regain their former height until modern times. The reason was almost certainly nutritional, for the Gravettians lived in the golden age of hunting.[12]

Life was less easy for their successors, broad-spectrum foragers who were obliged to supplement their diet with fish and small game. Dental caries testify to their increasing reliance upon a plant-based carbohydrate diet, and they were considerably shorter. Men averaged 165.3 cm as against 154.5 cm for women, a decrease of 8.8 and 7.3 cm respectively.[13] This was the prelude to what was once seen as the Neolithic revolution.

THE REVOLUTION THAT WASN'T

Prehistory began as a happy hunting ground for half-baked ideas. Amateurs and crackpots with preconceived notions ranged freely over territory later to be claimed by specialists in archaeology, anthropology, ethnology and linguistics. Distinguished gentlemen, ignorant of the local language, converted brief visits to some foreign shore into authoritative two-volume publications. The beliefs and customs of the local inhabitants were confidently extrapolated, and snippets garnered in leather armchairs were patched into learned fantasies such as the sacrificial priest-kings of James Frazer. Prehistoric folk wanderings were the order of the day, biological inequality was widely assumed, and long-headed Aryans roamed the prehistoric world, raising the tone wherever they went. The twentieth century saw the emergence of professional archaeologists who, slow as they were to shrug off the legacy of previous thinkers, nonetheless introduced the principle of meticulous scientific excavation coupled with cautious extrapolation from the facts.

Gordon Childe (1892–1957) was the sort of socialist who would be lined up against a wall in the aftermath of any revolution. Small, wiry, carrot-haired, odd-looking, awkward and intellectual, he stood out against any background. At the peak of his fame he would go about in heavy boots and an abbreviated pair of shorts while sporting a red tie and a wide-brimmed hat (he wore the same one for twenty years), with a black oilskin raincoat slung over one shoulder. He knew an astonishing number of European languages, but his disregard for pronunciation was such that he managed to be incomprehensible in most of them. Listeners who struggled to understand what he was saying must first decide what language he was saying it in. Childe wrote the almost obligatory book about the Aryans in 1927 but shied away from the topic when he saw where the Nazis were heading. Too impatient to achieve excellence as a field archaeologist, his achievement was to weave a staggering amount of archaeological data into a dynamic narrative which linked prehistory to the written record and filled the silent avenues of history with living people.

Childe noted that the beginnings of agriculture coincided with the appearance of polished stone tools, pottery and permanent villages of mud-brick houses. This happened about 10,000 years ago, and he coined the term 'Neolithic revolution' to describe it. The archaeologist who hit subsoil under layer after layer of pottery and sophisticated artefacts might well see this as a revolution, but the impression of sudden change was misleading: the interval between the first clear evidence of cultivation and the foundation of Jericho is estimated at around 1,700 years. These developments took place within the Fertile Crescent, a boomerang-shaped strip of land stretching from Palestine in the west to the estuary of the Tigris and Euphrates in the east. Gordon Childe proposed that climate change forced Neolithic peoples into a narrow strip of fertile land, hemmed in by mountains and desert, which just happened to contain the predecessors of our major cereal crops and farm animals. Later research suggests that cultivation developed independently in several parts of the world, but Childe's suggestion captures the three main explanations for the origins of agriculture: climate change, population pressure and serendipity. As we can now see, however, this was no revolution but a long, slow process of change.

The escape from what Childe termed 'the impasse of savagery' came from 'an economic and scientific revolution that made the participants active partners with nature instead of parasites on nature'.[14] Like many of his generation, he saw pain and suffering as the necessary prelude to a future in which pain and suffering would no longer exist. Gordon Childe retired to Australia, which he reached on his sixty-fifth birthday, and spent six months travelling around the continent, where he was greatly honoured. He wrote letters to all his friends before completing his journey in the beautiful Blue Mountains. Once there, he folded his faithful mackintosh, placed his well-worn pipe and glasses upon it and stepped over a thousand-foot precipice.[15]

THE DRIFT TO CULTIVATION

Once upon a time someone – perhaps a foraging mother with hungry children – came upon a clump of tall grasses nodding in the breeze. She stripped away grass heads plump with seeds, rubbed her hands together to remove the husks, and blew to expose the grains. The seeds were too gritty to chew so she spat on them, rubbed them between two stones and gave the resulting paste to her children. Later, perhaps, she slapped some of this paste onto a hot stone beside the fire. We learned to live on grass.

A starch-based diet changed the way we eat, and thus the whole course of our future development. Starch is cheap, abundant and easy to digest, and standard meals everywhere begin with a dollop of starch – whether in the form of potato, rice, maize, cassava, pastry or pasta. Starch is sticky and absorbent, and needs a lot of saliva to chew. This property has been used in ordeal ceremonies around the world. West African witch doctors gave a handful of dry rice to those suspected of wrong-doing and asked them to chew it before spitting it back into their hands. Dry rice signified guilt. In Anglo-Saxon England the equivalent ordeal was known as *corsned*. Menaced by Latin incantations and with a cross held over his head, the suspect was invited to eat a small barley cake or sacramental wafer. Guilt was proved if it stuck in his throat. Fear inhibits salivation, and you can easily understand how these ordeals work when you read the words of an American traveller in China who was threatened with a gun: 'My tongue began to swell, and my mouth to get dry. This thirst rapidly became worse until my tongue clove to the roof of my mouth.'[16] Starch slips down more easily when lubricated with fat or oil, and few will enjoy a meal which derives less than 30 per cent of its energy from fat. Oil-rich sauces give meals their characteristic taste whereas protein, being more expensive, is used sparingly. This is why, regardless of where you go, the meal on offer will consist of a dollop of starch lubricated with fat and garnished with protein.

About 23,000 years ago a small group of people built six brush huts beside Lake Galilee. The water level rose after they left, preserving organic debris in the waterlogged ground. Their huts were roofed with willow and oak saplings, and grass bedding was spread on sunken stone floors, strewn with the remains of more than 150 varieties of seeds and fruit, together with fish bones and the remains of gazelle, fallow deer and many smaller animals. A right-handed man, 173 cm tall, lay in a shallow grave. Between the dwellings lay a large basalt slab, firmly bedded in sand and pebbles. Microscopic analysis showed that this was the lower part of a quern used to grind a mixture of seeds, including emmer (a precursor of wheat) and wild barley mixed in with a small quantity of oats.[17]

As this snapshot reveals, grain was an important part of the diet long before the first settled communities appeared. More than 10,000 years went by before their successors, known as the Natufians, established the world's first township in Jericho. This was not, as you might imagine, a farming community surrounded by fields. Instead, it was a fortified base for people who lived by hunting, foraging, animal husbandry and shifting cultivation. Jericho had rich alluvial soil and was supplied with plentiful water from a nearby spring; enough to support and house some 2–3,000 people. Another early Neolithic settlement was Çatalhöyük, established in central Anatolia around 9,500 years ago. Oddly enough, at least to our eyes, it had no walls, no civic buildings and no streets. It was instead a sprawling mass of single-storey mud-brick apartments, accessed by a communal flat roof from which people descended by ladder into their own dwellings.[18] Privacy would have been unimaginable, as would the stench and vermin. Çatalhöyük was not a proto-city, it was an ad hoc arrangement which suited the needs of a community of hunters, pastoralists, foragers and shifting agriculturalists – people with no concept of civic life as we know it. If you and I walked the streets of Ur of the Chaldees, we would understand the temples, the palaces,

Figure 4: Çatalhöyük: artist's reconstruction.

the streets of the artisans; we would recognize the power structure and know how the system worked. By the same token, we would be utterly at a loss on the rooftops of Çatalhöyük. The physical basis of their lives would be evident, but their way of thinking would have been elusive and quite possibly incomprehensible. Cities made us, and we are their product, but there are other ways of being human.

THE AGRARIAN PHENOTYPE

Early settlements frequently exhausted the resources in their vicinity, obliging their inhabitants to tighten their belts or move elsewhere, and early townships were often abandoned. The inhabitants of these early farming communities were much shorter than the hunter-gatherers who preceded them, and their skeletons have the hallmarks of nutritional deficiencies. These include features of iron-deficiency anaemia, almost certainly due to hookworm, the commonest cause of anaemia today. Settled communities offered a safe haven for rodents, flies and blood-sucking insects, for water-borne and faecally transmitted infections, and for infections passed on by domestic animals. Palaeontologist Mark

Nathan Cohen argued that people did not turn willingly to cultivation of the soil but were forced into it by pressure of population and dwindling resources. Sedentary life entailed an environment that favoured the spread of infection and committed them to a food supply that was more abundant but also far less certain.[19] The Neolithic revolution, so-called, did not necessarily bring better living conditions in its wake, which may be why the journey from the early Neolithic settlements to the first great cities took longer than the journey from those same cities to the present.

Europeans had a mainly vegetarian diet, and they consumed a much wider range of plants than we do. Lindow man, sacrificed and thrown into a peat bog in north-west England in the first century AD, was a healthy person of around twenty-five, 170 cm tall and strongly built. He had recently eaten porridge made from barley, grass, wheat and herbs, with perhaps a few bits of pork.[20] Tollund man shared the same fate in Denmark at around the same time, and his intestine contained a purely vegetarian meal with around forty different types of seed, including barley and flax, together with false flax and knotweed. The barley and flax were probably cultivated, the rest were weeds.

Their descendants came to resemble the Germans described by Tacitus, who fermented barley juice to make an alcoholic drink. 'They change their plough-lands yearly,' he noted, 'and still there is ground to spare. The fact is that their soil is fertile and plentiful, but they refuse to give it the labour it deserves. They plant no orchards, fence off no meadows, water no gardens; the only levy on the earth is the corn crop.'[21] Tacitus may have been wearing rose-tinted spectacles, but there were obvious attractions to the German way of life. Who would prefer the drudgery of farm work to a free life in the wilderness? Who would attempt to extract crops from the same patch of ground, year after year, as against the lesser effort of burning another patch of woodland and scattering your seeds in the ashes?

As and when it developed, settled agriculture meant dependence upon grain, and dependence upon grain required organization. Harvests generated a large surplus of food at regular intervals, and this surplus needed to be stored, guarded and distributed. Soldiers appeared, protection rackets arose, and cities, administrators, priests and kings soon followed. As Adam Smith said in the *Wealth of Nations*, 'civil government . . . is in reality instituted for the defence of the rich against the poor, or of those who have some property against those who have none at all'. Civilization was founded on slavery.

History is written by the winners, and the winners lived in cities. City dwellers and the peasants who supported them formed a tiny fraction of the global population 5,000 years ago; the rest have no history. Their voice was expressed by the Arab historian Ibn Khaldun (1332–1406), whose refreshingly non-Eurocentric introduction to universal history is known as the *Muqaddimah*. In his view, the original state of mankind resembled that of the Bedouin peoples before the great Arab invasions of the seventh century: hardy nomads who moved around with their camels and subsisted on their milk and meat. They were lean and fit, accustomed to hunger and alert to every hint of danger. United by close ties of blood, they fought as one in battle. In contrast, city dwellers were soft, effeminate and cowardly, for sedentary life 'constitutes the last stage of civilization and the point where it begins to decay'. Waves of lean and hungry warriors emerge from the badlands to expropriate the effete and sinful occupants of cities, only to fall victim to luxury in their turn.[22]

As for those who were obliged to scrape a living from the soil, their heights remained about the same. Pooled data from 9,500 individuals buried in various parts of Europe in the first 1,800 years of the Christian era suggest that male height averaged around 170 cm, female height around 162 cm, and that these averages varied by little more than a centimetre over the entire period.[23] Agrarian society was polarized, and those at the bottom of the pyramid – the silent majority – lived at or near the margins of subsistence. Robert Malthus, a priest who worked in a rural parish in the 1790s before winning fame as a demographer, commented that 'it cannot fail to be remarked by those who live much in the country, that the sons of labourers are very apt to be stunted in their growth, and are a long while arriving at maturity. Boys that you would guess to be fourteen or fifteen, are, upon enquiry, frequently found to be eighteen or nineteen.'[24] Analysis of bones from a country churchyard in the village of Wharram Percy in Yorkshire, abandoned in medieval times, tells the same story. Ten-year-old children in Wharram Percy were 20 cm shorter than children of the same age today, and today's ten-year-olds are as big as fourteen-year-old children in medieval times.[25] The children of Wharram Percy were not much smaller than a sample of English children measured in 1833, suggesting that the increase in size is recent. James Tanner, the father of modern growth studies, noted that lifetime stunting is already established by the age of two, and that stunted children shadow the growth curves of healthy children thereafter.

The bodies of subsistence farmers were fashioned for hard work and lean rations, and their main product was grain. Bones are moulded by use and grow thicker in response to the pressure exerted upon them; muscle attachments also become more prominent. Palaeolithic hunters had travellers' legs and powerful throwing arms, but early Neolithic women were characterized by strong arms produced by grinding seeds, together with deformities of the knees and toes produced by rocking backwards and forwards in the kneeling position.[26] A study of women from central Europe over the first 5,500 years of cultivation shows greatly increased density of the bone in their upper arms consistent with heavy physical work such as hoeing or grinding corn. Even members of the Cambridge University women's rowing team failed to match them.[27] Occupational deformities of bones and joints are frequently found in rural cemeteries and testify to the suffering and endurance that went into producing them. This was the agrarian phenotype, and it varied little from the dawn of cultivation to the start of the phenotypic transition.

2

Charlemagne's Elephant

On 2 July 802, a weary elephant plodded through the streets of Aachen, much to the astonishment of its inhabitants. Aachen was the capital of an empire which straddled northern Italy, France, the Low Countries and parts of Germany, and Charlemagne became its emperor in Rome on Christmas Day, 800. He celebrated his new dignity by sending embassies to the East. One group contacted the patriarch of Jerusalem with offerings to the Holy Sepulchre and was given its keys in a token of deference. Three ambassadors went to Haroun al-Rashid, the legendary caliph of Baghdad (ruled 786–809).

Only one ambassador, a Jew named Isaac, survived to present his greetings to the caliph together with gifts of richly worked Flemish cloth. Haroun al-Rashid received him courteously and responded with the gift of an elephant. The elephant, whose name was Abul-Abbas, voyaged from Egypt to Libya and from there to Portovenere, south-east of Genoa. Here he waited until the passes were clear of snow before crossing the Alps, possibly retracing the route of Hannibal's elephants a thousand years earlier. From there he trudged a distance of 1,100 kilometres to Aachen, and survived several northern winters before his death on the shores of the North Sea in 810.[1]

All this was pure courtesy on the part of Haroun al-Rashid, who ruled the civilized world even as Charlemagne had insecure dominion over a remote and savage backwater. Even as Charlemagne struggled – in vain – to learn how to read, the written culture of Greece and Rome lived on in Arab libraries, and ancient and refined civilizations flourished in Asia.

A century had passed since the Arabs had first swept through north Africa and Spain; Charlemagne's own incursion across the Pyrenees in 778 had resulted in a fruitless campaign against the Moors and the massacre of his rearguard (by the Basques) at the pass of Ronces-valles. Arab fleets dominated the Mediterranean, and Ibn Khaldun boasted that the Christians 'can no longer float a plank upon it'.[2] The coastline of the western Mediterranean was incessantly pillaged by Barbary pirates, and places as remote as Ireland were raided for slaves. The major Mediterranean islands, Sicily included, were in Arab hands, although Greek fire had saved Byzantium itself from an Arab fleet in 709. Haroun al-Rashid glimpsed the golden city from the other side of the Bosporus when he commanded the Abbasid invasion of Asia Minor.

Byzantium, a bustling city of a million inhabitants, was the undis-puted focus of what remained of European civilization. It retained control of Anatolia, southern Italy, the Balkans and much of eastern Europe, although its navy was confined to the Black Sea and parts of the Aegean. Elsewhere, Europe had relapsed into barbarism. Endless forest, sparsely inhabited by heathen tribes resembling the German people described by Tacitus, stretched away to the east of Charle-magne's territory. Britain had receded into mist and legend, and weirdly tonsured Irish monks had yet to play their part in the revival of Christianity on the mainland. To the north, isolated communities along the Scandinavian fjords did little more than incubate obscure genetic diseases.

Unpromising though it was, this remote and barbarous region would become the birthplace of the Anthropocene. Many attempts have been made to explain why, and some reasons seem clear. The region was vast, fertile and underpopulated: the North America of its day. It had great mineral wealth. It was sufficiently remote to escape invasion while retaining links to the Mediterranean world and the thriving civilizations of the Middle and Far East. A half-forgotten memory of the Roman Empire lingered on in the Christianity of Rome, and a common language and culture prepared the way for the rediscovery of classical antiquity. The historian Kenneth Pomeranz pointed out in *The Great Divergence* that the industrial productivity and population of China increased at around the same time and in much the same way as in the West, but the Chinese – having no room to expand – became masters at extracting more and more from a limited resource. Theirs was an 'industrious' rather than an industrial revolution.[3] Europe alone had scope for expansion.

FEEDING EUROPE

North-western Europe was heavily forested and thinly populated despite its fertile soil. Roman Britain had around 750,000 acres under cultivation, as against 27 million in 1914. When Anglo-Roman Britain went into decline, the Anglo-Saxon invaders would be confronted by an overgrown wilderness. The biographer of St Brioc, a fifth-century saint, describes the establishment of a monastic community as the brothers 'cut down trees, root up bushes, tear up brambles and tangled thorns, and soon convert a dense wood into an open clearing . . . Some cut down timber and trim it with axes, others planed planks for the walls of their houses, many prepared the ceilings and roofs, some turned up the sod with hoes . . .'[4] It was a world of unremitting physical effort, of beasts flogged to the limits of endurance and of nights huddled by firelight under the silence of the stars.

Charlemagne's was a frontier society: brutal, expansionist, individualistic and self-seeking. His empire soon fell apart, but not before it had scattered the seeds of the language and culture it inherited from Rome along with the ideology and organization of Latin Christianity. The Church followed the sword into the uncharted forest, spearheading forest clearances, converting the survivors of conquered tribes and providing a framework for the civilizing process. The need for security gave rise to a warrior society armed with weapons that became progressively deadlier. Its chief offensive weapon was the heavy cavalryman, and the castle was its defensive equivalent. Castles began as earthen mounds topped with wooden towers, and evolved into armoured bases which sheltered the local warlord, protected the local church and provided a storehouse for meat and grain in times of trouble.

Each chieftain lived off his land with little motive to produce more food than necessary. The serfs got by on what was left and clustered into villages, separated from the ever-present forest by a ring of common land. Their core foods were grain, dairy products and occasional

Figure 5: Medieval serfs harvesting wheat with reaping-hooks under the command of a manorial supervisor.

meat; they supplemented this by foraging for nuts, plants and berries, and they caught birds, fish and small animals when they could – a practice outlawed as 'poaching' in later years. Most European farmers followed a two-field rotation, which meant that half of your arable land was ploughed each year, while the other half lay fallow. Their harvest yielded three to four seeds for each one sown, so a large proportion was needed as seed corn. Small variations in output could spell the difference between plenty or famine, and the annual harvest was occasion for triumph or despair. 'Peasants and crops,' said the historian Fernand Braudel, 'in other words food supplies and the size of the population, these determined the destiny of the age ... For each succeeding generation, this was the pressing problem of the day. Beside it, the rest seems to dwindle into insignificance.'[5] They farmed land in common, foraged in the surrounding wilderness and supported each other in times of hardship. There are many positive aspects to communal living, but a traditional farming society is a good match for any academic department when it comes to feud, frustration and ferocious battle for petty advantage.

OUR DAILY BREAD

Bread was the staple. The word 'lord' derives from the Old English *hláford*, from *hláf*, a loaf, and the *Oxford English Dictionary* explains that 'the etymological sense expresses the relation of the head of a household to his dependants who "eat his bread"'. 'Lady' derives from *hlǣfdíge*, the person who makes the bread. People prayed for their daily bread, but wheat was reserved for the wealthy; others ate rye, sometimes mixed with wheat to make maslin bread. The main alternative for the poor was oats, famously defined in Dr Samuel Johnson's *Dictionary* of 1755 as 'a grain, which in England is generally given to horses, but in Scotland supports the people'. This jibe had some truth, for wheat was not grown in Scotland until 1727, prompting Adam Smith to say that 'the common people in Scotland, who are fed with oatmeal, are in general neither so strong nor so handsome as the same rank of people in England'.[6]

Wheat and legumes are rich in protein, and provide a nutritionally adequate diet when taken in combination. Wheat requires richer soil than barley, its major rival in the Old World, and has important advantages. Supreme among these is its high content of gluten, a protein named for the Latin for glue, and from which we derive 'glutinous'. Gluten adds nutritional value and binds dough into an elastic mass which inflates as yeast generates carbon dioxide. Barley contains less gluten and will not bind so well, which is why it is used in liquid fermentation to make beer. Traditional wheat is soft-grained but was largely replaced by hard-grained North American varieties in the nineteenth century; these contain more gluten, produce lighter and crisper loaves and can be ground more finely by the roller mills that replaced the old mill-stones.

Wheat contains 60–80 per cent starch and 8–15 per cent protein, is more nutritious than most other grains and accounts for more than 20 per cent of global food consumption. Less nutritious cereals such as barley, rye or oats were grown on poorer or more northerly soils, but it was wheat that fuelled the later expansion of Europe. Seed crops were measured by volume rather than weight, and the measuring bucket was known as a bushel – which is why you can hide your light under one. One 'quarter' (8 bushels) of wheat was consumed each year per head of the population in the eighteenth century, enough for about 220 kg of bread, or roughly 2,000 calories per day.

Farmers faced two related challenges. One was to feed the soil, and the other was to feed their animals over the winter. This latter being impractical, most animals had to be slaughtered in the autumn; their meat was salted down or smoked for the winter. A 'hungry gap' came in the following spring and coincided with the Lenten fast and the injunction to eat fish. The alternative to this annual cycle, painfully discovered and slowly implemented, was to improve the soil, to feed the extra produce to your animals, and to use them for muscle power and a source of manure. The Flemish showed the way by introducing the four-field rotation – a sequence of wheat, turnips, barley and clover – in the seventeenth century. Turnips fed livestock over the winter, and clover fed them in the summer. Horses replaced oxen as the source of muscle power, and cows were reserved for milk and meat. Clover fed the land by fixing nitrogen, fields no longer lay fallow, crop rotation discouraged pests, and fewer animals had to be slaughtered for winter. Farming became more profitable, and professional farmers began to take over the common land.

The profitability of farming increased for many reasons, chief among them the transition from immemorial custom to a cash economy, coupled with a move towards private ownership of the land. This saw the rise of a new elite and the subsequent spillage of academic ink over the rise of the gentry. The trend was aided by the self-destruction of the British nobility in the Wars of the Roses. In 1450, the king, the Church and some thirty aristocrats owned 60 per cent of the 5 million hectares of farmland; by 1700 their share had fallen to 30 per cent.[7] The decline of the aristocracy created a power vacuum rapidly filled by a new class of self-made men: typical agricultural entrepreneurs, tough, tight-fisted, feet on the ground, upward bound. 'These which with grazing, frequenting of markets, and keeping servants not idle as the gentleman doth ... come to such wealth, that they are able and daily do buy the lands of unthrifty gentlemen.'[8] The first priority of the private landowner was to fence off his property, for common land made it impossible to improve soil, crops or livestock. Although scrawny enough by modern standards, the sheep of the time consti- tuted a valuable cash crop, and the wool trade was the first step towards the use of land for commercial profit; so much so that the Lord Chancellor still sits on a Woolsack (actually stuffed with horse- hair, as restorers discovered to their surprise in 1938).

The sheep that displaced people from country areas would have been almost unrecognizable to us. They were bred for wool rather than meat, and were 'small in frame, active, hardy, able to pick up a living on the scantiest food, patient of hunger . . . and [had] a starva- tion allowance of hay in winter'.[9] They were prized for their milk, and it was said that five ewes would give as much milk as one cow. Meat and dairy produce made no more than a marginal contribution to the traditional diet. Fernand Braudel estimated that poor people in Germany averaged a yearly allowance of less than 20 kg of meat per head at the start of the nineteenth century, as against 23.5 kg in France, equivalent to 50–60 grams per day. 'In nine-tenths of France,' as an observer said in 1829, 'the poor and the small farmers eat meat, and only salt meat at that, no more than once a week.'[10] The English ate so much meat that the French called them *Rosbifs*, but they could not match the American consumption of 81 kg each per year. 'Mon Dieu! what a country!' said a French visitor, 'fifty religions and only one sauce – *melted butter*!'[11]

Farm animals responded well to better feed and conditions. In *English Farming: Past and Present*, Lord Ernle contrasts the average weight of sheep and cattle sold at London's Smithfield Market in 1710 and 1795. The weight of beef cattle rose from 370 to 800 lb (168 to 363 kg), and sheep from 28 to 80 lb (13 to 36 kg). Ernle pointed out that 'the introduction of turnip and clover husbandry doubled the number and weight of the stock which the land would carry' and that 'the early maturity of the improved breeds enabled farmers to fatten them more expeditiously'.[12]

Subsistence farming was replaced by commercial farming over the course of a few centuries, a period that just happened to coincide with a collapse in England's population. There were around 4.7 mil- lion people in England at the start of the disastrous fourteenth century, but the loss of life from plague and famine was such that the population had only recovered to 5.2 million in 1700. By the latter date, however, England produced 50–100 per cent more wheat, milk and beef with fewer hectares, fewer cows and a massively improved economy.[13] A prolonged respite from population pressure made room for a revolution in food production.

3

The Road to Rabbit Island

In a pre-industrial society such as seventeenth-century England, a town of 1,000 people might witness fifty funerals a year. 'Never send to ask for whom the bell tolls,' said John Donne, 'it tolls for thee.' Fathers bury their sons faster than sons bury their fathers, and the bell tolls weekly. Nearly half the townspeople are under the age of twenty, and only thirty to fifty are over sixty. The town needs fifty or so births each year to make up for its losses, and there are around 150 married women of child-bearing age to provide them. Since the birth rate is limited, the death rate – which knows no limits – sets the size of the population. 'Nasty, brutish and short' was Thomas Hobbes' summary of life before civil government. Hobbes lived to be ninety-one, but this was exceptional for his time.

Table 1: Survival of hunter-gatherers and citizens
in seventeenth-century Breslau

	Hunter-gatherers	Breslau 1691
Survival to age 15 (per cent)	57	62.8
Survival from 15 to 45 (per cent)	64	63.2
Survival past 45 (average years)	20.7	19.8

(Gurven and Kaplan 2007, Halley 1691)

The survival of hunter-gatherers (table 1)[1] was surprisingly similar to that of the people of Breslau in 1691, as analysed by the astronomer Edmund Halley. In each setting almost one child in three died by the age of fifteen, the death rate was lowest during reproductive life, and those who reached the age of forty-five might expect to live for another twenty years. Gerontologist Caleb Finch points out that all mammals, regardless of size or length of life, have the same pattern of high infant loss, low mortality in reproductive life and an exponential rise in the death rate thereafter; he comments that 'no well-studied mammal has failed to show these changes'.[2]

The first British Census, of 1801, coincided with a brief respite in Britain's war with France. Conquering revolutionary armies had swept across Europe, and the old order of Church, state and aristocracy seemed on the verge of collapse. Some contemporaries saw the French Revolution as a dress rehearsal for the New Jerusalem, others as a glimpse into demon-haunted chaos. Dangerous ideas were in the air. Was this to be a false dawn or the prelude to limitless progress?

A country curate now entered the controversy. Thomas Robert Malthus (always known as Robert), the sixth of seven children, was brought up to believe in a rational universe presided over by a benign absentee landlord. We may imagine him in a Jane Austen sitting room, much valued by the adults for his wide reading, unassuming sincerity and charm. Elsewhere in the house children choke with laughter as they imitate his speech, for he was born with a hare-lip and cleft palate. The lip was stitched together and is neatly airbrushed out of his portrait, but the palate was beyond the surgical capabilities of the day. He went through life with an 'uncouth mouth and horrid voice' which was unable 'to pronounce half the consonants in the alphabet'.[3] As generally happens, this disability soon became invisible to those who knew him, for he was an entertaining conversationalist, but it set a cap on his ambitions. Robert told the Master of Jesus College (Cambridge) in 1786 'that the utmost of my wishes was a retired living in the country'.[4] So it was that, having distinguished himself in mathematics, he became curate to a small country chapel in Okewood (now Oakwood), Surrey, in 1793. While he pursued this quiet and blameless life, great events took place. It was a time of national crisis: a king had been guillotined on the other side of the Channel, revolutionary armies had thrashed the forces of reaction, and the Old Order was in full retreat. There were disastrously bad harvests in 1794 and

1795, and people were restless. Britain's safety depended upon a navy which had recently mutinied. A ferocious witch hunt against any manifestation of subversive thought was under way. An Anglican clergyman would know where his loyalties lay.

The *Essay on the Principle of Population* (1798) is one of the most effective polemics ever written. It tells of an unassuming, anonymous author who reads an interesting book (by William Godwin, Mary Shelley's father) at the urging of 'a friend' (actually his father). Captivated by the vision it offers, he stumbles upon a fatal flaw. Sadly, and much against his own inclination, he watches a dream fade into the cold light of day. He does not dispute the arguments of the philosophers or deny their attraction: he merely points out that they are incapable of realization. Argument generally precedes conclusion in the course of debate, but polemic is all about persuasion; Malthus is easier to understand if you work backwards from his conclusions. These are that radical secular progress is impossible, that poverty is both inevitable and beyond the reach of human intervention, and that all this was ordained by a wise and benevolent Deity.

There was nothing new in his ideas on population. Adam Smith estimated that the population of Britain and Europe had doubled over 500 years, whereas New Englanders had increased from 21,200 in 1643 to 500,000 in 1760 with no major contribution from immigration. This, as he pointed out, equated to a doubling time of twenty-five years, and implied that those who reached old age might have up to 100 children and grandchildren. Things would be very different in a falling economy, for 'many would not be able to find employment . . . but would either starve or be driven to seek a subsistence either by begging, or by the perpetration perhaps of the greatest enormities. Want, famine, and mortality would immediately prevail.'

Smith estimated that one child in two died before adult life, and that the children of the well-off were more likely to survive, whereas a woman in the poorer parts of Scotland might have twenty pregnancies for two living children. In China, or so he believed, population control was managed by infanticide such that 'in all great towns several [children] are every night exposed in the street or drowned like puppies'.[5] He need have looked no further than London, where Captain William Coram frequently walked through the slums of the East End.

The experience prompted him to set up the London Foundling Hospital in 1741 'to prevent the frequent murders of poor miserable children at their birth, and to suppress the inhuman custom of exposing new-born infants to perils in the streets'.[6] The hospital was faced by overwhelming demand: 3–4,000 infants arrived yearly, and 70–80 per cent of them died.

Malthus estimated that the offspring of a single breeding pair at the dawn of the Christian era would, if allowed to reproduce freely, produce a billion trillion humans within fifty generations, sufficient to populate this planet to a density of four per square yard, and to fill every planet in the solar system. Performed in reverse, this same calculation could be used to prove that we had a billion trillion ancestors fifty generations ago, but he omits to mention this. Instead he bases his argument on a syllogism: population increases faster than food production; lack of food creates misery; ergo, misery is inevitable. The assumptions underpinning this were that we would never be able to control our own fertility, and that food production would be unable to keep up with population. Both proved wrong.

His contemporaries liked and respected Robert Malthus and commented on his sweet and kindly disposition. He knew poverty at first hand. Okewood Chapel served a quiet rural area, and Malthus probably conducted about twenty-five burials over his period of tenure, performing his office as best he could while wretched little bundles were lowered into unmarked holes in the graveyard. Pity for the poor comes through in his writings. Even so, a philosophy which excludes the possibility of progress or helping the poor might incline you to pessimism. 'Moral evil', as he concludes, 'is absolutely necessary to the production of moral excellence.'[7] Malthus's views on population might seem dismal, but they are a spring morning by comparison with his moral theology.

The combination of a purely materialistic argument with a theology of despair (wisely omitted after the first edition) had a devastating effect upon its readers, and few clergymen have prompted quite so many people to lose their faith. Malthus nonetheless provided both Darwin and Alfred Russel Wallace with inspiration. 'I happened to read for amusement Malthus on *Population*,' said Charles Darwin, writing of the year 1838:

and being well prepared to appreciate the struggle for existence which everywhere goes on from long-continued observation of the habits of animals and plants, it at once struck me that under these circumstances favourable variations would tend to be preserved, and unfavourable ones to be destroyed. The result of this would be the formation of new species. Here, then, I had at last got a theory by which to work.[8]

Elsewhere he commented that his theory 'is the doctrine of Malthus applied with manifold force to the whole animal and vegetable kingdom'. There is indeed a curiously Darwinian flavour to a theology in which heredity and environment combine to determine which souls shall grow and which shall not, even as the Almighty moves between their ranks to make His divine selection.

THE DEMOGRAPHIC TRANSITION

Malthus based his gloomy arithmetic upon the assumptions that we will never be able to control our own fertility, and that food production must lag behind population. At first, events seemed to justify his predictions. Britain started the nineteenth century with 10.5 million people and ended with 37 million, despite sending another 11 million overseas.[9] The British Census of 1871 estimated that 1,173 babies were born each day, and that 40 per cent of these would emigrate.[10]

The western advantage was technological, for no one could withstand rifles, Gatling guns and explosive shells backed by steam engines, manufacturing power, communications and organization. People of European origin represented 33.6 per cent of the global total in 1933 as against 23.1 per cent in 1800.[11] Westerners dominated the planet, with direct or indirect control of almost every country on earth at the start of the twentieth century. Biological advantage was added to this, for they were better nourished, bigger and healthier than ever before, especially those who had emigrated: American and Australian soldiers looked like giants to the slum-dwellers of Britain in the First World War. Few paused to consider that this advantage might simply be due to better nutrition and freedom from disease. Even so, affluent white males feared for their future. They worried about the aspirations and political power of the working classes, the increasing assertiveness of women and the resurgence of non-European peoples.

The immediate concern, however, was a falling birth rate. This averaged around 33 per thousand when registration of births in England and Wales began in 1837, remained around 30 in the 1890s, but plunged to below 15 in the 1930s. The average family size had fallen to two in 1935–9, as against six in the 1860s.[12] Contemporaries were alarmed to see that talented people (educated women in particular) were failing to reproduce. This gave rise to two equally fearful prospects. One was that the British Empire, which dominated the oceans and held sway over 24 per cent of the world's surface area and 23 per cent of its population, was headed into a spiral of negative population growth. The other was that the lower strata of the population would out-produce the rest, thus (as they believed) sending evolution into reverse.

Warren Thompson mooted the concept of a demographic transition in 1929.[13] He predicted that Russia would grow by virtue of its abundant new lands and would equal the population of China and India by the end of the century. In other parts of the world, as he saw it, Malthusian factors would continue to determine the growth of the world's population. India, for example, would grow slowly because of uncontrolled famines and epidemics. Should the vast potential for growth of the developing world ever be realized, however, he argued that the challenge of the future would be to redistribute unused land currently occupied by the wealthier nations.

Kingsley Davis, writing in 1945, pointed out that people of European origin had multiplied seven-fold over the past 300 years, whereas the rest of the world had increased three-fold.[14] Europe had externalized its internal order, for its descendants now formed the global upper class and other groups supplied the lower orders. This situation contained the seeds of its own destruction, for Asia's teeming millions were set to double or treble by the end of the century. Were we heading for a 'beehive world' of 10–20 billion people? This might be prevented if the sociocultural constructs underlying the rise of the West could be transferred peacefully to the rest of the world, but a massive upheaval was in prospect.

The rise of the West was aided by two Malthusian holidays. The first resulted from depopulation in the fourteenth century and allowed breathing space for new developments in agricultural production. The second came when overseas migration and food imports eased population pressure. Even so, famine beckoned at the start of the twentieth century – until the inhabitants of Rabbit Island learned how to dodge the Malthusian trap.

4

The Invention that Fed the World

When Robert Giffen addressed the Manchester Statistical Society on 17 October 1900, he predicted that people of European descent would number 1,500–2,000 million by the end of the century, although they could not continue to increase at such a prodigious rate 'without a great deal besides happening of an astonishing nature'.[1] Sir William Crookes, distinguished scientist and researcher into the paranormal, had the same concern in mind in 1898 when he addressed the British Association on the subject of wheat.[2] People of European descent ate bread, and he estimated their number at 517 million with a projected increase to 819 million in 1941. But would there be enough bread to feed them? The frontiers of cultivation had already been reached in North America, Russia and elsewhere, and he estimated that wheat would be in short supply by 1931. Since no more land was available, the soil must be made to produce more.

Plants live on air, as the Dutch savant Van Helmont demonstrated. In 1692, he weighed 100 lb (45 kg) of oven-dried soil, placed it in a container and planted a willow tree weighing 5 lb (2.3 kg). Five years later the tree, which was regularly watered, weighed 169 lb (77 kg), but the soil was only two ounces (57 g) lighter.[3] It took three centuries to work out how this feat was achieved.

'For dust thou art and unto dust shalt thou return,' says the English Burial Service, unaware that our bodies, like the plants we eat, are woven from light and air. Most of our body is water, but our carbon content – 16 kg in a 70 kg person – was extracted from the air by plants. Nitrogen adds another kilo, which means that 96 per cent of our substance is ultimately derived from air and water. The rest is mostly mineral: 2.5 per cent as calcium and phosphorus, with an added contribution from potassium, sulphur, sodium, chlorine, magnesium and trace elements.

Plants convert the energy from sunlight into the carbon-based matter we know as food, and we reverse the process by breaking complex food molecules back into carbon dioxide and water. The energy content of the sun is endlessly renewable, but minerals from the soil must be replaced with the compounds of nitrogen, phosphorus and potassium that constitute our three main fertilizers.

Nitrogen makes up 80 per cent of the air we breathe, and the compounds it forms, proteins included, are essential to the chemistry of life. Plants and animals cannot access this abundant gas directly, for nitrogen circulates in pairs of atoms locked together by a triple bond so powerful that lightning is the only physical force capable of ripping it apart. Luckily for us, however, soil-based bacteria have evolved enzymes which can split this bond. Once separated, the atoms of nitrogen bind voraciously to other chemicals, and nitrogen is then said to be 'fixed'; all other life-forms are critically dependent on this.

Sir William's concern was that our numbers were increasing so rapidly that humans and domestic animals were taking nitrates out of the soil faster than they could be replaced. Mined sources of nitrate fertilizers were available, but were already running low; future projections made Malthusian meltdown seem inevitable. There was, as he pointed out, only one escape route: we must learn to harvest nitrogen directly from the air we breathe. Should this prove possible, he predicted that 'the chemist will step in and postpone the day of famine to so distant a period that we, and our sons and grandsons, may legitimately live without undue solicitude for the future'. On this timescale he was correct, and two or three billion people are alive today because Sir William's prediction was fulfilled.

Other developments contributed to the twentieth-century agricultural revolution, but the ability to convert atmospheric nitrogen into fertilizer was fundamental, for what is taken out of the soil must be replaced. The hybrid crops which gave us the green revolution were bred to feed on nitrates, and pesticides and other techniques increased the yield. Nitrogen fixation rescued the inhabitants of Rabbit Island from starvation, fed the population explosion of the twentieth century, gave the world a Malthusian holiday and created the conditions for the consumer phenotype. The story is worth telling.

In 1802 Alexander von Humboldt, bored to distraction by the social amenities of Lima, came upon the dusty remains of a vanished civilization on Peru's bleak coastline, complete with cities and aqueducts. The sea, as he noted, was surprisingly cold yet teeming with fish. The Humboldt Current, as it would later be called (to his annoyance, for he was not the first to describe it), runs deep under the Pacific before rising by the South American coastline, bearing nutrients that support one of the world's most prolific fishing grounds and an equally dense population of sea birds. Guanay cormorants had bred on Peru's offshore islets for so many millennia that their excrement was piled tens

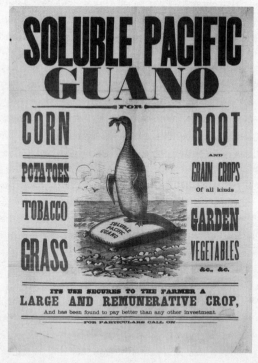

Figure 6: Nineteenth-century US advertisement for guano from the Chincha Islands.

of metres deep. This gave the islets a snow-crested appearance by day, turning to silver by moonlight.

Bird droppings, as car owners are aware, are not particularly soluble. Animals excrete nitrogen in the form of urea, which is soluble, but birds and reptiles excrete it in the less soluble form of uric acid. Rain will eventually leach this away, but rain hardly ever falls on the South American coastline, a climatological freak for which the Humboldt Current is responsible. Decades after Humboldt's visit, the value of nitrate-rich guano was finally appreciated. Merchant ships lined up beside the guano-tipped islands while indentured Chinese coolies, working under conditions of near-slavery, poured cascades of reeking dust into their holds. The ships trailed an ammoniacal reek around the world on their journey home.[4]

The great days of the guano trade ended when the coolies finally hit bedrock in the 1890s. Happily, more nitrate was at hand, for rain never falls on the Atacama desert, which borders Peru to the south. There, as Sir William Crookes would explain, 'for countless ages, the continuous fixation of atmospheric nitrogen by the soil, its conversion into nitrate by the slow transformation of billions of nitrifying organisms, its combination with soda, and the crystallisation of the nitrate' had given rise to a rich blend of nitrates, known locally as *caliche*. Sir William's account is disputed, but geologists acknowledge that it took some 10–15 million years for the deposits to accumulate.

The northern part of the Atacama then belonged to Peru, the southern part to Chile, and an intervening strip of land gave Bolivia access to the sea. Entrepreneurial Chileans soon started to mine deposits on land notionally owned by the other two countries, and it was not long before Chile's politicians identified an inalienable right to this previously disregarded wasteland. War followed, and Peru and Bolivia were trounced in the exuberantly titled 'War of the Pacific' (1879–83). Chile now had undisputed possession of the richest nitrate deposits on earth. Exports increased from 25,000 tonnes in 1850 to 1,454,000 tonnes in 1900 and 2,449,000 tonnes in 1911. Chilean citizens paid no tax.

AN EXPLOSIVE COMBINATION

Saltpetre (potassium nitrate) was used as a meat preservative until Europeans learned from the Chinese that a mixture of 75 per cent saltpetre, 15 per cent charcoal and 10 per cent sulphur has interesting properties. The chemical bonds formed by nitrogen are so strong that they come apart with considerable force, which is why nitrates form the basis of all chemical explosives. Gunpowder, for example, creates a self-propagating shock wave that travels at thirty times the speed of sound, emits white-hot gas and expands to 1,200 times its original volume. Since gunpowder needs careful handling, nineteenth-century chemists raced to discover more stable mixtures. They were notorious for blowing themselves up in the process: Emil Oskar, Alfred Nobel's younger brother, was killed by an explosion in the Nobel armaments factory in 1864.

The manufacturing goal was to absorb nitroglycerin in an inert medium that could be handled safely. Dynamite, upon which Alfred Nobel's fortune was founded, was nitroglycerin soaked in diatomaceous earth, a powder formed of the bodies of fossil algae. This earth comes from Krümmel, a remote location in the region of Hamburg later used for a nuclear power station. Nobel chose its site wisely, for the factory blew up twice, and a crate of dynamite destined for the Central Pacific Railroad exploded in the Wells Fargo office in San Francisco in 1866, killing fifteen people. Companies raced to get around Nobel's patent with other inert absorbents, but he stayed ahead of the game by inventing gelignite in 1875. Dynamite has the uncomfortable habit of leaking unstable liquid nitroglycerin from its solid matrix, but gelignite is safe to handle and will not explode without a detonator. Nitroglycerin proved unexpectedly useful as a medicine, however, for it could relieve the chest pain of angina. Alfred Nobel was among its users. 'Isn't it the irony of fate', he commented, 'that I have been prescribed nitroglycerin, to be taken internally! They call it Trinitrin, so as not to scare the chemist and the public.'[5] We use it still.

THE ELEPHANT AND THE WHALE

It is hard to imagine a world in which the First World War never happened and Hitler, Lenin and Stalin died in obscurity. It is almost equally difficult to imagine a world in which one country had a stranglehold over long-distance trade and travel, but Britain was in this happy (and much resented) position before 1914. Its navy was supreme, and Germany was almost powerless to defend the world's second-largest merchant marine. The attempt to build a navy of matching size guaranteed Britain's implacable enmity, and all for nothing: Germany's grand fleet remained at anchor throughout the war, offered inconclusive battle once and scuttled itself ignominiously in Scapa Flow in 1919.

The looming conflict between Germany's army and Britain's navy has been compared to a contest between an elephant and a whale. The American naval historian Henry Thayer Mahan depicted a comparable scenario in his book on *The Influence of Sea Power upon History*. Napoleon's army dominated the European mainland, but Britain ruled the seas. Strategists who devoured his book underscored the famous comment that 'those distant storm-tossed ships, never seen by the *Grande Armée*, were all that stood between it and world domination'. For twentieth-century Germany, dominant on land but heavily dependent upon the sea, this was – in Yogi Berra's immortal words – 'déjà vu all over again'.

The First World War was like a Greek tragedy in which the protagonists blindly court their own destruction. Germany's strength was the most powerful army in the world, and this was also its misfortune, for the man with a hammer sees every problem as a nail. Impressive though it was, this army required explosives made from nitrates that could only be obtained via sea routes controlled by the British. Since Germany was in no position to fight a lengthy war, it opted to take the offensive. First-strike capability was seen as the key to success, and the German army (which had learned how to load a train rapidly from Barnum's circus)[6] could get to the railheads faster than anyone else. The only snag was that their soldiers then had to slog their way to Paris with horse-drawn guns and waggons, just as in the days of

Napoleon. The German High Command lost touch with its advancing forces, and their forward momentum broke down at the Marne.

Generals decked out like barnyard roosters in peacetime now floundered out of their depth. 'I don't know what is to be done,' said General Kitchener to his foreign secretary on more than one occasion, 'this isn't *war*.'[7] Germany had no fall-back plan for an extended struggle, whereas Britain had the resources of the world at its disposal. Germany had imported one-third of Chile's nitrate in 1913, but now had none. The army had stockpiled munitions for six months and was getting through them much faster than anticipated. Emil Fischer, a leading scientist, and Walther Rathenau, a leading industrialist, joined forces in autumn 1914 to point out that the country would run out of munitions by the following spring.[8] Could German science rescue the situation?

THE COLOURS OF BLACK

Distillation of coal tar yields seven main products – benzene, toluene, xylene, phenol, cresol, naphthalene and anthracene – and industrial chemistry is founded upon them. All have carbon ring skeletons to which a vast array of other molecules can be attached, and they make a good starting point for the light-trapping molecules we know as dyes. The first synthetic dye, named mauve after the French name for the mallow flower, was discovered by William Perkin in 1856. This triggered a race to patent new dyes, but the shape of things to come was revealed when Perkin filed for alizarin, a synthetic version of the red dye in madder, on 26 June 1869 – only to discover that German competitors had filed their patent on 25 June. Some 50,000 acres of madder root were rendered worthless almost overnight, and Perkin retired in 1874 cursing the British education system for churning out gentlemen who spoke dead languages.

The Germans had their sights on a bigger target: indigo. This is the colour of blue jeans, originally made of denim (an anglicized version of *de Nîmes*, after the French town which produced it) and dyed with indigo from Genoa, known as *bleu de Gênes*, hence 'blue jeans'. Indigo was one of the world's most valuable crops, and the German chemist Adolf von Baeyer (1835–1917) had synthesized it in the laboratory in 1880. The problem was that every attempt to translate this discovery into an industrial process had failed, and the way in which this was finally achieved has some bearing on our story.

BASF (Badische-Anilin & Soda-Fabrik) was one of Germany's leading dye manufacturers at the end of the nineteenth century. Its custom was to plough all its resources into research and to pay its shareholders no more than 5 per cent in dividends. Heinrich von Brunck led the company in single-minded pursuit of indigo when he took over in the 1890s and poured millions of marks into the project over the protests of more conservative colleagues. The company attacked the problem on a scale never previously imagined: bench scientists identified the conditions under which a reaction might take place, engineers created them, and factories turned them into a product. As a result, the seventeen-year quest for indigo reached a successful conclusion. Germany's scientists filed more than 1,000 dye patents between 1885 and 1900, whereas Britain had eighty-six, and Germany had 85 per cent of the world market in dyes and pharmaceuticals when the First World War began.[9] Germany led the world in the industrial application of science and changed the course of the twentieth century in doing so.

THE BIG FIX

With months in which to find a substitute for Chilean nitrate, German scientists performed astonishing feats of chemical engineering at breakneck speed. Standard histories almost invariably get the story wrong, so let us pause to look at what happened.

The problem was this. Many existing industrial processes supplied fixed nitrogen in the form of ammonia (NH_3). This is a useful fertilizer – more so when two ammonia molecules are joined to form urea – but you cannot make explosives from it. Explosives require nitrates, which are made with nitric acid. Germany had plenty of ammonia in 1914, but no means of converting this to nitric acid on an industrial scale. Coal contains nitrogen, trapped in plants that died 240 million years ago. If you heat it in the absence of air, as in a blast furnace, nitrogen binds hydrogen to make ammonia ($N_2 + 3H_2 = 2NH_3$). The coal is turned into coke (used for steel production), generating coal gas as well as ammonia. Alternatively, you can heat coke and limestone to form calcium carbide, which binds atmospheric nitrogen at a temperature of 1,200°C. The product, known as cyanamide, releases ammonia on exposure to superheated steam. Germany had plenty of coal and limestone, but the energy costs of producing ammonia were high – and a better method was in prospect.

Fritz Haber (1868–1934) was born of secular Jewish parents. He lost his mother at birth and was never able to establish a satisfactory relationship with a member of the opposite sex, or indeed with his cold and distant father. His first wife shot herself with his service revolver, and the second divorced him. Haber, a passionate believer in the new Germany, had the disadvantage of being Jewish. He chose baptism in 1892 to escape this invisible exclusion zone, but also to signal his pride in being German. It was not enough, and never could be. Walther Rathenau said that 'in the adolescent years of every German Jew occurs that painful moment which he remembers all his life: the first time when he becomes aware that he has entered the world as a second-class citizen and that no achievement and no service can liberate him from this condition'.[10] This bitter comment sums up Haber's life. He was a late developer in academic terms and often at odds with his father, but his career took off when he was hired as an assistant to the chemistry department in Karlsruhe in 1894. Colleagues saw him as pushy, egotistical and easily provoked – a common response to people from minority backgrounds – but his energy and talent soon overcame all obstacles. His expertise in the new field of electrochemistry was such that he was sent to tour the USA in 1902 and report back on developments. His limited command of English was no problem, for all serious chemists then had to learn German. He had two textbooks and fifty scientific papers under his belt when he made full professor in 1906, but had yet to set his seal upon an important new scientific discovery.

His interest in nitrogen began in 1904 and became a passion when a rival dismissed his work with stinging contempt at a meeting in 1905. Haber now threw all his energy into fusing nitrogen with hydrogen. His special expertise lay in the effects of high pressure upon chemical reactions, and he co-developed a table-top apparatus capable of generating previously unthinkable pressures – up to 200 times atmospheric. This gave him the right combination of temperature and pressure to fuse the two gases, and he found an obscure catalyst to drive the process forward. BASF had been following his progress with some interest, and Haber invited their leading engineer, Carl Bosch, to see the new process in action. Bosch showed up with a colleague on 2 July 1909, whereupon the apparatus sprang a leak. Bosch couldn't wait, but his colleague stayed on until the apparatus was fixed. Hours later, liquid ammonia began to flow, and the man from BASF gripped Haber's hand in excitement.

The concept is beautiful. A stream of hydrogen meets a stream of nitrogen over a catalyst, and their fusion generates sufficient heat for the process to be self-sustaining. This allows it to run continuously, recycling hydrogen and nitrogen even as the ammonia is extracted. The product is remarkably pure, and nitrogen could now be fixed for 5 per cent of the cost of the electric arc, or 20 per cent of the cyanamide process. Could this be done on an industrial scale? Bosch returned to take a look and grunted that it could.

Fritz Haber was a deeply conflicted man, and Carl Bosch seems ordinary enough by comparison – so much so that he has not attracted the attentions of a recent biographer – yet he changed the world. Bosch had trained in metallurgy as well as chemistry – a combination that proved very important – and he was the perfect combination of a technocrat with a human dynamo. He drove the nitrogen project forward with demonic energy, wielding the considerable resources of BASF in a way that has been compared with the Manhattan Project. There was no thought of war in his head at the time – this was just his modus operandi. Haber got his Nobel Prize in 1918, despite furious protests about his involvement in gas warfare. Bosch's prize, which came in 1931, was the first ever to be awarded for technical achievement. He had certainly earned it, for the problems were formidable. So too was the achievement. Haber's experimental apparatus was 75 cm tall and 15 cm wide; it generated 1–2 kg of ammonia per day. Bosch's scaled-up versions produced 0.3 tonnes in 1910 and 75 tonnes by 1915.

This discovery did not solve Germany's problem in 1914, for

ammonia has no military value: explosives need nitrates, and nitrates are made from nitric acid. It so happened, however, that Wilhelm Ostwald, yet another Nobel-winning German chemist (and a committed member of the peace movement), had shown in 1902 that nitric acid can be obtained by mixing ammonia with air over platinum gauze. BASF had done little work on this before September 1914, suggesting that its intentions were genuinely peaceful. Bosch was now asked if he could take Ostwald's experiment from bench-top into full-scale industrial production, and *fast*. He responded that 'my answer could be, after a short evaluation, positive'.[11] He did indeed produce nitric acid on the scale required for military use by May 1915, and the guns did not fall silent.

Table 2: German fixed nitrogen production in thousands of short tons (2,000 lb / 907 kg), 1913–17[12]

	1913	1914	1915	1916	1917
Coke	121	(?)	(?)	(?)	134
Cyanamide	26	40	551	551	441
Haber-Bosch	7	14	34	68	113
Chilean nitrate	153	0	0	0	0
	307				688

Historians faithfully repeat the story that the Haber-Bosch process kept Germany in the war, but this is untrue. Germany got its ammonia from cyanamide, and Haber-Bosch never made a major contribution. The key development was not to produce more ammonia, but to convert this to nitric acid by scaling up the Ostwald process. Here again, Bosch played a central role. His first major factory at Oppau in the Rhineland was just within range of French bombers, and this prompted him to create a massive new industrial complex at Leuna, near Leipzig. The research skills and industrial capacity of an entire nation had been mobilized for war, and the state partnered with industry in pouring funds into new technologies. It was the birth of the military-industrial complex and – ultimately – of the phenotypic transition.

THE POLITICS OF HUNGER

Hunger is the time-honoured way of sapping morale in wartime, and both sides used it to good effect in the First World War. Germany imported 20 per cent of its food calories in 1913,[13] and the deficit now had to be met. Farm workers joined the army but still had to be fed, and nitrates were needed for munitions. Meat production is highly inefficient – 90 per cent of the calories fed to pigs are lost– and more than 5 million pigs were sacrificed in the *Schweinmord* of spring 1915. Hastily conserved in cans, the meat frequently spoiled. Others profited. 'There was a time', said Rear-Admiral Consett, British naval attaché to Scandinavia,

> when meat was so scarce in Copenhagen that butchers' shops had to be closed down: special fast trains packed with fish, the staple article of diet among many of the Danes, carried it to Germany when fish was unprocurable in Denmark ... coffee, the favourite beverage of the Swede, was unobtainable in Swedish restaurants at a time when Sweden was exporting large quantities to Germany.[14]

As ever, the burden of hunger was unequally distributed. Bread, fat and sugar were rationed in 1915, and long queues of shivering women formed outside food stores before dawn. They jumped around to keep warm; a sight described, with bitter humour, as the 'polonaise'. The civilian daily energy ration hovered at around 1,500 calories for most of the war, reaching a low point of 1,100 in July 1917. The black market supplemented this, and those who could grew potatoes. The potato crop failed in 1916, however, and a 'turnip winter' followed.

A nutritionist who attempted to live on the official ration saw his weight fall from 76.5 to 57.5 kg within six months. It is estimated that hunger caused up to three-quarters of a million civilian deaths. Three women died in Germany for every two in Britain, and the excess mortality persisted for several years afterwards.[15]

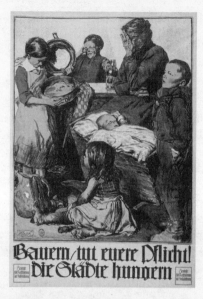

Figure 7: A distraught mother sits with five hungry children around a table. One holds an empty bread box. 'Farmers, do your duty!' says the poster. 'The cities are starving.'

Hunger prompted the desperate gamble of unrestricted submarine warfare, in the hope that the Allies would be forced to surrender before the Americans came into the war. Civilian morale held up well while the war lasted – Germany seemed set to win at the start of 1918 – but the blockade was prolonged for six months after the war had ended. This was done with obvious punitive intent and it would never be forgiven.

The Haber-Bosch process may not have rescued the German war effort, but the ability to fix atmospheric nitrogen and to transmute ammonia into nitrate fertilizers showed us how to escape starvation in the twentieth century. To save the world and gain a Nobel Prize in the process might seem the stuff of dreams, but Fritz Haber's end was not a happy one. His attempt to pay off Germany's reparations by extracting gold from seawater was a failure, German society became more overtly anti-Semitic, and he found himself an outcast in his own country. He resigned as Head of the Kaiser Wilhelm Institute in Berlin in 1933 and went into voluntary exile, moving restlessly from one hotel or sanatorium to the next. He even looked into the possibility of an academic position in Cambridge – a university that became home to many Jewish exiles from Germany – and enquired about British citizenship. 'My most important goals in life', he wrote to an English friend, 'are that I not die as a German citizen . . .' He was increasingly plagued by angina pectoris and succumbed on 29 January 1934 in a hotel bedroom in Switzerland.[16]

Carl Bosch, meanwhile, went from strength to strength. His main factory complex at Leuna was untouched when the war ended and would soon produce more nitrates than Chile, although production slumped during the Great Depression. The leading chemical and pharmaceutical companies in Germany had partnered closely in wartime, and seven joined forces in 1925 to form IG Farben, the biggest chemical company in the world. The CEO of Standard Oil paid them a visit in 1926, and it took his breath away; it 'was a world of research and development on a gigantic scale such as I had never seen'. The company president was promptly summoned to the spot. 'I had not known what research meant until I saw it,' he said, 'we were babies compared to what they were doing.'[17]

Carl Bosch ran this vast enterprise, and two projects absorbed his energies in the 1930s: the production of synthetic gasoline and synthetic rubber from coal – both central to Hitler's plans for another war. Bosch fell out of favour when he remonstrated with Hitler as to the loss of so many Jewish scientists – prompting the famous retort that if German science could not manage without Jews, Germany would have to manage without science. Disenchantment followed. Bosch retired to Sicily and died there two weeks before Hitler invaded France. He had a prophetic vision on his death-bed. All would go well for Germany, he said, until Hitler invited calamity by invading Russia. 'I see terrible things,' said Bosch. 'Everything will be totally black. The sky is full of airplanes. They will destroy whole Germany [sic], its cities, its factories, and also the IG.'[18] Bosch's dying vision was wrong in one respect, for BASF, Bayer and Hoechst were each bigger than IG itself by the 1960s. Haber-Bosch may not have prolonged the First World War, but Bosch's genius certainly did, and synthetic oil and rubber underpinned the

German army's performance in the war that followed. His was the unique distinction of prolonging two world wars.

PLENTY AND WANT

The world changed after the First World War. The old deference was gone, women had the vote, and populist parties were in the ascendant. Working people in the industrial nations still subsisted at a level of material poverty that is hard to imagine today, but change was in the air, and expectations were high. They ranged from a socialist nirvana to a consumer paradise.

The first, brief flowering of the consumer society came in America after the war. Paul Nystrom, professor of marketing at Columbia, signalled the change in a book called *Economic Principles of Consumption*, published in 1929. Consumption, as he observed, was an unfamiliar concept; forty books had this word in their title before 1910, and thirty-seven were about tuberculosis. Nystrom considered that poverty exists when a family has to spend more than 50 per cent of its income on food. This accounted for 73 per cent of an English family budget in 1796, as against 38.2 per cent of an American budget in 1918–19. By this time the wartime boom was such that US shipyard workers asked for time off in order to spend their money. A consumer society might be defined as one in which people have more money than they need but not as much as they want, and Henry Ford was its prophet, for he knew that if you pay people well to make cars, the people who make the cars will buy them. The motor car ushered in the era of the common man, but it also reinforced status. You can all have a car, but you can't all have a Cadillac. Wealth generated aspiration, aspiration generated desire, and the consumer escalator rolled upwards.

Productivity increased in line with wages, and the horsepower disposed of by each worker rose from 2 to 4.5 between 1899 and 1925. The working day grew shorter, and this created the phenomenon of leisure. Machine production, said Nystrom, is 'the most outstanding development of our age ... and it is perhaps only natural that the machine and its processes should dominate our leisure time as well as our working hours'. Machines now superseded muscle at work and at play, and Nystrom went on to moralize that 'flabbiness and laziness is evident in both sexes and may be seen in the growing tendency to ride instead of to walk, to participate in sports as spectators rather than players and to shirk responsibility and effort in every form'.

By his definition, Nystrom estimated that 2 million American families lived in poverty in 1929, and he claimed that their babies were one-third as likely to reach their first birthday as those of the better-off.[19] The situation was deteriorating as he wrote. People collapsed from hunger in the streets of Chicago in 1933, and the director of the newly created Office of Defense estimated in 1941 that 45 million Americans did 'not have enough to eat of the foods we know are essential to good health'.

Things were worse in Britain. John Boyd Orr qualified as a teacher before the first war and was assigned to a school in the notorious Glasgow slums. He saw at a glance that his task was hopeless. You could not teach anything to children who lived on tea, bread and butter and came to school without breakfast. Lice crawled on their heads and clothing. He resigned on day two and went on to teach 12–14-year-olds in a deprived but less destitute locality. These children were destined to start a life of manual labour at the age of fourteen, and there seemed little point in offering them much formal education. Stung by sneering remarks about his school, he did, however, offer extra coaching to his four brightest pupils and entered them for a bursary examination. They gained four of the six places. Wearied by watching the waste of human potential, he decided to put himself through university, choosing medicine because it had the best employment prospects. A fellow student paid his own way through medical school by working night shifts at the coal face.

As luck (or the low status of nutritional science) would have it, he was offered the chance to set up an institute of nutrition in Aberdeen. War supervened, and he won three medals for bravery as a medical officer before taking up his new position. The institute was designed to help produce better farm animals; the possibility that the same nutritional principles might be extended to humans does not seem to have been considered. His chance came in 1927, when milk was being tipped down the drain because of overproduction. Boyd Orr proposed that it should be given to schoolchildren instead. A seven-month trial

Figure 8: School milk (1929).

made the benefit obvious, and milk was routinely offered at British schools until Margaret Thatcher removed it (for children over seven) in 1970.

Boyd Orr's energies now focused upon human nutrition, and he formed a committee in the 1930s to report upon the nutritional status of people in the UK. It found that 50 per cent were inadequately nourished. Up to 10 per cent suffered from generalized starvation – serious deficiency of all the nutritional elements – and 40 per cent from specific deficiencies. Rickets was widespread. The report was political dynamite, and an irate minister of health summoned Boyd Orr in order to inform him that government policy had abolished poverty. Boyd Orr stood his ground and broadcast his findings on the BBC despite a threat to have him struck off the Medical Register. His co-authors melted away under the onslaught, but he went ahead and published. The government not only bowed to the inevitable but – in a very British solution – now offered him a knighthood! Nutrition became a national priority during the food shortages of the Second World War, and his policies did much to ensure the future health of babies born in wartime. I was one. He became the first director of the Food and Agriculture Organization (FAO) and was awarded the Nobel Peace Prize.[20]

THE CONSUMER PHENOTYPE

The West did not run short of wheat in 1931, as Sir William Crookes had predicted. Many did, however, experience hunger or worse, for stark famine swept eastern Europe between the wars, and cannibalism marked the terrible Volga famine of 1921. Germany's huge chemical plant at Leuna switched from munitions to fertilizers after the First World War, and BASF had developed an industrial process for converting ammonia to urea, a more convenient source of nitrogen, by 1922. Technical improvements apart, today's methods of nitrogen fixation and fertilizer production were up and running a century ago. Germany's monopoly of the Haber-Bosch process ended at Versailles, but other countries lacked the infrastructure and skills to capitalize upon the gift, and it would take another war to mobilize the method's full potential.

The Second World War jerked America out of depression, and the US economy was organized, streamlined and directed much as Germany's had been in the First World War. Both industry and agriculture benefited, and a dramatic effect upon wheat yields was soon seen around the world (figure 9).

Global use of nitrogen-based fertilizer increased 125-fold between 1900 and 2000, by which time 50 kg was added yearly to each hectare of crops, equivalent to 14 kg per head of population. Nitrogen fixation accounts for 1.3 per cent of all fossil fuel consumption, and 40 per cent of the nitrogen in our bodies is there by courtesy of Haber and Bosch; the world could not support more than 6 billion people in the absence of their process. The combination of high-yield crops with plentiful doses of pesticides and fertilizer increased the global cereal harvest from 741 million tonnes in 1961 to 1.62 billion in 1985.[21] Nitrogen fixation had lived up to Sir William Crooke's expectations, but at a huge cost in terms of environmental degradation. Since even the new

Wheat Yields in the UK, 1270–2014

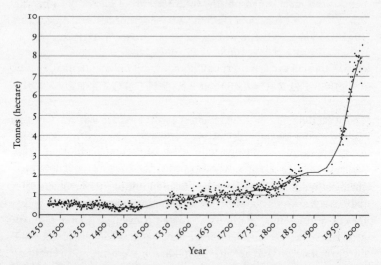

Figure 9: Haber-Bosch transformed wheat yields in the post-war world, as seen in the UK. Data from https://ourworldindata.org/yields-and-land-use -in-agriculture.

crops are inefficient nitrogen users, insertion of a gene that enables them to utilize it more efficiently might help farmers to stop poisoning the environment.[22]

The western world enjoyed a thirty-year Golden Age between 1950 and 1980, and the global economy expanded six-fold in the second half of the twentieth century. Economic growth averaged 3.6 per cent per annum over this period, as against 1.6 per cent between 1820 and 1950, and 0.3 per cent before that.[23] Wealth spread around the world, and a combination of cheap energy, rising wealth, medical knowledge and cheap food caused the global population to jump from 2.3 billion in 1945 to 7.2 billion in 2015 – all within my lifetime. The consumer phenotype was founded upon food abundance.

THE CONSUMER
PHENOTYPE HEADS EAST

Western historians have traditionally portrayed Asia's past as an endless Malthusian cycle of overpopulation, stagnation, ignorance, apathy and famine. More recent analysis has refuted this. There was surprisingly little difference between life expectancy, population growth and nutrition in eighteenth-century China and Europe, and China was possibly closer to a market-driven agricultural economy. The 'great divergence' came as Europe followed a capital-intensive route with ready access to fossil fuels, whereas China followed a labour-intensive route. China experienced devastating famine in 1959–60; an estimated 30 million people died because of Chairman Mao's doctrinaire ignorance and a Soviet-style approach to collective farming. By Nystrom's criterion (50 per cent of family income spent on food), most Chinese remained in poverty. Rationing had been in force for twenty-five years by 1978, and rural families spent 67.7 per cent of their income on food, as against 59.2 per cent for city families.[24]

A global food crisis seemed imminent in the 1960s and 1970s, and the 1974 World Food Conference in Rome noted that poor weather conditions in 1972 had caused the first fall in global food production since the Second World War. Many countries relied upon reserves held by the food-exporting countries, notably the US, and these reserves were so depleted that the world relied on current harvests in 1973 and 1974. 'For the third successive year', as the subsequent report noted, 'food supplies in 1975 were dangerously dependent on a single year's production.' The conference also noted that 'the majority of the world's undernourished people' were concentrated in South-East Asia – mainly, China.[25]

China's population rose from 660 million in 1961 to 870 million by 1972, the year of President Nixon's celebrated visit, and the country seemed on the verge of ecological disaster. The outcome of Nixon's visit, however, was that China made an immediate investment in thirteen of the world's largest and most advanced ammonia–urea production facilities, with more to follow. By 1979 China had become the largest consumer and exporter of nitrogenous fertilizers, its

Biomass change, 1960–2010

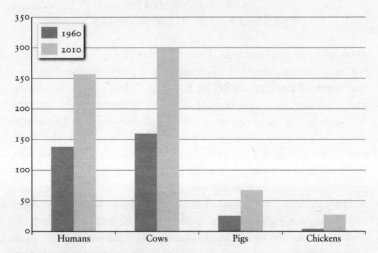

Figure 10: The estimated biomass of humans and three sources of meat in 1960 and 2010, expressed as millions of metric tonnes. One tonne of human biomass equated to twelve Americans or seventeen Asians in 2005, and the energy converted to excess weight could feed another 473 million adults.[26]

population was responding to the one-child policy, and its economic situation was about to be transformed. Once again, Haber-Bosch had saved the day.

Food affluence produces characteristic changes in eating habits which are collectively known as the nutritional transition. Features include a smaller fraction of disposable income devoted to food, and an increasing proportion of expenditure on former luxury items such as meat (figure 10).

The nutritional transition is associated with a switch from small-scale, locally sourced food to large-scale commercial farming based upon cheap fuel and intensive use of fertilizers and insecticides. China saw a shift from the traditional rice bowl regions in the south-east to its northern grasslands, which now support huge herds of cattle. It became the world's largest producer of sheep (twenty times more than Australia), the second-largest producer of beef and the fourth-largest of milk. Wheat production increased dramatically, and the southward flow of wheat calories overtook the northward flow of rice calories for the first time in a thousand years. Hidden costs include overgrazing and degradation of grassland, a falling water table and contamination of groundwater and rivers by animal wastes.

China's vastly expanded food production goes into feeding itself, but some of the environmental fallout has been exported; Brazil grows soybeans to feed Chinese animals on land reclaimed from the Amazonian rainforest. As ever, China's wealth is unevenly distributed, and the 2002 FAO report found that 120 million people were still undernourished. China could easily live well and within its own resources by eating less meat, and its current inability to do so threatens environmental retribution.

As for the future, our current Malthusian holiday cannot be expected to last. We can generate fixed nitrogen, but we have not solved the problem of disposing of it. Phosphate is a finite resource which has to be mined; 'peak phosphate' will be reached in the 2030s according to some estimates. The race between population and resources is far from ended, and the UN estimates that sub-Saharan Africa will increase its population from 1.0 billion to 2.1 billion between 2015 and 2050. Its ability to feed this number is in serious doubt.[27] Yet another concern is that intensive farming drains the soil of micronutrients which fertilizers cannot replace.[28]

In summary, the inhabitants of Rabbit Island have to date confounded Malthus' expectations. Charlemagne's elephant entered a world that was remote and backward by the standards of Haroun al Rashid's Damascus, yet this was where our escape from natural selection began. Overpopulation and famine threatened when the frontiers of cultivation were reached at the start of the twentieth century, but this was countered by a revolution in food production. More and more people could now enjoy a Malthusian holiday, and the consumer phenotype spread around the world.

PART 2

Plasticity

5

The Discovery of Human Plasticity

Food production, industry and science worked hand in hand to transform the dimensions of human existence, and the remainder of this book will be concerned with the change in these dimensions. To begin with, however, I will look at the way in which previous generations have asked this question, for their answers still haunt our thinking. In particular, it is odd to note that profound pessimism as to our future pervaded biological thinking at the start of the twentieth century, even as humanity stood poised for the greatest and most far-reaching transformation in its existence since *Homo sapiens* left Africa.

DEGENERATION

The concept of degeneration is deeply embedded in western culture. Classical authors believed that humanity had deteriorated from its Golden Age, and post-Renaissance thinkers were appalled to learn that the high civilizations of Greece and Rome had fallen into near-oblivion. The malaria-ridden peasants of southern Europe knew nothing of the history under their feet and bore little comparison to the glorious statues of antiquity. Eighteenth-century Europe viewed its rediscovered past with envy, and Edward Gibbon sincerely believed that civilization had reached its apogee in the first and second centuries AD.

Religious orthodoxy taught the same lesson. Its sacred texts stated that humankind had been created, and its theologians estimated that this had taken place some 200 generations previously. Eighteenth-century biologists must then explain how the descendants of a single breeding pair came to vary so widely.

Johann Friedrich Blumenbach (1752–1840) studied at Göttingen to such good effect that he became a professor at the age of twenty-six. He remained there for the next sixty-two years, spry, decorous, affable, beloved as a teacher and famed for the clarity and wit of his books and lectures. Fathers sent their sons and grandsons to study under him. *On the Natural Variety of Mankind*, published in definitive form in 1795, was his most celebrated work.[1] His faith taught him that life had been created, but the paving stones of Göttingen testified to life-forms that no longer existed. Life must therefore have recovered from at least one cycle of destruction, and Blumenbach concluded that some formative force must exist in nature, a force that had acted in the past and was active still.

His starting point was that all animals were created perfect – a perfect Creator could scarcely do otherwise – and that any deviation from this state could only be downhill. Downhill, no doubt, but not entirely random, for the changes he referred to as 'degeneration' matched a creature to its environment, and he spoke of degeneration much as we might speak of variation. Our domestic animals were in his view the most 'degenerate' of creatures – simply because they had encountered the widest variety of external conditions. The badger-dog, as he pointed out, seems remarkably like 'an original purposed construction to meet a deliberate object of design'. The 'badger-dog' is familiar to us as the dachshund, bred to pursue badgers down their burrows. Since humans have been exposed to the same degree of environmental variation as our domestic animals, we are therefore equally degenerate, and he cites the delightful suggestion that we are descended from the household pets of some long-vanished master race!

Blumenbach classified humanity into five racial groups, but was at pains to describe the existence of considerable overlap: 'one variety of mankind does so sensibly pass into the other, that you cannot mark out the limits between them'. Races differ because of climate, diet and behaviour, but he emphasized that this should not be taken to imply that they were unequal. His thinking was remarkably modern in this respect.

Religious orthodoxy taught that the first humans had been created. But where? Blumenbach set out to locate the Garden of Eden. His search was based on the assumption that Adam and Eve were created perfect, and that humanity had subsequently degenerated from this state of perfection. Since 'degeneration' was due to climate, diet and behaviour, those races which travelled furthest from their starting point would show the greatest variation. Conversely, those who stayed closest would bear the greatest resemblance to mankind's original form. How might this resemblance be recognized? By Blumenbach's logic, perfection meant beauty, and beauty should be sought in the skull, since this houses our higher faculties. All that remained was to find the most beautiful skull.

Blumenbach was not the first to seek the Garden of Eden, for many contemporaries were engaged in the same task. Asia was the most popular location: Buffon placed Eden on the eastern shores of the Caspian Sea, and Immanuel Kant suggested Tibet. Others favoured Persia, Kashmir or northern India. Thus it was that Blumenbach looked east, and his criterion was beauty. The rest was easy, for the people of the Caucasus – the area between the Black Sea and the Caspian Sea – have been noted for their beauty since records began, and every visitor to his extensive collection remarked on his most beautiful skull, which had belonged to a woman from Georgia.

Blumenbach considered that European skulls bore the closest

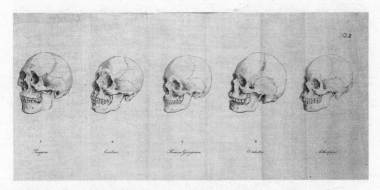

Figure 11: Skulls from Blumenbach's collection, with his 'most perfect' Georgian skull in the middle. Although routinely said to represent his five main racial groups (Mongolian, Native American, European, Malay and black African), the skulls actually came from Siberia, the Caribbean, Georgia, Tahiti and West Africa.

resemblance to this original, which is why the term 'Caucasian' featured on immigration forms in the early part of the twentieth century. 'I gave to that variety the name of the Caucasian mountains', said Blumenbach, 'because it is in that region that the finest race of men is to be found, the Georgian race, and if it were possible to assign a birth-place to the human race all physiological reasons would combine to indicate that place.'[2] Daft indeed, and deeply rooted in magical thinking, but it set the scene – innocently enough – for what would later become tragedy.

Blumenbach's successors pursued his ideas further into the realm of myth. 'In our school days', wrote the American anthropologist W. Z. Ripley in 1899, 'most of us were . . . told that an ideal race of men swarmed forth from the Himalayan highlands, disseminating culture right and left as they spread through the barbarous West.'[3] The Aryans, as it was then believed, mingled disastrously with lesser breeds of men. Since they could still be distinguished by their appearance, however – notably the skull – the race could potentially be reconstituted, as the Nazis attempted to do. Blumenbach's naive attempt to locate the Garden of Eden ended in tragedy. The economist John Maynard Keynes said that 'practical men, who believe themselves to be quite exempt from any intellectual influences, are usually the slaves of some defunct economist. Madmen in authority, who hear voices in the air, are distilling their frenzy from some academic scribbler.'[4] Hitler distilled his frenzy from generations of forgotten racial scribblers.

EVOLVING BACKWARDS

Jean-Baptiste Lamarck (1744–1829) became professor of inferior animals at the Natural History Museum in Paris as the French Revolution was getting under way. He worked his way through drawers of fossil molluscs and found that some could be arranged in lines of descent reaching down to the present day, whereas others had become extinct. Extinction was a major challenge to the eighteenth-century concept of an ordered universe, since it implied that an infallible Creator had produced a flawed design. Lamarck suggested that the missing creatures had not died out; instead they had *moved on* to higher forms. This could also happen in reverse: 'If the environment remains constant, so that the condition of the ill-fed, suffering or sickly individuals becomes permanent, their internal organisation is ultimately modified, and these acquired modifications are preserved by reproduction among the individuals in question, and finally give rise to a race quite distinct from that in which the individuals have been continuously in an environment favourable to their development.'[5]

Regression – reverse evolution – became entrenched in the Victorian imagination, long before Darwin proposed that evolution was travelling in the opposite direction. Animal breeders were familiar with 'throwbacks'; highly bred animals that reverted to a more primitive form. Human examples abounded in works of popular fiction, whose villains were characterized by body hair, deep chests, long arms, deep-set eyes with prominent brow ridges, frightening physical strength, impulsiveness and credulity. The anthropologist Cesare Lombroso classed criminals as throwbacks, capable of training but incapable of reformation, and sex workers were evidence of regression to a stage when morals were unknown. The Victorians saw further evidence of degeneration in a falling birth rate, in the stunted growth of the urban poor and in the downhill trajectory of healthy immigrants from the country. Zoologist and one-time director of the National History Museum Ray Lankester is quoted as saying:

> any new set of conditions occurring to an animal which render its food and safety very easily attained, seem to lead as a rule to degeneration; just as an active healthy man degenerates when he becomes suddenly possessed of a fortune; or as Rome degenerated when possessed of the riches of the ancient world. The habit of parasitism clearly acts upon animal organisation in this way. Let the parasitic life once be secured, and away go legs, jaws, eyes and ears; the active and highly-gifted crab, insect, or annellid may become a mere sac, absorbing nourishment and laying eggs.

Naturalist Alfred Russel Wallace harped on the moral dimension when quoting this, and commented that the prospect of degeneration teaches us 'the absolute necessity of labor and effort, of struggle and difficulty, of discomfort and pain, as the condition of all progress', where the alternative could so easily be, as Lankester put it, 'to degenerate into a contented life of material enjoyment accompanied by ignorance and superstition'.[6]

Darwin's theory of natural selection was based around biological variation but (in the absence of gene theory) he struggled to explain how variation came about in the first place. Some of his explanations were frankly Lamarckian, as when he made the unconvincing suggestion that humans lack a tail because our ancestors rubbed it away by sitting down, or that babies born to the labouring classes have larger hands than those born to professionals.[7] Others looked to climate as a source of variation, for this was then believed to influence the character of a population as well as the colour of its skin. North-western Europeans were said to be hardy and warlike because of their bracing weather conditions, whereas the (supposedly) soft and easy lives of Mediterranean people inclined them to be sensual and relaxed. The real basis for this perception was malaria, just as the apparent indolence of people in the American South was due to hookworm and vitamin deficiency. Lacking this type of explanation, early anthropologists exaggerated the influence of climate; some even believed that white immigrants to the USA would eventually come to resemble Native Americans.[8]

NATIONAL DETERIORATION

At the start of the twentieth century we were poised to add forty years to our lifespan, and to grow taller and healthier than ever before. The outlook for the growth and development of *Homo sapiens* had never been brighter, yet the leading biologists of the day were profoundly pessimistic about the future. Schooled as they were in evolutionary thought, they were dismayed to see that the operations of natural selection no longer applied to modern society, and that the least fit members of society (from their point of view) were reproducing faster than the rest. They thought that civilized behaviour had sent evolution into reverse, and that humankind was heading downhill.

In January 1903, Major-General Sir Frederick Maurice (1841–1912) wrote an article in the *Contemporary Review* which a medical journal – *The Lancet* – characterized as sensational. The article was entitled 'The National Health: A Soldier's Study' and it described the poor physical condition of the men who came forward to fight in the Boer War, the Empire's most recent savage war of peace. In Manchester, for example, 11,000 men offered themselves for enlistment in the first enthusiasm of war. Of these, only 1,000 were fit for active service. Manchester was an extreme instance, but Sir Frederick estimated that only 40 per cent of potential recruits were physically capable of fighting for the Empire.[9]

A committee of the Privy Council was promptly established to consider Sir Frederick's allegations. The committee interrogated sixty-eight witnesses and declared that the physique of the population was not deteriorating, concluding instead that 'the calling of a soldier has

Figure 12: Many volunteers for the First World War were under the regulation height of 63 inches (160 cm), and special 'Bantam' regiments were formed of men of 58 inches (147 cm) upwards.

ceased to attract the class of men who formerly enlisted'.[10] The impli-
cation that men of a better class had stepped forward for military
service in some previous golden age was, of course, pure nonsense.
Nelson's navy had to snatch its recruits from the streets, and Wellington described his heroes as the scum of the earth. It was, however,
true that, in the words of the previous inspector-general of recruiting,
the population from which military recruits were drawn was 'very
largely rubbish', for they came from the most disadvantaged levels of
society.

In retrospect we can see that Britain in the full flower of its imperial glory would now be classed as a Third World nation. In 1900, 63
per cent of people died before the age of sixty, and life expectancy at
birth was forty-five years for men and forty-nine for women. Visitors
to London were shocked by the co-existence of appalling poverty with
complacent affluence, just as visitors to India are shocked today.
William Thackeray reflected on Henry Mayhew's early studies of the
London poor and commented that:

> these wonders and terrors have been lying by your door and mine ever
> since we had a door of our own. We had but to go a hundred yards off
> and see for ourselves, but we never did . . . We are of the upper classes;
> we have had hitherto no community with the poor. We never speak a
> word to the servant who waits on us for twenty years.[11]

Dr Thomas Barnardo (1845–1905) started his medical training at
the London Hospital in Whitechapel, the most deprived area of the
capital, and established a Ragged School which opened his eyes to the
surrounding poverty. He was dining at his London club when someone mocked the idea that destitute children were sleeping rough in
the streets of London. Suitably fortified with alcohol, the diners ventured into the mean streets; a sleeping urchin, betrayed by a naked
foot protruding from beneath a street barrow, was yanked into view.
Barnardo began to set up shelters for homeless children. An eleven-
year-old boy known only as Carrots was turned away by an overcrowded
shelter, only to be found dead in the street two days later. No one
was refused admission after that.[12] By the age of thirty Barnardo had
established a school, a series of children's homes, facilities for children to learn a trade and (needless to say) a mission church. Many

other middle-class men and women discovered urban poverty for themselves in the years to come, and city missions (both religious and secular) appeared in the slums of the affluent nations.

The stunted specimens that lined up in front of the recruiting sergeant came from nurseries such as these, too pitiful even to qualify as cannon fodder. It is easy to dismiss Sir Frederick as a typical product of the military mind, but he felt cheated by the committee on physical degeneration. It 'left on the minds of the members and the public an impression that the prime object of the inquiry was to investigate whether, as compared with the past, the nation was degenerating physically'. In contrast, his intention was to show that a considerable stratum of the population was 'physically inefficient, and that this inefficiency was mainly due to remediable causes'.

The property-owning classes of nineteenth-century Europe were haunted by the spectre of the unwashed masses which surged through the streets of Paris in 1789 and 1870. Repression is a dangerous game, however, and timely concession took its place when Bismarck introduced state socialism in the 1880s. This began as a series of insurance-based social welfare reforms designed to pre-empt the more enticing proposals of the socialist programme. In Britain, the social reforms undertaken by a victorious Liberal Party in 1906 combined similar prudential concerns with more progressive aspirations. In time, these measures began to take effect. Sir Frederick Maurice quoted the professor of hygiene at Birmingham University as saying that: 'all the work hitherto accomplished has practically done nothing to reduce the terrible waste of infant life, the veritable slaughter of the innocents, which annually takes place.' Little did the reformers dream of the potential they were about to unlock.

THE MYTH OF
THE IMMUTABLE SKULL

Western thinking about human biology in the early decades of the new century reflected the realities of global power. Westerners dominated almost every corner of the planet, confident in the belief that women were not the equal of men and that insurmountable inherited differences divided the human race. This prejudice was on full display when western nations refused to accept a Japanese amendment affirming racial equality at the Treaty of Versailles in 1919.[13] Racist thinking was at that time based upon classification of the skull, and it was taken for granted that its shape is invariant and hereditary. 'The general proportions of the head', said Ripley in 1899, 'seem to be uninfluenced either by climate, by food supply or economic status, or by habits of life; so that they stand as the clearest exponents which we possess of the permanent hereditary differences within the human species.'[14]

Remove the head from the human skeleton, said anthropologist William Howells, and you decapitate physical anthropology; no theory of racial difference could be founded on the scapula. The myth of the immutable skull was debunked by the anthropologist Franz Boas (1858–1942), a founding father of American anthropology who pioneered its four-fold division into archaeology, linguistics, physical anthropology and cultural anthropology. Born of secular Jewish parents, he was a lithe man with a penetrating gaze who studied in Heidelberg at a time when Jews showed every sign of assimilating into the wider German culture, and he boosted his Teutonic credentials by fighting duels. It was not enough, and he became a staunch opponent of racist ideology.

His landmark study of the children of European immigrants did much to undermine it. There was a massive influx of immigrants into the USA from southern and eastern Europe around the turn of the twentieth century, and many considered them of inferior stock. Boas wondered if some of their supposedly 'racial' characteristics might reflect the environment in which they had been raised, and he applied for funding to compare the children of immigrants passing through Ellis Island with the American-born offspring of first-generation immigrants. The study began in 1908, and 120,000 individuals – an enormous sample by the standards of the day – had been examined by his team when the results were published in 1912. The shape of the skull was judged by the ratio of width to length, known as the cephalic index, and considered an inflexible marker of race. Boas' findings showed this to be an illusion. To take one example, the skulls of children born to Sicilians in the US were distinctly broader than the heads of children born in Sicily. Conversely, broad-headed European

Figure 13: US immigrants being processed at Ellis Island, 1907.

Jews who moved to the US were producing children with longer heads, and two supposedly distinct European 'races' showed signs of converging towards a common American type. Children of immigrants born in the US were taller than those born in Europe and generally had longer skulls and narrower faces. Markers of ethnicity such as hair and eye colour might be unchanged, but their bodies were becoming American. Boas reported to the immigration authorities that 'the adaptability of the immigrant seems to be very much greater than we had a right to suppose'.[15]

Contemporaries were unimpressed, and Madison Grant, a lawyer turned amateur anthropologist, had much greater influence with his book *The Passing of the Great Race*. Published in 1916, this came complete with coloured maps to show the route taken by the Nordic races after leaving the Himalayas and made no mention of Boas. The maps implied that 'the master race' had passed through the Middle East and central Europe like a dye through a chromatograph, leaving no trace of its passage, and had reached the borders of the North Sea without serious contamination. Sadly, as he noted, only 90 of the 420 million inhabitants of Europe were of Nordic stock, and their descendants seemed destined to vanish without trace in the melting pot of North America. Adolf Hitler claimed the book as his Bible, and defendants used it in the Nuremberg trials to show that Nazi thought was not confined to Germany. Boas' astringent critique prompted Grant to seek his dismissal from Columbia University.

Many later studies of immigrants to the USA took their cue from Boas, and with similar results. Regardless of ethnicity, American-born children consistently tended towards longer bones in the legs, slimmer hips and broader shoulders. Since these same characteristics emerged from comparison of fathers and sons attending Harvard, almost all of whom came from long-established American families, it seemed that American-born immigrants simply mirrored a change in the population as whole. Even so, the concept of bodily plasticity was not considered 'quite acceptable' until the 1980s.[16] It was already quite evident by then that a changing phenotype is rooted in early development, and this went on to become the broader concept of 'developmental plasticity',[17] which we will consider in later chapters.

Max Planck said that 'a new scientific truth does not triumph by convincing its opponents and making them see the light, but rather because its opponents eventually die, and a new generation grows up that is familiar with it'.[18] In 1962, Carlton Coon, president of the American Association of Physical Anthropologists, learned that his delegates wanted to vote on the motion that all races are of equal intelligence. He side-stepped the issue by suggesting that it made no sense to vote on a matter of scientific fact, and that the jury was still out when it came to the issue of race and intelligence. His book *Origin of Races*, published in the same year, proposed that the major branches of the human race had evolved from *Homo erectus* at different times and on separate occasions and had thus attained different rungs of the evolutionary ladder. The hostile reception to this thesis showed that Coon was out of step with his times. Even so, the American Anthropological Association did not pronounce on the subject of racial equality until 1998, and then with the proviso that it did 'not reflect a consensus of all members of the AAA'. The statement affirmed that 'at the end of the twentieth century, we now understand that human cultural behaviour is learned, conditioned into infants beginning at birth, and always subject to modification' but did not explain why it had taken the best part of a century to reach this not-as-yet unanimous conclusion.[19] Eighty-six years after Boas' study of immigrants, it offered no indication that such a thing as developmental plasticity exists.

6

Matrix

We are nine months older than we think, and this prologue is where the phenotypic transition begins. When Americans take the Pledge of Allegiance, they place their hands over their hearts to signify that they pledge their lives to the nation. Ancient Romans placed their hand over their testicles to pledge the lives of future generations when they took an oath in a court of law; this is the literal meaning of 'testify'. A male-dominated world believed that future generations were contained in the seed, and that a woman's body merely provided the soil. This is why the protagonist of this parody of the eighteenth-century novel *Tristram Shandy* begins the story of his life at the instant in which the homunculus – the miniature, preformed version of himself then seen as the agent of inheritance – undertook the momentous journey from his father to his mother. 'Now when once the sexes have obtained the *summa voluptas*', he wrote, 'millions of the animalcules above-mentioned are shot, point-blank into the uterus . . . away they go, jostling, kicking and biting, till one of them has the good fortune to arrive at the small hole in the side of the ovum, into which it enters, and leaves its tail sticking in the passage.' In the manner of Laurence Sterne, the original author of *Tristram Shandy*, this is parodying the prevalent belief that the vital principle was male. Today, we too are encouraged to believe that character and fortune are determined at the moment of conception – albeit with a matching contribution from the mother – and we forget too easily the soil in which that seed will germinate.

Better living standards mean that more children are likely to survive. The nineteenth-century population boom was the result. Childhood mortality fell – 39 per cent of deaths in England and Wales were

84

under the age of five in 1841, as against 1 per cent in 1999 – and parents found that they had more children to support. The need to regulate female fertility became increasingly urgent, and the birth rate began to fall towards the end of the nineteenth century. More care and attention could now be lavished on each child, and the first clear evidence of accelerated growth, earlier sexual maturity, increasing body size and increasing longevity dates from around 1870. And it was founded in the female body.

MEN ARE MODIFIED WOMEN

There could be no better demonstration of the inherent plasticity of our phenotype than the common origin of two sexes from an identical ground plan. Eugen Steinach was an Austrian experimentalist who gained international respect before the First World War for his groundbreaking work on the physiology of sex, and notoriety after the war for an operation which he claimed could reverse the ageing process. His early work showed that the physical and behavioural consequences of castration in rats could be prevented by implanting the testes elsewhere in the body, thus confirming that the gland releases sex hormones into the bloodstream. He also showed that the physical and behavioural characteristics of young male and female rats could be reversed by transplanting testes into the females and ovaries into the males. The transsexual animals took on the size and shape of the opposite sex, adopted the same pattern of timidity or aggression and engaged in futile attempts to mate with animals of their own sex.[1]

The genes in a fertilized egg are identical in the two sexes, save that males have one X chromosome instead of two. This is partnered by a weedy-looking Y, named for its appearance under the microscope. The Y chromosome is a male conversion kit and contains no essential information apart from the control elements which make the switch from female to male. The default mode being female, maleness is determined by genes on the Y chromosome which tell the gonads to produce testosterone while switching off development of the female reproductive system. The gravitational pull is nonetheless feminine, and masculinity is aptly described as 'a prolonged, uneasy and risky venture . . . a kind of struggle against inherent trends towards femaleness'.[2] Sex is an elaborate strategy for shuffling genes, and men are a convenient way of shaking the dice. Women could easily maintain a testosterone-free species if provided with a well-equipped sperm bank. Deep down, men know this.

NATURAL FERTILITY

The novelist David Lodge commented that literature is mostly about sex and not much about having children, and that life is the other way round. From a biological perspective, however, unproductive sex is a human trademark. Our big brains are responsible, for they only begin to approach adult size two years after birth, and more years are required before they can be operated with adult competence. Children need to be cared for over this extended period, and mothers need support while caring for them. A long-term partnership with the presumed biological father is a well-tested solution, and sex is the glue that holds it together. In this we differ from other species, for women ovulate in private and are sexually active even when pregnant. Men have bigger penises and smaller gonads than other primates, which tells us – as if we didn't already know – that human sex is about much more than reproduction.

Female fertility is surprisingly flexible. Anthropologists in the second half of the twentieth century found that hunter-gatherer groups were well able to balance their fertility against resources. Women of the !Kung San of the Kalahari, for example, generally had their first menstrual period at the age of sixteen, their first child at around the age of twenty and gave birth to five or six children at intervals of two to three years: two to three of these survived to adult life.[3]

A contrasting pattern of natural fertility was seen in twentieth-century Hutterites, a small community that survived the turmoil of religious and political upheaval in Europe at the start of the sixteenth century and eventually settled in North America. Hutterites live a simple, austere communal existence with their sights firmly fixed on Heaven. Birth control is anathema but modern medicine is not, and almost all of them marry. Only one divorce and four desertions were recorded between 1880 and 1950. Some (mostly men) left the colony,

Figure 14: Hutterite women and children at the Stand Off colony, Alberta, Canada, 1946.

but they generally came back into the fold. Their numbers multiplied, new colonies budded off by a process quaintly referred to as 'swarming', and many ended up in Canada.

The Hutterites are a delight to demographers, who see them as a natural breeding experiment. This was Malthus unchained, for famine was averted by their system of mutual support and ready access to unploughed land, and disease was kept to a minimum by a healthy lifestyle and the resources of modern medicine. In 1880, 47 per cent of Hutterites were under the age of fifteen, only 2.7 per cent were over sixty, and the ratio remained relatively unchanged until the 1950s; the low proportion of older people simply reflected a very high rate of reproduction. Hutterite women married as they approached the age of twenty, and 97 per cent of them gave birth – an extraordinarily high rate, given that up to 10 per cent of women are infertile in most societies. On average, they had 10.4 children each, with a maximum of around 16. A typical Hutterite mother had the theoretical possibility of 100 grandchildren and 1,000 great-grandchildren,[4] although a recent slow-down suggests that birth control is becoming acceptable.

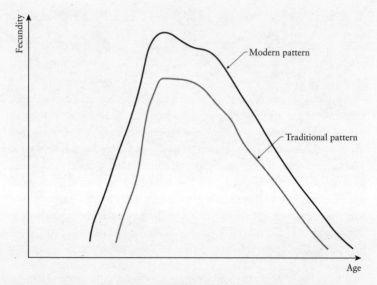

Figure 15: Previous checks on the fecundity of women included late puberty, prolonged breastfeeding, poor living conditions and earlier menopause. Based on Frisch.[5]

The !Kung and the Hutterites bracket the range of natural fertility, with a span of five to ten children in the absence of birth control. But why were the !Kung so much less fertile? Their reproductive lifespan was reduced by late puberty and early menopause, a difference equivalent to two fewer pregnancies (figure 15), but the main reason for the difference between !Kung San and Hutterites appears to lie in the spacing between their pregnancies, and we will come back to this in a moment.

Other communities fall between these extremes. The Yanomama Indians of Venezuela, another much-studied group, have a total fertility rate of about 8. This high rate – possibly related to improved nutrition following their discovery of the banana – is balanced by selective infanticide of female babies. In contrast, premodern or severely deprived modern communities required a high birth rate in order to balance high infant mortality. In 1940, the Muslim population of Palestine had a birth rate not far behind that of the Hutterites, for example, but 43 per cent of the Palestinian babies died young, as against 9 per cent of the Hutterites.[6]

Female fertility has been honed by natural selection to offer the most efficient balance between resources and environment. A woman who is worn out by repeated pregnancy cannot raise the optimum number of viable children, and natural selection will weight the scales accordingly. Ironically, the *BRCA 1/2* genes, notorious for predisposing women to breast and ovarian cancer, also appear to increase reproductive success. Women in the Utah Population Database who were born before 1930 and carried these mutations had more children (on average 6.2 vs 4.2), shorter birth intervals and a longer child-bearing period than those who did not, but an 85 per cent greater mortality in post-reproductive life. The reason for their increased fertility is unclear,[7] but this finding, if confirmed, could explain the persistence of a lethal gene in the population and would be an example of *antagonistic pleiotropy*, a phenomenon whereby genes which enhance evolutionary fitness in early life confer a corresponding disadvantage in later life.

A woman who adjusts her reproductive performance to her environment will produce more children in times of abundance and fewer in times of dearth. The relation between fertility and the flow of food energy was emphasized by the scientist Rose Frisch, who made her name in the 1970s by linking a woman's fertility to the amount of fat in her body. She later deduced the existence of a 'fat hormone' which interacts with the menstrual cycle, long before leptin was discovered in 1994. Her work on puberty, based on analysis of growth records, suggested that menstruation begins when a critical level of body fat has been reached; it would certainly make biological sense to delay ovulation until sufficient energy stores are in place to support a pregnancy. In pursuit of this elusive threshold, Frisch went on to note that women in hard training – runners and ballet dancers, for example – stop menstruating when their fat stores fall below a critical level, which she estimated at around 17 per cent of body mass. Oestrogen provides a link between energy stores and the reproductive cycle, but Peter Ellison, a more recent professor at Harvard, believes that the body's 'decision' to trigger puberty probably relates to integrated signals of growth rather than to the single cue of fat deposition.[8] Whatever the mechanism, female reproductive capacity is tailored to its environment by evolution and social custom, and so is the phenotype of their children.

CHILDBIRTH

Childbirth is far more dangerous for human mothers than for any other species. The distance that modern societies have travelled in this respect was shown when WHO estimated in the 1990s that the chances of death in childbirth ranged from 1:8,000 for a fifteen-year-old girl in western Europe to 1:8 in Gambia. In previous centuries women everywhere experienced the same risk of death in childbirth as they do in poorer parts of Africa today.

The voices of mothers are rarely heard in the historical record. An exception, entitled *Maternity: Letters from Working-Women*, was published by the UK Women's Co-operative Guild in 1915. At times almost unbearably moving, this chronicles without self-pity the struggles of women who attempted to raise a family on an average income of 20 shillings a week. 'The mother wonders what she has to live for,' says one: 'if there is another baby coming she hopes it will be dead when it is born.' Another writes, 'Many a time I have sat in daddy's big chair, a baby two and a half years old at my back, one sixteen months and one [of] one month on my knees, and cried for very weariness and hopelessness.' 'I don't really believe the children (with the exception of the oldest boy) have suffered much, only they might have been so much stronger, bigger, and better if I had been able to have better food and more rest.' 'No one but mothers who have gone through the ordeal of pregnancy half starved, to finally bring a child into the world to live a living death for nine months, can understand what it means . . .' Of the 348 mothers who contributed, 42.4 per cent had stillbirths or miscarriages and 21.5 per cent of pregnancies ended like this. Of 1,396 live births, 8.7 per cent failed to reach their first birthday.[9]

Obstructed labour, often associated with rickets, was a much-feared complication in Victorian times and provided a stimulus to the introduction of caesarean section. Rickets is due to lack of exposure to sunlight (common in industrial cities of the past) plus inadequate diet and resulted in the softening of the pelvic bones, which warped

ELEVEN CHILDREN BORN, ALL LIVING.   FATHER A FISH-HAWKER.
This family is not connected with the Women's Co-operative Guild.

FIFTEEN CHILDREN, FOUR LIVING.   FATHER AN IRON-MOULDER.
The family is not connected with the Women's Co-operative Guild.

Figure 16: Illustrations from *Maternity: Letters from Working-Women* (1915). Top: the woman shown here – incredibly – raised eleven children and dressed them smartly for their photograph. Bottom: This mother gave birth to fifteen children, eleven of whom are represented by gaps in the line-up.

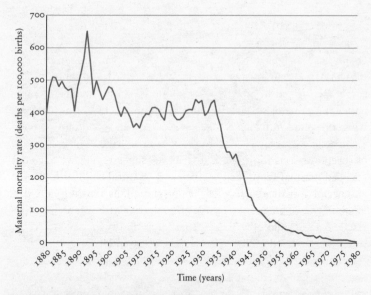

Figure 17: Maternal mortality in childbirth, Britain, 1880–1980.[10]

in a way that obstructed a baby's head and meant a fearful death for the mother. I was lucky enough to have Malcolm Potts, a great expert in human reproduction, as my college tutor. He witnessed an obstructed labour in a medical mission station in rural India and watched in horror as the doctor, a deeply religious man, reached for a long-obsolete device used in Victorian times to crush the foetal head. 'What chance does a second baby have in Bihar?' said the missionary by way of explanation. The introduction of forceps delivery and caesarean section alleviated the horrors of obstructed labour.

This apart, the 'Four Horsemen' of maternal death were infection, haemorrhage, convulsions and illegal abortion,[11] and the precipitous decline in maternal deaths after 1935 shown in figure 17 was associated with the introduction of effective antibiotics and drugs which prevented uncontrolled haemorrhage. Effective contraception and legalized abortion saved women from the septic knitting needles of back-street abortionists.

THE FRUIT OF THE APPLE

People have struggled to find an evolutionary explanation for the fact that humans are uniquely inefficient in giving birth. An international survey performed in 2012 suggested that the best outcome of pregnancy (in terms of survival of both mother and child) was achieved when one child in five is delivered by caesarean section.[12] Although fashions in caesarean section vary and obstructed labour is only one of several reasons for doing it, the survey suggests that we have not attained optimal reproductive efficiency. 'Natural childbirth' (in the absence of a medical safety net) is no solution, as shown by the dismal outcome of pregnancy – three times the first-year infant mortality rate and a 100-fold increase in maternal mortality – in an American sect which rejected all forms of medical intervention.[13]

Adverse social circumstances have a major influence upon the outcome of pregnancy, and it is not surprising that working-class mothers in London ran into so much difficulty a century ago. Poor diet, stunted growth, chronic or recurrent infection and lack of medical attention undoubtedly contributed to their misery. We do, however, need to ask why today's healthy and well-nourished young women should require surgical assistance when every circumstance might seem to favour a straightforward delivery.

The Bible relates that Eve is punished for her transgression, the punishment being that 'I will greatly multiply thy sorrow and thy conception; in sorrow thou shalt bring forth children.' The standard explanation for Eve's Curse is known as the Obstetric Dilemma. Briefly stated, this argues that our upright posture obliges mothers to have a narrow pelvis, whereas the need for a big brain obliges the baby to have a big head. The fit between the two is tighter than in almost any other species, and childbirth is only possible because the foetal skull compresses under pressure and the mother produces a hormone which softens her pelvic outlet. In the absence of medical assistance, a foetus that cannot pass through its mother's birth canal is condemned to die. So too is the mother. Why has the invisible hand of natural selection failed to solve such an obvious problem? One point to note is that (whatever your girth) the hip joints themselves are only a hand's-breadth apart. This minimizes side-to-side movement as we walk, and helps us to run efficiently. It has been argued on theoretical grounds that a wider spacing would not be much of a disadvantage, for the female pelvis is wider than the male, and a slight waddle might seem a small price to pay for safer and easier pregnancy. Conversely, the brain is only 30 per cent of its adult size at birth, and even a small reduction would greatly ease its passage into life. Since evolution did not select for either alternative, we must widen our search for a solution to the Dilemma.

One is the cliff-edge model.[14] Obstructed labour affects some 3–6 per cent of pregnancies worldwide, arguably because maternal genes determine the size of the pelvis, whereas genes from the father influence the size of the foetal head. Since a smaller head increases the mother's chance of surviving pregnancy whereas a bigger head favours the foetus, this creates a potential conflict of interest. We may picture two bell-shaped curves edging closer together: the closer the fit, the more viable the baby, but only up to a 'cliff edge', at which disaster supervenes. The authors argue that routine use of caesarean section acts against natural selection, and will cause a 10–20 per cent increase per generation in the proportion of babies that cannot be delivered naturally.

It is an intriguing proposal, but open to debate: human childbirth does not lend itself to simple conclusions. Where, for example, is the evidence that the circumference of a baby's head is a critical determinant of its survival after birth? Nor is the size of the baby unrelated to the size of the mother, for *maternal constraint* comes into it. This was famously demonstrated by inseminating Shetland mares with Shire stallions, and Shire mares with Shetland stallions. Mercifully for the Shetland mares, offspring size is strongly influenced by the size of the mother, and they were able to give birth successfully.[15] Maternal constraint seems to explain why first-born children are on average 200 g lighter at birth than their siblings, and why the birth weight of half-siblings correlates more strongly with the size of the mother than that of the two fathers. Equally, birth weight in surrogate pregnancy is influenced more by the size of the surrogate mother than that of the woman who donated the egg.

The Obstetric Dilemma is far from solved. The foetal quest to grow

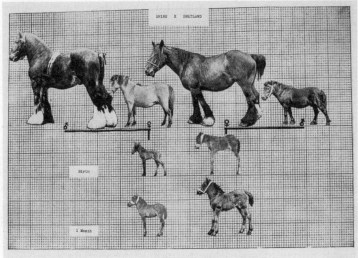

Parents and offspring of reciprocal Shetland-Shire crosses.

Figure 18: Maternal constraint: the foal resulting from a cross between a Shire stallion and a Shetland mare (left) is considerably smaller than the foal of a Shire mare and a Shetland stallion.

rapidly and the maternal quest to give birth safely may pull in opposite directions, but the best outcome for both is a healthy infant delivered at term. Given the complex nature of the trade-offs involved, it is perhaps not surprising that the quest for an optimal outcome might sometimes stray over a cliff edge. The inference that routine caesarean section might change the future child-bearing capacity of our species seems unduly simplistic, however, and any solution to the Dilemma must allow for the fact that the human phenotype is changing so rapidly.

The outstanding characteristic of human pregnancy is flexibility of means in achieving its outcome. Mothers have carried babies successfully through feast and famine since time began, enduring every imaginable variety of hardship along the way, and their ability to adjust to surrounding conditions while preparing a child for the world it is about to enter is a remarkable example of phenotypic plasticity. A pregnancy can only be thought of as normal in the context of the environment in which it unfolds, and nothing in our evolution could have prepared us for the world we live in now.

THE RATCHET

James Joyce said that history is a nightmare from which he was trying to awake. Childbirth certainly was a nightmare for mother and child in the past and has only become relatively safe within living memory. Our phenotype reflects the world we live in, and both mothers and children have been changing over several generations. A ratchet effect largely accounts for this, for taller mothers have bigger babies, and bigger babies grow taller. James Tanner, the father of modern growth studies, showed that adult height increased at a rate of around 1 cm per decade between 1880 and 1950 in the USA and four European countries, and that average birth weight increases by around 200 g for every 5 cm of maternal height.[16] Taller mothers largely account for the increasing trend in birth weight.

Adjustment for height shows that undernourished Victorian women were able to produce babies of near-normal birth weight by today's standards. Evolution clearly made it possible for hungry mothers to maximize the chances of the next generation under the most adverse of circumstances. What evolution could not possibly have prepared mother and baby for, however, were the consequences of a chronic excess of food. An oversupply of glucose occurs in the babies of mothers with poorly controlled diabetes, for example, and these are not only large at birth but more likely to gain weight in later life. A similar effect can be seen in the children of mothers who are considerably overweight, or who gain too much in pregnancy. The likely reason is that the foetus adjusts to an oversupply of nutrients (glucose in the case of diabetes), thus creating a lasting predisposition in later life. Over-nourished motherhood may thus, by a less welcome ratchet effect, transmit obesity to the next generation.[17]

The children of well-nourished mothers grow faster and reach sexual maturity earlier. Data from Oslo show that average age at first menstruation fell from 16.5 to 12.5 years between the nineteenth and twentieth centuries, and that a girl's first period came a week earlier for every calendar year of birth.[18] This was associated with increasing height, an exaggerated pubertal growth spurt and an easily recognizable change in our physical proportions, and it gave birth to a new phenomenon: adolescence.

PUBERTY

Achilles was the nonpareil of Greek heroes. As a youth, he was offered the alternatives of long life and happiness or a short life and undying fame. He opted for the latter. Prophecy said that the Greeks would be unable to conquer Troy without him, but that he himself would not return. Thetis, his divine mother, tried to evade this fate by dressing him as a girl and packing him off to the court of King Lycomedes of Skyros, an island far out in the Aegean. Once there, he took advantage of his situation to father a son upon Deidamia, the king's daughter, apparently without this coming to her father's attention. Odysseus came looking for him, posing as a trader, and produced a display of trinkets for the maidens to admire; a spear and shield were placed casually alongside. Achilles alone found these of interest and betrayed himself by grabbing the weapons when Odysseus caused the alarm to be sounded and the real ladies fled.

The biological interest in this fable is that the great warrior (although evidently potent) had no beard, and that his voice had not as yet broken. We should not place undue reliance upon a legend, but puberty undoubtedly started later then than now. The emperor Augustus had his first shave when he was twenty-three, and the shaving ceremony that welcomed Roman citizens to manhood generally took place at between twenty-one and twenty-three years (they presumably sported designer stubble before then).

At puberty, the bones of the female face stop growing, whereas continued growth of the facial bones gives men craggier features and boxier jaws. This gives women a more child-like (paedomorphic) appearance, with smaller, oval and more symmetrical faces. Their cheekbones are thrown into greater prominence, and their eyes appear larger. Most boys are far from beautiful at the onset of puberty, but there are striking exceptions. Teenage boys played female parts in

Shakespeare's plays, and Oscar Wilde suggested that the 'Mr WH' addressed so passionately in the Sonnets was one. Adolescent youths were known as ephebes in ancient Greece, and no stigma was attached to the romantic interest they awakened in older men.

The ancient Greeks divided male life into seven periods, or hebdomads, corresponding in Latin translation to *puerulus*, *puer*, *adolescens*, *juvenis*, *junior*, *vir* and *senex*, a succession famously adopted by Shakespeare. The first period ended when you shed your milk teeth, the second when boys emitted semen; adolescence ended when your beard had grown (a landmark still reflected in our celebration of the twenty-first birthday); men were considered ready for marriage at twenty-eight; by thirty-five they were mature in judgement, from forty-two to fifty-six they attained their prime, after which they became Shakespeare's 'lean and slippered pantaloon', feeble in mind and body. By seventy this 'strange eventful history' terminated in second childishness and mere oblivion. It would be wrong to read too much into these ancient categories, but they do suggest that maturity came later and senescence earlier than now.

Growth acceleration over the past century means that children now enter puberty up to four years earlier. Hormones released at puberty unleash a secondary growth spurt, which is ended by fusion of the growth plates in our long bones. The children of the upper classes reached this point earlier in previous centuries, and sons of aristocratic parents attending the Carlschule in Stuttgart from 1772 to 1794 were nearly 7 cm taller than sons of bourgeois parents by age fifteen, despite the same school diet. This difference had almost vanished when the pupils were measured again at the age of twenty-one, suggesting that middle-class boys entered puberty later but caught up with the aristocrats.[19] Well-to-do adults were not much shorter than us at the beginning of the nineteenth century; Rushworth, the doltish landowner in Jane Austen's *Mansfield Park*, wonders out loud why women should show any interest in a rival who was less than 5 feet 9 inches (175 cm) in height.

Earlier puberty became a headache for choir masters. The boys who formed J. S. Bach's choir in Leipzig from 1740 to 1745 generally experienced a break in their voice at around sixteen to seventeen years, although some remained altos or sopranos to the age of nineteen or twenty. These highly trained voices were lost at an earlier age as time went by, and broke some three and a half to four years sooner in 1959 than in Bach's time.[20] The vocal cords are folds embedded in the larynx that descend and lengthen in pubertal boys due to enlargement of the cartilage that forms the Adam's apple. The pitch of a voice depends upon their length and tension and deepens as the cords thicken in response to testosterone. The resulting increase in bulk creates the same increase in resonance as the copper filament wound around the bass strings on a piano.

Increasing size appears to have affected the adult singing voice. The Gregorian chant was pitched in the tenor range; the tenor, as the name indicates, was the singer who 'held' the note. This fashion was not restricted to Europe, for traditional singing styles around the world place a strong emphasis on the higher register, with little role for baritones or basses. The bass voice did not find a role until the Flemish school of singing became popular around 1450; the Italian courts embraced the new style but were obliged to import Flemish singers since their own could not offer the same range. Deeper registers did not come into wider use until the nineteenth century. Fashion undoubtedly came into this, but it seems likely that increasing body size enlarged the male larynx, thus extending the range of the human voice.

Past fashions favoured the higher ranges, and the introduction of female sopranos in the second half of the sixteenth century was a significant development in the history of singing. Even so, the superstars of the time were the castrati – boys castrated before puberty for the sake of their singing voice. Their voice is lost for ever, despite some poor recordings at the start of the twentieth century, but two centuries of music enthusiasts rejoiced in the sound they produced. Consider, for example, the performance of Pacchierotti in Forli in 1776. His supreme aria – which told of a son preparing to sacrifice himself for his father – reduced the audience to tears. As he approached his climax, the orchestra faltered and fell silent. The affronted singer advanced front stage to demand an explanation and found that the conductor was too overcome with emotion to continue.[21]

The castrati were generally emasculated between the ages of seven and twelve years after a faint induced by pressure on the carotid

Figure 19: Pacchierotti's skeleton was exhumed recently for scientific investigation. He was 191 cm tall, with advanced osteoporosis and highly developed respiratory muscles.[22]

artery. Many came from desperately poor backgrounds and were volunteered by their parents in the hope of fame and fortune.

All too often this sacrifice was in vain, since only around 10 per cent went on to become professional singers. Real success was only possible for the most gifted, and only then after endless hours of practice. The castrati combined the advantages of supple pre-pubertal vocal cords with an adult-sized chest and exquisite respiratory control. Although ornamentation and affectation were central to their repertoire, fame did not depend upon hitting the high notes, but upon their range and fluency, together with the colour and expression they could infuse into those lost voices.

Puberty is commonly equated with the first menstrual period or emission of sperm, but these are simply milestones in a hormonal reconfiguration of the phenotype that takes years to complete. This begins around the age of eight, before which boys and girls develop in much the same way. Their skeletal growth and body composition diverge thereafter in response to sex steroids from the adrenal cortex, a phenomenon known as *adrenarche*. The growth spurt begins earlier in girls but ends sooner, which is why they are shorter. As the ovaries kick in with oestrogens, the pelvis widens, and the pelvic brim splays to provide added mechanical support when walking. Girls lay down more fatty tissue, their breasts bud, and their sexuality flowers. Boys have a later but more sustained acceleration in growth, which leaves them taller, broader in the shoulder and relatively longer in the leg. Their faces get craggier, they lay down more muscle relative to fat, and their brains (according to some) work differently.

A recent review of twenty-two subsistence-based traditional societies found that the growth spurt preceding puberty came much later than in modern times and ranged from ten to thirteen and a half years as against our typical age of eight. Menstruation followed, typically after a gap of four years.[23] The Gainj people of Papua New Guinea were outliers in this survey; for them, puberty came around the age of eighteen, and their first pregnancy at around the age of twenty. These were short people who grew slowly and ate a spare diet – no doubt representative of many of our ancestors.

The children of the affluent mature earlier, presumably for nutritional reasons. Since the ovulatory cycle takes time to become fully established, teenage girls have more anovulatory cycles – menstruation without ovulation – than adults. The chances of pregnancy increase from about 14 per cent per cycle for a modern adolescent girl having unprotected sex to around 25 per cent in a woman in her mid-twenties.[24] Girls were married off early in past societies, partly as a guarantee of virginity, and girls of high social status were as fertile then as adolescent girls today. On 28 January 1457, Margaret Beaufort, wife of Edmund Tudor, gave birth to the future King Henry VII at the age of thirteen. The delivery was traumatic, and she did not conceive again despite two further marriages.

One anomalous feature of human puberty is that sexual characteristics appear in advance of fertility, whereas other primates only

develop breasts when pregnant. Women from the Bundi people of
Papua New Guinea did not menstruate until eighteen to twenty years
of age under traditional conditions, and the mismatch between the
early appearance of sexual features and the late development of full
fertility might – or so it has been suggested – have enabled Bundi girls
to gain sexual experience and form bonds with male partners at low
risk of pregnancy.[25] Sex before full fertility may not have been uncommon in previous generations.

The tragic history of Catherine Howard throws an interesting light
on this. Catherine was born to impoverished aristocrats in the early
1520s – she was not important enough for her date of birth to be
recorded – and packed off to live with her grandmother, the dowager
duchess of Norfolk. Later, she shared a dormitory in Lambeth Palace
with other teenage girls. No one bothered to keep an eye on them,
and male visitors were frequently admitted. Catherine engaged in
heavy petting with her music tutor at around the age of fifteen, and a
gentleman called Francis Dereham later took his place in her dormitory. By her own account, 'finally he lay with me naked and used me
in such sort as a man doth his wife many and sundry times but how
often I know not'. She went on to become a hanger-on at the royal
court and was attracted to Thomas Culpeper, a royal favourite,
before she had the misfortune to catch the eye of Henry VIII himself.
She was perhaps seventeen when she became his fifth wife on 28 July
1540 – the day that Thomas Cromwell was executed. It was not a
good omen. Her reckless affair with Culpeper caught up with her,
and she was executed on 13 February 1542. Late puberty and its
associated subfertility might perhaps account for the casual licence of
the girls in the dormitory and their apparent low risk of pregnancy.

BIOLOGICAL CONSEQUENCES OF
MANAGED REPRODUCTION

Managed reproduction is an essential feature of modern life and
could potentially affect the phenotype of future generations. *In vitro*
fertilization (IVF) is an extreme example of interference with natural
selection, for it allows otherwise infertile women to bear children,

while introducing the potential for gender selection or genetic manipulation. Some forms of male infertility can be treated by direct injection of a sperm into an egg, a technique responsible for the birth of 2.5 million children each year. Not unexpectedly, the sons of fathers with impaired spermatogenesis are more likely to be infertile themselves, which means that future generations could see the emergence of male lines which cannot propagate without the help of a laboratory.[26]

Meanwhile, women who conceive naturally now do so later in life. In 1968, for example, 75 per cent of births were to mothers under the age of thirty, as against 40 per cent in 2013. Despite aspirations for natural childbirth, delivery is treated as a medical procedure, up to a third of deliveries are by caesarean section, breastfeeding is an option rather than a necessity, and the infant will be exposed to an environment abounding in calories but depleted of challenges to its immune system. Babies born by caesarean section have a higher risk of type 1 diabetes, for example, possibly because they were not exposed to the normal microbial flora of the birth canal.

In past societies, childbirth could only be limited by delaying marriage – Malthus's 'prudential restraint'. Increasing prosperity then made it possible for people in the middle of the twentieth century to marry earlier than at any period before or since. Parental age has increased steadily since then, and the risks of miscarriage, pre-term birth, low birth weight and stillbirth rise with maternal age. Around 9 per cent of intended pregnancies in women aged twenty to twenty-four end in spontaneous abortion, for example, as against 20 per cent for ages thirty-five to thirty-nine, and 41 per cent for ages forty to forty-four. Children born to older mothers have an increased risk of Alzheimer's disease, hypertension and some forms of cancer.[27] Chromosomal abnormalities are also more common, and the risk of Down's syndrome rises exponentially above the age of forty to approach 10 per cent by the age of fifty.

Men are sperm factories, and the possibility of transcription errors leading to mutation is greatly magnified by the astronomical rate of cell division in the testis. Sperm undergo around 150 germ-line replications by the age of twenty, rising to 610 by the age of forty, and the risk of a new mutation doubles for each 16.5-year increase in the age of the father. Noting this, the geneticist J. B. S. Haldane proposed that the rate of genetic mutation in sperm has been one of the drivers of natural selection. Adverse consequences of increasing paternal age include an increasing risk of schizophrenia, of autism spectrum disorders[28] and of a variety of rare genetic conditions.[29] These risks should not be exaggerated, for older men routinely father healthy children, but sperm banks set a prudential upper age of forty years for prospective donors.[30]

High paternal age is not a new phenomenon. In Iceland, for example, the mean paternal age at conception was thirty-five between 1650 and 1950, dropped to twenty-eight in the post-war period and moved back into the thirties in the twenty-first century. The earlier pattern reflected a rural community in which men did not marry until they had a farm of their own; late marriage was common in Ireland for the same reason. Greater paternal age is not necessarily a disadvantage, however. Telomeres are protective sequences of DNA which seal off the ends of chromosomes and shorten with each cycle of cell replication; shorter telomere length is a marker of ageing. In contrast to other dividing tissues, sperm have telomeres that lengthen with age, and this feature is passed on to their offspring. A multigenerational study in the Philippines confirmed that children of older fathers have longer telomeres. This effect is reinforced by the age of the paternal grandfather (but not the maternal grandfather) at the time of the father's birth. Telomere length is associated with increased life expectancy and a lower risk of arterial disease (but a higher risk of cancer) in later life. Since increased telomere length is associated with older fathers, the authors propose that it is a cue to the safety and stability of the environment into which the child will be born. Augmented telomere length, passed on from generation to generation, could potentially provide a mechanism for increasing longevity.[31]

Despite the evident disadvantages of later pregnancy, the human phenotype – and the society that fosters it – is changing so rapidly that the chronological benefit of later birth could outweigh the biological disadvantage of maternal age. It has, for example, been argued that a female child born to a Swedish woman of twenty in 1980 would have done less well than a child born to that same woman in 2000 at the age of forty. According to this argument, the biological disadvantages of delayed motherhood would be outweighed by the societal trend towards increasing height, health, intelligence and longevity, not to mention greater educational opportunity. This hypothetical comparison has its limits, for cross-sectional analysis shows, not unexpectedly, that those with very young or very old mothers generally do worse. The benefits peak for mothers who give birth in their thirties: their daughters are taller, and their academic attainment greater, than in other age groups. The study concluded that the positive time trend for the population as a whole has cancelled out the potential disadvantage of rising maternal age, although not for the oldest mothers.[32]

MENOPAUSE

In premodern times women reached peak fertility around the age of twenty, by which time some 60 per cent of married women had already given birth. Other things being equal, they went on to produce a baby every second year into their early thirties, falling to one in every three after the age of forty and dwindling to zero by the age of fifty. Why should this be?

A woman is born with all the eggs (ovarian follicles) she will have. The egg which produced me was one of 2 million or so formed when my mother was in my grandmother's womb, 105 years ago. Follicles die off rapidly, so my mother was down to perhaps 300–400,000 when she began to menstruate. Fertility ceases with ovulation, but the menopause is preceded by years of subfertility characterized by anovulatory cycles, declining levels of oestrogen and irregular bleeding. The evolutionary benefits of the menopause seem clear, for (biologically speaking) twenty years of fertility are sufficient for a woman to produce the children she needs, and her remaining time is better spent helping them to raise children of their own.

One-third of a modern woman's life is post-menopausal. Early menopause is associated with malnutrition or poor health, and women in poorer countries enter menopause earlier than those in an affluent environment. Smokers reach menopause one to two years earlier, and there are strong associations between early menopause and poor socio-economic status. Improved socio-economic circumstances probably explain why the age of menopause is still increasing in affluent parts of the world, with a median age of fifty-four in Europe.[33] Later menopause is associated with social advantage, good health, increased longevity, a reduced risk of cardiovascular disease, a reduced risk of osteoporosis and delayed decline in intellectual function. Conversely, it carries an increased risk of breast, uterine and ovarian cancers.

THE SOCIAL RATCHET

The first phase of the phenotypic transition was from around 1870 to 1950, and its effects were mainly due to the catch-up effect of rising prosperity among the socially disadvantaged. Size is channelled through the body of the mother, and both pelvis and foetus have grown steadily bigger. In periods of prosperity, daughters outgrow their mothers, become fertile earlier, and produce bigger babies which turn into taller women with a wider pelvis. The ratchet can also operate in the opposite direction, for as UNICEF pointed out in 1998 'young girls who grow poorly become stunted women and are more likely to give birth to low birth-weight babies. If these infants are girls, they are likely to continue the cycle by being stunted in adulthood and so on.' Maternal weight also comes into the equation, and 10–20 g is added to the weight of the child for every additional 100 g in the weight of the mother. As a result, the obesity epidemic has caused this particular scourge to be passed on from one generation to the next.

This completes our brief circuit of a woman's reproductive life. Several things stand out. One is that the familiar milestones are so dependent upon the right sequence of complicated events that you can only wonder how they happen at all. Another is that pregnancy is a dynamic situation, and that both mother and baby have a remarkable ability to adapt. The reproductive career of a woman can be influenced by intergenerational signals passed on by her mother, by signals exchanged with her foetus, and by her own state of health and nutrition. Social advantage or disadvantage carry over from one generation to the next, a legacy that has proved hard to eliminate in even the most egalitarian of societies. Superimposed upon these are social influences such as age at marriage and pharmaceutical pseudo-pregnancy induced by the contraceptive pill. The regulation of female fertility has done more to promote the equality of the sexes than anything else in history, and nowhere else have we intervened so directly to counterbalance our escape from natural selection. The matrix is where the phenotype is forged, and its influence lasts for a lifetime.

7

Life before Birth

The most exciting period of our existence has ended by the time we are born, for the single cell we came from divided some forty-two times before we saw the light of day; another five cycles would in theory be enough to generate all the cells in the adult body. All living things are vulnerable during periods of rapid growth, and the Victorians were well aware that a mother's health and behaviour could affect her baby. They were also familiar with the cascade of poverty whereby an impoverished mother produced stunted offspring who gravitated towards the lowest stratum of society. They called this 'the residuum', and its inhabitants were considered to be virtually beyond the reach of science, religion or charity. Strangely enough, the importance of this formative period in the womb was overlooked for much of the twentieth century.

Access to cheap gin caused an outbreak of alcohol addiction in eighteenth-century London, memorably recorded by William Hogarth in *Gin Lane* (figure 20). This outbreak gave rise to widespread concern, and a committee appointed in 1735 by magistrates in Middlesex commented that 'unhappy mothers habituate themselves to these distilled liquors, whose children are born weak and sickly, and often look shrivel'd and old as though they had numbered many years'.[1] Alcohol was seen as a leading cause of intergenerational degeneration, and the physician W. C. Sullivan said in 1899 that:

> We are familiar with the fact . . . that the chronic alcoholism of one or both parents frequently appears as the first moment in the degenerative career of a family; that it represents a state of artificial degradation of the organism, capable of transmission in augmented force to the

Figure 20: A detail from William Hogarth's *Gin Lane*.

descendants, and culminating in some four generations in the extinction of the stock.[2]

John William Ballantyne, a leading authority of the day, published two volumes in 1904 which summarized the current state of knowledge concerning growth and health of the foetus. He listed, among other things, the harmful effects of alcohol, tobacco, opium, lead, mercury and chloroform, plus numerous examples of infections that can be passed from mother to child.[3]

Experimental evidence had confirmed these observations, and the danger of alcohol to the next generation is mentioned in many biology textbooks. Aldous Huxley used this knowledge when he wrote *Brave New World*, published in 1932. Natural birth has long been superseded in this vision of the future. Women who volunteer to become egg donors are well rewarded, their eggs are fertilized and processed in the laboratory and the foetus is maintained in a nutrient medium. The lower orders of society are produced in cloned batches generated by the mysterious Bokanovsky's Process, and graded doses of alcohol are used to impair the intelligence of mass-produced Gammas, Deltas and Epsilons. How strange, therefore, that the dangers of alcohol to the foetus were largely forgotten until the foetal-alcohol syndrome was rediscovered in the 1970s!

The foetus itself was virtually ignored. Shryock's magisterial *Development of Modern Medicine*, published in 1936, lists the achievements of public health in terms of declining maternal and neonatal mortality, but nowhere mentions the possibility that the life and health of the mother could affect the unborn child. He seems to have shared the prevailing belief that the foetus is a 'perfect parasite' safely insulated from the external world behind a placenta that could filter out infections or toxins.

All this was about to change. By the 1970s, the medical community had been forcibly reminded that infections, alcohol, smoking, poisons, drugs and nuclear radiation could affect the developing foetus. Why had it taken so long for these risks to be recognized or rediscovered? One reason is professional, for obstetrics was now a surgical speciality which focused its attention upon the technique of delivery rather than upon the outcome. Viable babies left the delivery suites in increasing numbers, but who was to look after them? The obstetrician's responsibility ended with delivery, paediatricians rarely ventured into maternity hospitals, and care of the newborn was generally left to the midwives. My wife – the smaller of twins – was born in the 1950s at around twenty-eight weeks of gestation; she weighed 900 g. A doctor took her parents aside and told them that she was more likely to survive if they took her home and looked after her themselves. The advice was doubly fortunate, for hospitals then treated premature infants with high doses of oxygen that could cause blindness. Her parents (both chemists) took their children away, constructed their own incubator and fed them by pipette. Neonatal medicine had yet to be recognized as a speciality in its own right, and we can only speculate as to the number of newborn children who paid the price for fifty years of medical complacency.

THE AWAKENING

Roger Bacon, a medieval monk, said that there are four grounds of ignorance: 'trust in inadequate authority, the force of custom, the opinion of the inexperienced crowd, and the hiding of one's own ignorance with a parade of superficial wisdom'. Not to be outdone, modern science has added two more: training in the wrong speciality, and failing to read the work of your predecessors. Never was this more strikingly demonstrated than in the odd story of the impregnable foetus.

A series of events shook this complacency. The first was a major outbreak of rubella ('German measles') in Australia in 1940. Protected by its isolation – the long sea voyage had the same effect as quarantine – Australia had not been exposed to the virus since 1925. It now swept through a country which was mobilizing for war, and where young people were crowded into camps and barracks. A year or so later the eye surgeon Norman Gregg realized that infants with an unfamiliar variant of congenital cataract were lining up in his outpatient clinic. Those affected were sickly and stunted, and mental retardation was common. The link to maternal rubella was suggested by two mothers discussing their pregnancies in his waiting room. It took courage for Gregg to suggest that a 'harmless' virus could cause congenital malformations such as these: the medical wisdom of the day maintained that maternal infection was unable to cross the placenta.[4]

Another example of foetal vulnerability resulted from events in Holland in 1944. The liberation of north-western Holland (which includes Amsterdam) seemed imminent, but the occupation period was extended by more than six months when British troops failed to capture the bridge at Arnhem. The Dutch mounted a railway strike in support of the Allies, and the occupying forces responded by cutting off food supplies. The embargo was lifted in November 1944, but unusually severe winter conditions made it impossible to supply the region by canals and waterways. The food ration fell from 1,800 calories per day to 1,000 and dropped to 400–800 between December 1944 and April 1945.

A study published in 1947 noted that babies born during the famine were some 200 g lighter at birth, but that the weight deficit was soon regained post-natally; the possibility of long-term consequences does not seem to have been considered.[5] Many years later, American investigators saw the famine as an opportunity to test the effects of foetal malnutrition upon development of the brain, and their findings, published in 1975, concluded that what they called mental competence at nineteen years of age had not been affected,[6] although adverse effects would later be suspected when survivors reached their fifties. The studies that followed showed that mothers who experience famine late in pregnancy give birth to undersized babies who regain weight on an adequate diet – and are less likely than controls to suffer from obesity in later life. Conversely, mothers who faced starvation in early (but not late) pregnancy had normal-weight babies who were predisposed to adult obesity. Other delayed consequences included diabetes, heart disease and schizophrenia.

On Christmas Day 1956, a baby girl was born without ears in Stolberg, Germany. The father, a company employee, had given his wife samples of a new treatment for morning sickness. Thalidomide was considered safe enough to sell over the counter, and 3,049 German children were born with birth defects, often horrific, before it was taken off the market. The drug caused multiple defects, especially in developing limbs, and 10,000 children were affected worldwide; another 8,000 may have perished before birth. As so often happens, the company went into denial, incomplete information was supplied (thalidomide was marketed as a safe sleeping tablet in Japan for a year after it had been withdrawn in Germany), and the regulators dithered; a press campaign was needed before action was taken.[7]

Meanwhile, the foetal-alcohol syndrome described by Middlesex magistrates in 1735 was rediscovered in 1971, and the *British Medical Journal* commented in 1973 that 'no reasonable doubt now remains' as to the harmful effects of smoking in pregnancy. Hazards included growth delay, prematurity, perinatal death and possible intellectual impairment. No one recalled that Ballantyne had written seventy years earlier that 'there seems to be no shadow of doubt that there is a very large infantile mortality in postnatal life among the offspring of women workers in tobacco'. Cumulative evidence of foetal vulnerability finally focused attention on the possibility that experience before birth might have lasting effects upon the phenotype of adults.

MY END IS IN MY BEGINNING

Anders Forsdahl was born to a district doctor in the Finnmark, the most northern county of Norway, and became a doctor in his turn from 1963 to 1974. Life was harsh in the far north at the start of the twentieth century, and 14 per cent of children died in the first year of life as against 7 per cent in the rest of Norway. Although this no longer applied when Forsdahl picked up his stethoscope, Finnmark's mortality from cardiovascular disease was 25 per cent higher than in other parts of Norway. Forsdahl began to wonder if children born into poverty were more prone to heart disease in later life, and he went on to show an impressive statistical correlation between the two. Past conditions in northern Norway, as he pointed out, had been 'bad enough to be called catastrophic'. Furthermore, neighbouring Finland, which had been equally hard hit, was experiencing a major epidemic of coronary disease as he wrote. Could coronary risk be a legacy of childhood deprivation? If so, he suggested that heart disease was about to soar in newly affluent parts of the world and would fall in countries that already enjoyed affluence. Both predictions were amply confirmed. Even so, his views were heresy at a time when medical dogma maintained that coronary disease affected the middle classes and was due to executive stress and a high cholesterol intake.[8]

David Barker (1938–2013), a British paediatrician turned epidemiologist, entered the debate. According to established belief, heart disease in the UK should have concentrated in areas of middle-class affluence. Instead, it mapped to areas of long-standing social deprivation such as the industrial regions of south Wales, Lancashire and the north. What is more, this distribution could almost be superimposed upon a map of neonatal mortality in England and Wales for 1907–10. All this pointed to a link between maternal deprivation and heart disease, but how might he prove it? For this he needed survivors. Since low birth weight is another marker of maternal deprivation, Barker resolved to look for adults who had been underweight at birth. But where might he find birth records dating back fifty years or more? His team began a search through dusty archives up and down the country.

He was helped by the fact that at the start of the twentieth century the British Establishment had seen evidence of racial decline in a falling birth rate and in the poor physical condition of volunteers for the Boer War, nearly two-thirds of whom were unable to run a hundred yards while carrying a rifle. The medical officer for health for the county of Hertfordshire was in distinguished company when he commented that 'it is of national importance that the life of every infant be vigorously conserved'. No coincidence, therefore, that he appointed Ethel Margaret Burnside to supervise health and midwifery services in Hertfordshire in 1911. A tall woman with 'a very imposing presence, a penetrating voice and a dominant personality', she was not to be trifled with. While she reigned, midwives and health visitors kept meticulous records of the birth weight and early progress of every child in the county, right up until she retired in 1948.

Barker paid a hasty visit to the chief archivist of Hertfordshire when he became aware of this gold mine, only to be told that the records contained personal details and could not be consulted for another fifty years. By extraordinary chance, Barker's own family had been evacuated to the Hertfordshire village of Much Hadham during the Second World War. His sister was born there in 1943, and she too was on the register. This detail softened the heart of the archivist, who agreed to release the records on condition that a perfectly secure home could be found for them. Barker's University of Southampton did indeed have a secure vault (constructed to house the papers of the Duke of Wellington), and the treasure was duly transferred. Barker's research over the following years led him to the conclusion that

> as a group, people who are small at birth or during infancy remain biologically different throughout their lives. They have higher blood pressure and are more likely to develop type 2 diabetes. They have different patterns of blood lipids, reduced bone density, altered stress responses, thicker left ventricular walls, less elastic arteries and different hormonal profiles, and they are ageing more rapidly.[9]

Maternal deprivation could indeed have a lasting effect upon the phenotype.

Why might this be? Forsdahl and Barker focused upon maternal poverty, but other reasons for low birth weight include malnutrition, anaemia and life at high altitudes. Babies may also be small because of an inadequate blood supply from the placenta. It soon emerged that, regardless of the underlying cause, underweight babies share many of the same characteristics. Peter Gluckman and Mark Hanson concluded after an extensive review of such studies that 'despite the variety of models examined, there is a remarkable consistency in the phenotype that emerges in adulthood. The common features include a tendency to insulin resistance, increased blood pressure, vascular endothelial dysfunction, altered lipid and carbohydrate metabolism, a tendency to obesity and small muscle mass. We have termed this the *survival phenotype*.'[10]

Gluckman and Hanson argue that the survival phenotype prepares a foetus for life in a world of hardship, and call it a *predictive adaptive response*. Since the same set of responses also predispose to the immediate survival of a foetus – surely its leading priority – the predictive component is open to debate. For obvious reasons this is hard to test, but retrospective analysis of a Finnish population over the period 1751–1877, when 42 per cent of children died before the age of fifteen, suggested that babies born in years of plenty were more likely to survive periods of hardship.[11] The strongest pigs in a litter do better than the runt, and a silver spoon in the cradle is generally a favourable omen.

We are entitled to doubt whether the survival phenotype does confer a lasting advantage to those born into a lean environment, but there is no doubt at all that early deprivation can and does affect the whole trajectory of life, although conditions after birth can also have a lasting legacy. Famine in early pregnancy predisposed to obesity in later life in survivors of the Dutch Hunger Winter, for example, but not in those of the Leningrad siege. The likely reason is that the Dutch children were well fed after birth, whereas the Russians remained on short rations.[12] As Forsdahl suggested and others have shown, early deprivation followed by relative abundance in later life is a particularly dangerous combination.

THE STRATEGY OF THE GENES

The triumphal march of twentieth-century biology passed a number of major landmarks along the way. One was the development of gene theory in the early part of the century, followed by the demonstration that natural selection can be understood in terms of gene variation. The gene itself remained a hypothetical entity until Watson and Crick gave it a structure in the 1950s. The revolution in molecular biology that followed suggested that life itself could be explained in terms of the interaction of large molecules, and so indeed it can. As this book will argue, however, analysis of individual genes can no more explain the development of complex traits than analysis of individual neurons can explain the workings of a brain.

This was not how it seemed at the time, however, for molecular biologists believed that they had hit bedrock, and that there was nowhere further to go. When analysis of the entire genome came into prospect in the 1990s, its explanatory powers seemed boundless. James Watson said of it that he 'wanted to know what it meant to be human'. I well remember a lecture by a distinguished geneticist who informed an audience of physicians that the genomes of their patients would soon be read like barcodes, enabling diseases to be diagnosed and treated before they happened. Similar genetic determinism informed the film *Gattaca* (a name confected from the initial letters of the four nucleotide bases in DNA), whose protagonist had a genome scan at birth which foretold the precise date of his death from heart disease.

Faith in genome scans declined as these became more widely available. They can tell you a lot about simple traits related to specific genes, but they are far less informative when it comes to the complex traits which make up the more important elements of a phenotype. Genetic analysis can inform your baseline probability of multifactorial disease, but the extent to which these probabilities will be realized will depend upon how you live. You might be unusually susceptible to lung cancer, for example, but your chances of getting it will largely depend upon whether you smoke. Your risk of heart disease or diabetes is far more closely linked to your environment and lifestyle than to your genes. Witness the fact that life insurance companies have yet to ask for a genome scan before selling you a policy. We are indeed the expression of our genes, but the way in which those genes will find expression reflects their environment.

Even so, genetic determinism occupied the academic high ground at the start of the twenty-first century, and those with an interest in the developmental origins of health and disease (DOHaD was its unappealing acronym) found themselves at the margins of mainstream science. Worse still, its exponents were drawn from the low-kudos specialties of epidemiology, clinical medicine and animal physiology. Even so, they furnished mounting evidence to show that the first thousand days of life (before and after birth) can have a lasting effect upon the phenotype.

A striking feature of our changing phenotype is that people raised in the same environment bear a strong generic resemblance to one another, as for example in what I have called the Palaeolithic and agrarian phenotypes. It seems increasingly clear that genes work together in response to their environment, but genes are almost infinitely diverse. Why then should they choose to shape us in much the same way?

The idea that the same genes can fashion different phenotypes was foreshadowed by Richard Woltereck, a contemporary of Johannsen, in the early part of the twentieth century. Woltereck worked with single-celled freshwater organisms called *Daphnia*, otherwise known as water fleas. He noted that these develop a tiny helmet when raised in an environment shared with predators, a species-wide response apparently unrelated to individual genetic variation. Woltereck concluded that certain patterns of variation are built into all members of a species, and he called these *norms of reaction*.[13]

Similar ideas were taken up by the geneticist Conrad Waddington around the mid-century. He was concerned with an apparent paradox that had bothered Charles Darwin. Suitably updated, this goes as follows: natural selection favours any variant that improves survival in a given environment, and will therefore select for the most efficient gene variant. Selecting for one variant should, however, have the effect of discarding the alternatives, thus eliminating the possibility of future variation. This means that natural selection should – in theory at least – foreclose on the possibility of future evolution. Waddington's solution to this paradox came in *The Strategy of the Genes*, published in 1957.

He suggested that natural selection operates at two levels, and that the conventional evolutionary mechanism of gene mutation is supplemented by a range of overarching responses to environmental challenges. A hedgehog reacts to every threat by rolling itself into a ball, for example, and he argued that natural selection has equipped us with similar reflex reactions. These resembled Woltereck's norms of reaction (although he does not cite him), and could, for example, explain why an undernourished foetus adopts the same 'survival phenotype' in response to a variety of threats. Since built-in responses of this type do not depend upon individual genes, a species can react to its environment while preserving genetic variation, thus resolving Darwin's dilemma. This, as I understand it, was Waddington's strategy of the genes.

Waddington referred to this supplementary override system as *epigenetics*, resurrecting an obsolete biological term in doing so. The most effective way of adjusting a phenotype is to modify its early growth, and he surmised that the growth of a foetus could be channelled into standard pathways in response to signals from the mother's world – with lasting consequences. Epigenetics has acquired far more precise connotations since then, but we should not lose sight of Waddington's original reason for coining it, which was to define 'the interactions of genes with their environment which bring the phenotype into being'.[14]

To summarize thus far, embryology was a relatively neglected speciality in the first part of the twentieth century, and the notion of the impregnable foetus crept into medical thinking almost by default. This complacency was rudely disturbed by the realization that viruses, drugs, alcohol, tobacco, maternal starvation and material deprivation can each have lasting effects. The 'foetal origins' hypothesis, as it was initially known, was superseded by the broader concept that sequential influences upon development shape our adult phenotype, and an understanding of the ways in which the genes involved in development interact with our environment is beginning to emerge. It is time to look at some consequences of this interaction.

8

Growing Tall

Pity the eighteenth-century soldier. Herded into line and marched to within 20 metres or so of ranks of equally terrified men glimpsed through acrid clouds of black smoke as you blast away with heavy and inaccurate firearms that take an age for shaking hands to load again. Feet clogged with mud, you advance, fire, retire and reload, locked into a place beyond terror by mindless drill and a conviction that those behind you are more to be feared than those in front. No one did this willingly, and the recruiting sergeant was obliged to dip into the poorest and most hopeless levels of society. Suitably cowed by incessant drill and discipline, these unwilling recruits stepped like automata into gaps left by the cannon balls. When fear overwhelmed discipline, the ordered ranks broke and ran like rabbits, much to the frustration of their generals. 'Dogs, would you live for ever?' bellowed Frederick the Great on one such occasion. Generals of the period had little respect for the cannon fodder at their disposal, described by the Duke of Wellington as 'the scum of the earth – the mere scum of the earth. It is only wonderful that we should be able to make so much out of them afterwards.'[1]

Clockwork soldiers were obliged to carry heavy muskets, needed arms long enough to operate a ramrod and had to be able to march in step, a Prussian innovation dating from around 1700. Drill became the alpha and omega of military discipline and required people of standard size. This is why the first systematic records of height were made by recruiting officers; women were rarely if ever measured. Eighteenth-century soldiers were astonishingly short by modern standards, and elite troops were greatly prized for their height. Frederick William, father of Frederick the Great, was noted for his zeal in collecting tall men for his Guards regiment. These were sent to him as gifts, and even kidnapped.* One tale relates that he saw an unusually tall young woman in the street. Having ascertained that she was single, he sent her round to the barracks with a note instructing that she be married to one of his soldiers. She passed the note to an older woman of unprepossessing appearance whom she met on the way. Napoleon's Imperial Guard stood around 183 cm tall, and his habit of posing beside them may have enhanced the legend of his own short stature. With some help from British propaganda, it has been claimed that he was only 157 cm in height, thus giving rise to psychological treatises about the Napoleon or 'short man' complex. Unfortunately for this hypothesis, the Englishman who measured him for his coffin recorded that he was 171 cm tall, and the French physician who performed his autopsy measured him at 169 cm. Since Napoleon was fifty-one at the time, not to mention dead, a couple more centimetres could be added to his stature as a young man.

The life of an eighteenth-century soldier was brutal enough, but seamen fared worse, prompting Dr Samuel Johnson to wonder why anyone with the option of jail would ever go to sea. Height was less important, for a low centre of gravity was no disadvantage on board ship, and Nelson's mariners were snatched from the streets. The Marine Society, set up in the mid-eighteenth century to recruit London boys over the age of twelve for naval service, targeted 'vagabonds, the major part of them overwhelmed with Filth and Rags, in danger of perishing through Cold, Hunger, Nakedness or Disease'. At the age of fourteen, these boys were the height of a modern nine-year-old.[2]

Growth triggers puberty, and puberty triggers the adolescent growth spurt. The children of the upper classes accelerated away from the rest in their early teens and generally remained taller. Aristocratic recruits attending the military academy at Sandhurst in the first half of the nineteenth century averaged 174.4 cm by age nineteen, only 3 cm below the British average at the end of the twentieth century.

---

* White (1993) cites a letter from a seaman called James Richardson to King George III dated 31 May 1767. Richardson, 180 cm in height, was kidnapped while taking a stroll ashore in Memel and enlisted in the Prussian army. King George secured his release.

Comparison of age-matched recruits to the Marine Society and Sand-hurst showed a difference of 22 cm by the age of sixteen.[3] The British upper classes were even taller than Americans and were matched only by the upper echelons of the German aristocracy. There could scarcely be a better demonstration of the influence of privilege upon the pheno-type. There are no records of female height at this period of history, but working-class women will have averaged around 152 cm if we assume them to have been 5–7 cm shorter than men.

Height has proved to be the royal road to historical investigation of the phenotype, eagerly seized upon by economists who want to meas-ure the biological impact of economic change. This chapter will look at some of the lessons we have learned.

MEASURING PEOPLE

Louis-René Villermé (1782–1863) was born to well-to-do parents in a small village near Paris, and his medical studies were interrupted when he was drafted into Napoleon's army as a surgical assistant. He saw terrible things during his time in Spain, and his thesis on 'Effects of famine on health in places which are theatres of war' contained a graphic account of the effects of hunger on the civil population during the campaign in Extremadura. This brutal campaign eroded the humanity of the Spanish population by fighting and famine, and Francisco Goya's etching entitled *And they are like wild beasts* shows women fighting with bestial ferocity to protect their families. The experience had a lasting effect on Villermé, and he devoted himself to investigation of those at the wrong end of the social spectrum – weavers, cotton spinners, silk workers and convicts – after a brief spell in civilian medical practice. He found that big cities were death traps, and that Parisians were twice as likely to die as people in wealthy country districts. As for poor city folk, their mortality is greater 'to a degree of which we have no inkling'.[4] Villermé was no advocate of radical social reform – France had burned its fingers on this – but he saw every reason for the wealthy to show compassion towards the poor, a view not generally shared by the wealthy.

He analysed the height of 100,000 Napoleonic recruits (mean height

162 cm) and found striking differences between the heights of men from different regions of France. In the wealthy Département of Bouches-de-la-Meuse, for example, only 6.6 per cent of recruits were rejected, 2.4 per cent for being too short, and 4.2 per cent on the grounds of ill-health; their mean height was 168 cm. In contrast, the average was 156 cm in the poor and mountainous Département of Appenins, where 30 per cent were rejected for short stature and 9.6 per cent for ill-health. The same pattern appeared wherever he looked; the taller the people, the lower the rate of infirmity, and his overall conclusion was that 'human height becomes greater and growth takes place more rapidly, other things being equal, in proportion as the country is richer, comfort more general, houses, clothes and nourishment better and labour, fatigue and privation during infancy and youth less'. Furthermore, 'all the advantages go to the tall men'.[5]

People raised in poor environments were shorter in the legs and took longer to complete their growth – up to the age of twenty-three in Villermé's estimation. A detail which Villermé appears to have missed is that recruits are taller in the morning than in the afternoon, due to compression of the spaces between their vertebrae. In the eighteenth century, Reverend Wasse of Aynho in Northamptonshire – who presumably had time on his hands – observed that his own height decreased by about 2 cm after sitting at his desk for five hours or more, quite enough to discourage the recruiting sergeant. Villermé attributed differences in height entirely to nutrition, but others contested this. Paul Broca (1824–80), better remembered for his work on the speech areas of the brain, wrote that: 'The height of Frenchmen, considered generally, depends not on altitude, nor latitude, nor poverty or riches, neither on the nature of the soil nor on nutrition, nor on any of the other environmental conditions that can be invoked. After these have all been successively eliminated, I have been brought to consider only one general influence, that of ethnic heredity.'[6] This was the opening shot in a long debate.

Villermé's observations confirm that the inhabitants of the French countryside were pitifully stunted, and that the city poor were even worse off. In rural society everyone had a place – if only at the bottom – and there was some concept of collective responsibility. Things were different in the cities. There, as in Freud's tripartite division of the personality, the superego was represented by a community's professed social and religious aspirations, the ego was the rising middle class with its robust mechanisms for self-advancement, self-approval and exclusion of others, and the id resided at the borders of consciousness, a seething cauldron of hellish danger, abandoned hope and inadmissible desire. Appropriate no doubt for polite concern, religious forays, social reform, sex tourism or punitive repression, but above all alien: you might visit, but you never belonged. The city mob haunted the imagination of the European ruling classes from the French to the Russian Revolution.

At the start of the nineteenth century, Europe was a dense mosaic of overlapping languages, but the continent began to resolve itself into nation-states, each with its own founder myth and racial origins, for people were now defined by their nationality as never before. Modern states needed to be managed, and this required a ceaseless flow of information about their citizens. Where was the new wealth coming from? How did you tax it? The military mind worried about citizen recruits; businessmen wanted the most efficient use of their workforce, and the ruling classes wondered how to control their seething masses. And they each began to ask questions about the phenotype.

Adolphe Quetelet became a Belgian when his country was carved out of Holland in 1831–2, and became one of the first and ablest explorers of this new order. 'The more advanced the sciences have become,' he noted, 'the more they have tended to enter the domain of mathematics, which is a sort of centre towards which they converge.' He added that 'it seems to me that the theory of probabilities ought to serve as the basis for the study of all the sciences, and particularly of the sciences of observation'. Quetelet was a polymath, at home in sciences ranging from astronomy to the new discipline of social statistics. Probability came to the fore wherever he looked. In the exact sciences, for example, attempts to pinpoint the trajectory of a planet were limited by the accuracy with which its position could be measured. Measurement error is not random, as he noted, since the estimates arrange themselves into a bell-shaped curve with an apex that provides a closer approximation to the truth than any single measurement. A similar bell-shaped curve emerged from the rough and tumble of biological measurement and found major uses in descriptive statistics such as the height, weight at birth or age at death of Belgian men.[7]

Quetelet and his contemporaries were looking for something beyond measurement: this was the biological archetype, an ideal from which individuals might deviate but towards which populations aspired. The average was not just the middle of the heap: it showed you what the heap was trying to achieve. Armed with this new magic wand, Quetelet found unexpected order emerging from chaos wherever he looked.

The height and weight of Belgian boys in 1835 was on the 3rd percentile of a modern population

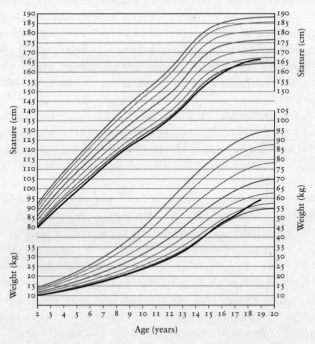

Figure 21: The height and weight of Quetelet's children, as plotted on a modern growth chart.

Adult weight, for example, was twenty times weight at birth, and his pioneering studies of human growth led him to conclude that 'weight increases as the square of the height'.[8] From this came the measure which was known as the Quetelet Index until it was renamed the Body Mass Index (BMI) by Ancel Keys in 1972.

GROWING TALLER

Americans were the tallest people in the world at the start of the twentieth century but were later overtaken by western Europeans, possibly because of an influx of shorter immigrants to the USA. Britain peaked soon after the Second World War, only to be left behind by the people of Scandinavia and the Netherlands. Accelerated growth reached the Far East in the second half of the century. The Japanese gained around 2 cm per decade in the post-war period, reaching a plateau among children born in the 1960s, whereas the South Korean peak came with children born in the 1980s. The Chinese have overtaken the Japanese, but the Japanese are still 5 cm taller than the people of India and Bangladesh, and people in parts of sub-Saharan Africa are shorter than they were fifty years ago.[9] As this snapshot demonstrates, height is a sensitive marker of economic conditions.

The head is one-quarter of a newborn baby's length, but one-seventh of the length of an adult. Growth is staged; the head grows first and fastest, the trunk and viscera grow next, and the long bones of the arms and legs come last. The adolescent growth spurt mainly affects the legs, and legs have a major influence on your height. You can check this for yourself by going online to order a men's suit. The standard inside leg measurement for men below 175 cm comes out at 42–3 per cent of their height, whereas the trousers of a man 190 cm tall represent 45–7 per cent of his total height. Analysis of the long bones from Americans who died between 1800 and 1970 revealed that both arms and legs grew longer over this period; legs grew faster than arms, and the greatest relative increase was below the knee.[10] This apart, there are also ethnic differences: people of west African descent have longer legs relative to their height than Europeans.

Height discrimination is built into our language, as when we speak

PLASTICITY

of a person's standing, stature or status (or erect statues to them). We look up to some people and down on others. Like glossy feathers, height is a marker of health, and it is also associated with leadership, authority, sexual preference and salary. Height and leg length are deeply engrained markers of social status, perceived at an almost subconscious level. Physical differences such as these were readily visible when nutrition favoured the dominant classes, and the height, grace and refined features of the nobleman could be contrasted with the squat coarseness of the peasant. Since aristocrats were not always tall, they also insisted upon a rigid dress-code to distinguish them from the lower orders. Michel de Montaigne was a short man, as judged by the 150 cm doorways in his tower, and bitterly regretted the fact. 'Where smallness dwells,' he remarked,

> neither breadth and roundness of forehead, nor clarity and softness of eyes, nor the moderate form of the nose, nor small size of ears and mouth, nor regularity and whiteness of teeth, nor the smooth thickness of a beard brown as the husk of a chestnut, nor curly hair, nor proper roundness of head, nor freshness of colour, nor a pleasant facial expression, nor an odourless body, nor just proportion of limbs, can make a handsome man.

Montaigne was not without vanity, as this loving description might suggest, and he was wounded to the quick when he attended the royal court flanked by retainers, and a courtier asked him where his master was.[11]

Isabella Leitch, a twentieth-century pioneer of growth and nutrition, received a first-rate research training in the laboratory of the Nobel laureate August Krogh in Copenhagen but could not find a post on her return to Scotland despite her doctorate – no doubt for reasons of gender. She became an associate librarian in Boyd Orr's institute in Aberdeen, where her talent was soon recognized. She was interested in the time-honoured observation that the legs of the poor are disproportionately short. Artists and fashion designers have long known this, and Leitch commented in 1951 that 'high-class fashion journals depict women with an extreme length of limb, and decorative art does the same for both men and women . . . When the artist wishes to depict the lower orders [with comic intent] he draws people with exaggeratedly

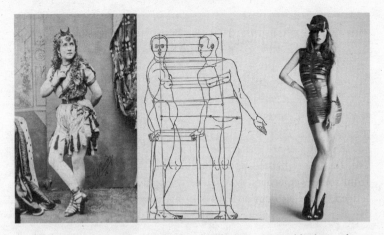

Figure 22: Human proportions as sketched by Dürer resemble those of Adah Menken, a scandalous American beauty of the 1860s. Cheryl Cole, a contemporary pop icon, is 155 cm tall but has much longer legs.

short legs and makes them fat.' 'In romantic literature,' as she pointed out, 'the hero and heroine are always long limbed. If the heroine is small . . . it is always expressly stated that she is "perfectly proportioned".'[12] She noted that 'a very small increase in the ratio of leg length to total height has a surprising effect on appearance', and later studies have shown just how right she was. She included a measure of leg length in a nutrition survey undertaken with the support of the Carnegie Trust in 1937 and showed that social disadvantage was clearly reflected in the ratio of sitting to standing height. Better-fed children are taller because their legs are longer, and this means that their adult proportions are different. Cheryl Cole may be short at 155 cm, but she is certainly not stunted (figure 22).

Fashion reflects this. A woman who is 163 cm tall typically has an inside leg measurement of 74 cm, representing 45 per cent of her height. If shown a female figure in silhouette, people of either sex prefer longer legs, opting for 78 cm or 48 per cent of total height.[13]

Leonardo's famous Vitruvian man, drawn within both a square and a circle, follows the advice of the Roman architect Vitruvius, which was to draw the body eight times the length of the head.

Figure 23: Dürer's proportions varied with social class. The engraving on the left shows a *Young Couple Threatened by Death* (c.1498). To the right, *Peasant Couple Dancing* (1514).

Drawing manuals still instruct the novice to divide the upright body into eight parts, counting head length as one eighth and setting the halfway point at the crotch. Albrecht Dürer routinely followed the 'eight head rule' for heroic subjects, but drew peasants seven head lengths tall to make them look squat and stocky.

The effect of varying body proportions is shown in a classic and much-loved drawing manual published by Andrew Loomis in 1943 (figure 24). The 'academic proportions', in which, as Loomis points out, the ratio of the head to the body is 1:7.5, yield a dumpy, nondescript appearance with the crotch below the mid-point. This is what most of us look like. Reduce the head ratio to 1:8, increase body width from 2 to 2.3 heads, lengthen the legs ... and you end up with someone you might wish to resemble. Accentuate these characteristics, and you enter the world of fantasy.

Although rapid growth of the long bones takes place in adolescence,

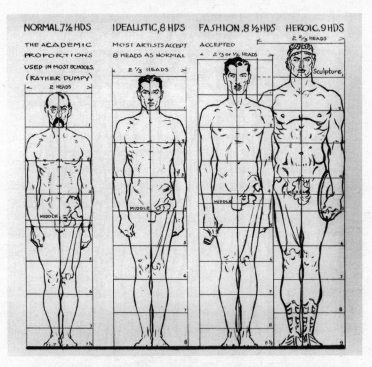

Figure 24: Human proportions, real and enhanced. From Andrew Loomis, *Figure Drawing for All It's Worth* (1943).

final height is predetermined by development in early infancy. Examination of bones from a Victorian cemetery which provided the last resting place for children from a deprived area showed a distinct lag in growth of the long bones as compared with children today. The deficit was already apparent by two to four months of age. No wonder the poor had short legs.[14]

THE PURSUIT OF THE AVERAGE

Americans looked enormous to people from other parts of the world in the nineteenth century, but even members of the elite were small by today's standards. In 1888, men at Amherst College were on average 172.5 cm tall and weighed 61.2 kg, with a BMI of 20.6. The record weight of 91.2 kg was set by a student called Harlow.[15] In 1869, Harvard sent four of its best oarsmen to compete with Oxford over the Boat Race course on the Thames; Oxford won a closely contested race by a narrow margin. It helped that they averaged 78 kg, as against 71 kg for the Americans. Oxford oarsmen averaged 99.5 kg in 2009.

American students were routinely weighed and measured at many East Coast universities: male measurement began in the 1860s, and female measurement in the 1880s. The motivation remains unclear but had eugenic overtones; Ivy League students were almost exclusively white, and of northern European origin. For some, they would become the highest expression of eugenicist Madison Grant's Great Race.

The Harvard Venus, as the female came to be known, was notable for her fashionable wasp waist; the young ladies probably inhaled vigorously when measured. Male Harvard students had an average height

Figure 25: Composite figures of white American male and female students of the 1890s, based on measurements collected by Dudley A. Sargent, Peabody Museum, Boston. Note the facial designation of gender by modelling the chin.

of 173 cm in 1856–65, rising to 178 cm in 1906–15. They were 3.5 cm taller than their fathers and 4.5 kg heavier, with broader shoulders and narrower hips. Girls were 1.8 kg heavier and 2.9 cm taller than their mothers; thicker around the waist but narrower across the hips.[16]

In 1916, women at Wellesley College were delighted to discover that their composite measurements approximated to those of the Venus de Milo, although none was a perfect fit. This was not unusual, and Sargent himself commented that 'among the many thousands who have been measured at the gymnasium, not one has fulfilled every requirement'. The search for the perfect Venus, egged on by the newspapers, culminated in the American Venus Contest held in Madison Square Garden in 1922. Each of the five finalists was taken into a side room and invited to strip naked for inspection by the five male judges. When one contestant protested, the head judge insisted that the nude body is more beautiful. 'Yes indeed,' chorused the other four, no doubt somewhat breathlessly; 'by all means. It certainly is.'[17] Fashions were already changing, however, and the Greek ideal was judged too heavy around the hips and thighs. The *New York Times* proclaimed in 1923 that the 'true American Modern Venus' should be 170 cm tall and weigh no more than 50 kg; Venus had a BMI of 17.2. Things had changed when the *New York Times* reported on 5 June 2018 that the Miss America pageant had decided to dispense with the swimsuit competition. 'We are not going to judge you on your outward appearance,' said the chairwoman, somewhat improbably.

The cult of measurement spread far and wide. In 1941, the US Department of Agriculture set out to determine the dimensions of the American female. This was designed to aid the mass production of garments, since, as the report noted, everyday observation testifies that women display 'an almost bewildering variety of shapes and sizes'.[18] More than 10,000 white women aged eighteen to eighty years were measured in fifty-five ways, and varied more in their horizontal than in their vertical dimensions. Their mean height was 160 cm with a tidy bell-shaped spread of around 38 cm, but the equivalent spread for weight (average 60.5 kg, BMI 23.6) was skewed towards the higher values and ranged from 36 to 91 kg.

In 1945, the artist Abram Belskie and gynaecologist Robert Dickinson used measurements from 15,000 men and women aged twenty-one to twenty-five – all of them white – to construct two ala-baster statues, soon to be known as Norma and Normman (figure 26). These are taller, longer in the leg and distinctly fleshier than their Harvard predecessors, and they have a disturbing resemblance to Nazi propaganda. Norma, still innocent of pubic hair, prompted more interest, and a $100 bond was offered to any woman who could match her dimensions. A total of 3,863 entries were submitted, of which only 1 per cent were a good match; the prize went to a twenty-four-year-old theatre cashier.[19]

These surveys all pointed to the same conclusion: the average is a fiction. Paradoxically, anyone who approaches the statistical average is a statistical freak. Todd Rose, author of *The End of Average* (2016), recounts that the US Air Force was confronted by an outbreak of unexplained crashes towards the end of the 1940s. This was the dawn of jet aviation, and pilots were stretched to their limits. To allow for this, cockpits had been carefully designed on the basis of 140 physical measures in 4,000 selected pilots. The problem was that the average pilot didn't exist; the cockpit designed to fit them all didn't actually fit any of them.[20]

Physical evaluation of freshmen continued to be a rite of initiation

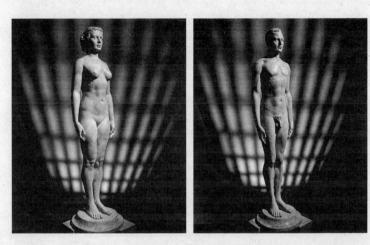

Figure 26: *Normman* and *Norma* (1943). Sculptures of composite young white Americans by Abram Belskie and Robert Latou Dickinson.

at many leading universities. Photographs now replaced measurement, and students of either sex were expected to pose for them nude or semi-naked. The practice was finally discontinued in the 1960s, by which time the college archives were packed with nude or semi-nude pictures of prominent Americans ranging from John F. Kennedy to Hillary Rodham Clinton. When the story finally hit the headlines, the institutions concerned had no idea why they had been photographing their students in the first place. The quest for the American phenotype had ended.

A FACE TO MEET
THE FACES THAT YOU MEET

The bones of our arms and legs grow rapidly in well-nourished children and adolescents, and so do our skulls, whose vaults have grown taller in recent generations.[21] Our jaws have grown lighter because we give them less to do. The jaw is the only part of the head that performs mechanical work, and jaws are powerful. Try clenching your incisors, and then your back teeth. The two main muscles acting on the jaw are the masseters and the temporal muscles. The masseters are the ones that bulge when you clench your back teeth, and express resolve when film characters are under stress. The temporal muscles pass under your cheekbones to reach the temples and can also be felt there when you use your back teeth. The lower jaw operates like a pair of tongs held close to the hinge, which means that we bite into things at a considerable mechanical disadvantage. Even so, our teeth bring considerable force to bear, transmitting 77 kg through the molar teeth in an average adult, and ranging up to 125 kg.[22]

The jaw performs mechanical work, and its shape reflects this. Palaeolithic hunters used their teeth for cutting and tearing and brought their incisors together like a pair of clippers. In contrast, people who live on grain crush it between their back teeth and have a pronounced overbite. Anglo-Saxon skulls have ground-down molars because the coarse flour produced by primitive milling techniques contained small seeds and millstone grit, and the dental arch of people in a medieval plague pit is shorter and broader than in modern individuals. Sir Arthur Keith argued in 1925 that a softer modern diet had reshaped our faces. In his words, 'the cheeks, which are high and prominent when the biting muscles – the masseter and internal pterygoid – are well developed, become reduced and sunken, giving us our narrow, hatchet-shaped faces – our oval cast of countenance'.[23] More recent analysis has confirmed the influence of softer food upon the conformation of the skull.[24]

Dentistry is one of the blessings of modern life, and modern life has made a lot more work for dentists. Ancient hunter-gatherers generally had excellent teeth, with little evidence of dental caries; these came with farming because dental bacteria feed upon carbohydrates, releasing lactic acid, which eats away at tooth enamel. A high-sugar diet exposed our teeth to decay, even as soft food gave us a lighter jaw and crowded our teeth together. The first molars erupt around the age of six, the second around the age of twelve, and the third molars or 'wisdom' teeth emerge between the ages of seventeen and twenty-five. These are vestigial organs: we don't have room for them, and they frequently cause problems by pushing in. Dental impaction affected fewer than 5 per cent of people in traditional farming communities,[25] but 85 per cent of the wisdom teeth we produce today will need to be removed. Some of our domestic animals have shown the way forward by losing their third molars,[26] and, since one in three of us do not develop wisdom teeth, we may be evolving in the same direction. The size and shape of our jaws also affect the alignment of our teeth, and malocclusion – failure of the teeth to come together in an effective bite – has become more common. Comparison between dental casts made from Austrian conscripts in the 1880s and those from modern recruits shows that modern jaws are narrower and longer, with greater overbite and higher malocclusion scores.[27]

It may not seem surprising that use should shape our jaws, but it is less easy to explain why use and disuse should affect our eyes. I often wondered how short-sighted people got by before there were glasses, and the answer is that – for the most part – short-sighted people did not exist. Myopia is a condition in which distant objects appear out of focus, whereas close objects are clearly seen, and it affects 20 per cent of school-age children in Europe. It has now become epidemic in South-East Asia. Standard eye examination of Chinese children showed that the prevalence of reduced visual acuity (myopia being the commonest cause) was 28.5 per cent in 1985, 41 per cent in 1995, 49.5 per cent in 2005 and 56.8 per cent in 2010. City children are most affected, with rates of 81 per cent in Singapore, 86 per cent in Taiwan, 96 per cent in Seoul and 95 per cent in Shanghai.[28] Close eye work is traditionally associated with myopia, and Jewish boys who spend their youth studying the Talmud are four to five times more likely to develop it than their sisters. Competitive schooling increases myopia, whereas regular exposure to outdoor life offers some protection. In all events, an increasing proportion of young people no longer have natural vision, possibly for avoidable reasons.

We will take another look at our changing face in a later section.

9

Performance

There was little call for physical education before the nineteenth century, which was when military officers began to worry whether city clerks could be made into fighting men, and the German craze for gymnastics took hold. This did not meet with universal approval, and students at Harvard complained in 1826 'that they were fatigued, and sometimes overcome, rather than invigorated at the gymnasium, and were unfit for study for some hours afterwards'. An influx of German immigrants followed the unsuccessful political upheavals of 1848, and gymnastic associations arose in many American cities. The gymnasium was a standard feature of American education by the 1880s, and physician Dudley A. Sargent (1849–1924) introduced a way of strengthening muscles by machines of his own devising, mostly operated by weights and pulleys. He also supervised the collection of anthropometric data from leading educational institutions.[1]

Sargent qualified as a doctor at Yale and moved to Harvard in 1879. One of the first students who came to him for advice was a young man called Theodore Roosevelt, a compulsive over-achiever who suffered from asthma, weighed 61 kg and was described by a contemporary as 'thin-chested, spectacled, nervous and frail'. Undeterred, he gained 5.4 kg as a result of his exertions in the gym and was a runner-up – although quite badly knocked about – in the Harvard lightweight boxing championship.* In 1880 he called upon Dr Sargent for a medical examination and was gravely informed that he had overstrained

---

* Lightweight then meant under 140 lb (63.5 kg); the current definition of 135 lb (61.2 kg) was introduced in 1886.

his heart and must avoid any form of physical exertion. No doubt mindful of the young Achilles, Roosevelt said, 'Doctor, I'm going to do all the things you tell me not to do. If I've got to live the sort of life you have described, I don't care how short it is.'[2]

Physical culture became a central focus of education in Britain's top schools during the nineteenth century, partly to divert sexual energies and partly to produce the requisite officer material. The Duke of Wellington is supposed to have said that the Battle of Waterloo was won on the playing fields of Eton, but organized team sports had yet to be invented in the late eighteenth century. George Orwell was more realistic when he wondered how many battles Britain had lost there. British public schools did, however, help to shape many of the world's competitive team sports, designed for gentlemen amateurs who should not strive too obviously for success. People grew much taller and stronger in the twentieth century, and a changing phenotype was reflected in their sporting prowess.

HIGHER, FURTHER, FASTER

The modern Olympic Games began in 1896, in the hope that, as in ancient Greece, they might bring competing nations together in a moment of peace. They reflected prevailing assumptions as to the racial superiority of Europeans, apparently confirmed when Britain won fifty-six gold medals in the London Games of 1908. The gentlemanly insistence upon amateur status, which ended in 1986 after decades of hypocrisy, handed an obvious advantage to the privileged classes. Even so, the door was left ajar, and talent would eventually push it wide open.

The original ethos of the games was long forgotten by 1952. The Cold War had turned the event into a testosterone-charged facedown between opposing ideologies, and the testosterone was increasingly dispensed by syringe. The games went on to become a high-profile media circus after the Tokyo Olympics of 1964 made worldwide television. 'Fifty years ago,' as Norton and Olds said in 2001, 'sport was largely participatory, regionally-based, generalised and semi-professional. Today it is largely spectatorial, global, specialised and highly-paid.'

Furthermore, as they also point out, 'contemporary sport cannot survive without media and media cannot survive without sport'.[3]

An athletic record is the supreme expression of the human phenotype, and the record book has shown astonishing improvement over the past century. Some of the reasons are technical. Sprinters of the *Chariots of Fire* vintage used holes in the ground rather than starting blocks and were slowed by cinder tracks. Improved training techniques also made a big difference, as did the recognition that the apparent limits of the human body could be exceeded. Emil Zátopek, the sporting sensation of the mid-century, was sixteen years old when the Nazis annexed the Czech borderland in 1938. Seven years later, the Red Army was welcomed with open arms by an unsuspecting nation, and Zátopek joined the Czech army to concentrate on his running. His style seems ludicrous today; arms flailing, head lolling on his shoulder and a face like a devil in torment, but as an American competitor said, 'before Zátopek, nobody had realized it was humanly possible to train this hard'.[4] In the 1952 Olympic Games in Helsinki he achieved the extraordinary feat of winning the marathon as well as the 5,000 and 10,000 metres. Films show the raw excitement his running generated among spectators; it was the apotheosis of the common man. Zátopek retired with eighteen world records and three Olympic ones but would not have qualified as an entrant for the 10,000 metres in 2016. If he had competed in the final, he would have trailed the winners by three minutes. Sadly, his life finished in obscurity: he was rejected by the communists for supporting the Prague Spring of 1968, and his previous support for the Party disqualified him as a hero of Czech independence.

Zátopek was not the only great athlete to be eclipsed by later competitors. How, then, can we account for the steady improvement in athletic performance, as shown, for example, by the steady improvement in the men's sprint record?

A specialized phenotype may not guarantee success in athletics, but it certainly helps. The favoured physique at the start of the twentieth century was of the all-purpose variety, tall, lean and well-muscled; brute strength was considered a plebeian attribute. Today's elite athletes self-select for a narrowing range of physical characteristics, for minor variation becomes all-important when you are striving for peak

Men's 100 metres sprint records

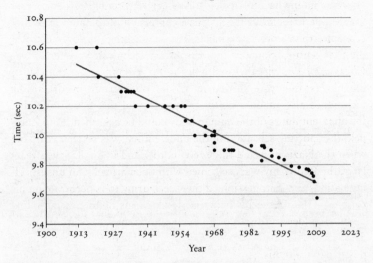

Figure 27: World 100 metres record holders at the start of the twentieth century would have struggled to beat today's schoolboy champions.

performance. This can be seen in the changing physical dimensions of the athletes. A comparison between Olympic athletes in 1928 and 1960 showed that the distance runners were unchanged, for example, whereas 400 metre runners and jumpers were 8–10 cm taller and 10 kg heavier; the biggest difference was in the throwers, who were 8–12 cm taller and 25 kg heavier.[5] Anabolic steroids may have contributed to the increase in body mass.

Sporting events can be divided into those that are 'open-ended' – the more muscle mass the better – and those that are not. The throwing events are open-ended, and the average weight of competitors has accelerated rapidly. The same applies to contact sports. In 1994, Bill Tobin, manager of the Indianapolis Colts American football team, said:

> twenty years ago we never felt we'd have this many big people who
> could run this fast. It wasn't much further back that 250 lb [113 kg]

was big for a lineman. Now it's not big enough to play. With advances in nutrition, weights, kinesiology and development techniques at an early age, we could see the day when 300 lb may be the minimum and 350 lb [159 kg] may be the standard.

The average weight passed 136 kg in 1998. Rugby has gone the same way. In the 2015 World Cup the Welsh backs averaged 99.5 kg and were heavier than the New Zealand forwards in 1987.[6] Muscle mass and speed are just as essential in American football, but rugby players keep going for eighty minutes, and the need to combine endurance with bulk and mobility means that they will never get quite so big.

Increasing mass moving at higher speed carries a greater potential for injury. If my car collides with a car of twice the weight, I am four times more likely to be injured. This applies to the human body. Smaller people, regardless of ability, are more likely to get hurt, and injury is an ever-looming problem for all contact athletes. The English Rugby Football Union has kept records of injuries since 2002, and its report for 2013–14, although soothingly presented, shows that the number of severe injuries had increased by about a third over the course of a decade, and that there were 12.5 episodes of concussion for every thousand hours of match play. Twenty-three professional players were forced to retire through injury. The higher the level, the greater the risk, and twenty-four players were invalided out of the opening stages of the 2015 Rugby World Cup, making injury an ever more important consideration. The public wants gladiatorial events, and injuries are whisked efficiently off the pitch once the cameras have panned in on the anguished expressions of the players. The ever-increasing demand for massive athletes implies an ever-diminishing pool of possible candidates and makes it hard to achieve such bulk without recourse to drugs.

Different combinations of agility, muscle power and endurance will determine the sport in which you are most likely to excel. Such variables include the ratio of fast- to slow-twitch muscle fibres, the density of mitochondria and metabolic determinants such as oxygen consumption, lactate accumulation and recovery time. Since these are under genetic control, there has been an avid quest for sports genes: but – as in every other aspect of the phenotype – the influence of individual genes is limited. When newspapers announce a gene 'for' this or that, they merely report a statistical association. Gene variants certainly do segregate with different types of athletic ability, but it is the combination that matters – for genes are also team players. Great athletes need the right genes, but they become great because they have the grit and motivation to show that, of 7 billion people, they are the best.

The relationship between physique and sporting success is best shown by comparing the height and weight of leading sportsmen (forgive the male bias) with that of the background population. Professional soccer players, for example, do not differ greatly from other young men other than in the size of their ego. Leg length is more important in Olympic athletes. In 1928, as in 1960, the ratio of leg length to height was greatest in the jumpers, followed in descending order by long-distance runners and middle-distance runners. The 400 metre runners were tallest of all, but height is less critical in the sprint events because muscle mass gives greater acceleration and can – to some extent – compensate for shorter stride length.[7]

You run by throwing yourself forward, best seen as sprinters hurl themselves from their blocks at the start of a race. Our centre of gravity is located in the pelvis, just above the mid-point of the body, and a runner chases his or her centre of gravity down the track. Longer legs and a higher centre of gravity translate into a longer stride, and the longer stride will win if legs move at the same rate. Usain Bolt, currently the fastest man in the world, is 195 cm tall, weighs 94 kg (BMI 24.7); at full speed in a race he is travelling at 45 km per hour: his feet touch the ground forty-one times in the 100 metre dash.

People of different ethnicity represent overlapping samples of the human gene pool, and differences in the resulting phenotype emerge at the extreme limits of athletic endeavour. Those of European descent had a height advantage in the early decades of the last century, and this – plus ready access to sporting facilities – allowed them to dominate sporting events. Athletes of African-American descent then displayed their mastery of the sprint events. The first African-American to win the Olympic 100 metre event was Eddie Tolan in 1932, followed by Jesse Owens (who won three other gold medals) in

Berlin in 1936. African-Americans are generally of west African origin: fourteen of nineteen Olympic sprint champions since 1932 and the past twenty-five world record holders trace their descent from this region; 494 of the 500 fastest times ever recorded before 2007 were set by athletes who share this background.[8] Oddly enough, no one actually born and raised in west Africa has won the Olympic title.

People of African descent have on average longer legs, narrower pelvises and a 3 per cent higher centre of gravity than people of European descent. This is just how you would redesign the human body if you wanted it to run faster, and has been estimated to translate into a 1.5 per cent speed advantage. Conversely, the Olympic 100 metres freestyle swimming event has been dominated by people of European descent. Johnny Weissmuller (better known for playing Tarzan in the movies) set a new world record for the event in 1922, beating the previous record held by the Hawaiian swimmer and surfing pioneer Duke Kahanamoku. Since then, every record holder has been of white European descent. Social discrimination may play a part, but analysis of human dimensions suggests that there is more to it than this. Swimmers, like runners, achieve their momentum by falling forwards, and a swimmer's centre of gravity is just that bit higher in people of European descent, a small but crucial advantage.[9] If you stand Michael Phelps, who has won twenty-two Olympic medals for swimming, next to Usain Bolt, for example (figure 28), you will see that they have much the same height and BMI (1.93 vs 1.95 metres, BMI 23.7 vs 24.7). Legs dominate with the runner, however, and trunk and arms with the swimmer. Michael Phelps has arms like oars; his span (normally the same as your height) is 208 cm, his size 14 feet work like flippers, and his long trunk helps to minimize drag.

Regardless of ethnicity, height is a key prerequisite for both swimmers and runners. No one under 190 cm has set the 100 metre freestyle swimming record since 1981. Much the same applies to sprinting, and only two recent record holders, Maurice Greene (1999, 175 cm) and Tim Montgomery (2002, 179 cm), have been under 180 cm.[10]

It is a different story in distance running. Since 1968, Kenya has won sixty-three Olympic medals in long distance track events, twenty-one of them gold. The majority of these athletes have come from the Kalenjin, a highland tribe who live 7,000 feet above sea

Figure 28: Sprinter and swimmer: Usain Bolt and Michael Phelps. Notice the difference in trunk length.

level, especially those from the Nandi Hills. Meanwhile, whole continents have been notable for their absence from the winner's rostrum. When Liu Xiang, born in Shanghai and 1.89 metres tall (weight 85 kg, BMI 23.8), cruised to victory in the high hurdles in Athens in 2004, he became the first Asian man ever to win an Olympic track or field event. This will change, for everyday observation is enough to show that the Asian phenotype is changing fast.

Even as the records fall, the human body has become increasingly polarized between the athletic and the sedentary. The sedentary are ever less active, with reduced muscle mass relative to fat. At the professional end of the spectrum, your phenotype determines your potential, and the gap between physiology and pharmacology has been narrowing rapidly.

10

Designer Phenotypes

Ruth Handler noticed in the late 1950s that her daughter enjoyed giving her dolls adult roles. The result, reputedly inspired by a German sex toy, has sold more than a billion copies. Barbie's success bore little relation to the accuracy of its depiction of a woman's body; toys need not resemble what they represent – but the distortion tells us how the original is desired or perceived. Barbie has two highly rated features of the consumer phenotype: increased height and enhanced leg length, together with another ardently desired feature – extreme

Figure 29: It can be done! Candice Swanepoel takes on Barbie.

144

thinness. She is too thin to menstruate (not a requirement in a doll), and her legs are up to 50 per cent longer than her arms, as against a 20 per cent difference in an adult woman.[1]

Barbie's success remains something of an enigma. She evidently tapped into something important to growing girls in a way that bulked-out superheroes never quite achieved with boys. It might have something to do with her poise, for Barbie is serene, unruffled, smiling, autonomous, in control and (although adult) almost entirely sexless: Ken is a fashion accessory rarely taken out of the cupboard. The fashion houses certainly did not need to be told that affluence is associated with longer legs, and the result could be seen on catwalks long before the coltish legs of teenagers proliferated in the streets of our cities. Catwalk models have impossibly long legs and limited sex appeal. Analysis of the height and weight of national models, international models and supermodels in relation to American women aged eighteen to thirty-four showed, predictably, that the models clustered to the taller and thinner end of the spectrum, with eleven supermodels – whose yearly income averaged in excess of $5 million in 1999 – at the extreme end of the distribution; only one American woman in 200 had the dimensions – let alone the looks – to be eligible.[2]

Fat is the archetypal marker of conspicuous consumption. When food is in short supply, excess weight is desired in women and a marker of status in men. Conversely, when everyone eats too much and takes little exercise, fashion requires women to look half-starved and men to be bursting with muscle. Analysis of *Playboy* centrefolds over the decades shows that they have become progressively more scrawny, preserving the same ratio between their body measurements, but losing the voluptuous curves favoured in earlier times. Men, meanwhile, filled out; Clive James memorably compared Arnold Schwarzenegger to a condom stuffed with walnuts. In each case the desired phenotype has diverged progressively and conspicuously from the population norm. Women with slim bodies and men with rippling muscles appeal to the opposite sex, but only within certain limits: starved females and over-bulked males run into diminishing sexual dividends, even to the point of repulsion. Despite this, some members of either sex are willing to pursue the fantasy of self-image to the point of self-destruction.

REDESIGNING THE PHENOTYPE

A tall, skinny, self-conscious young man went up to Cambridge University in the 1980s. To his surprise and delight, his body filled out to the point at which he could row for his college. He switched to Oxford for the second half of his medical course, and his physique gained him admittance to the University Boat Club. His height, 185 cm when he entered Cambridge, was now 196 cm and his weight had increased by 14 kg. In his own words, 'I had gone from being quite a tall but scrawny undergraduate to being a guy who was head and shoulders above the rest of the year, thickset, big shoulders, big arms, big legs and big hands and feet, and girls you can work the rest of it out.' As a member of an elite rowing squad he found no lack of female company, even though he did not achieve his ambition of rowing in the Blues boat.

Nemesis came a few years later when he scrubbed for the operating theatre and found that extra-large surgical gloves no longer fitted his hands. He exchanged a glance of horrified realization with the senior surgeon. Next morning, he himself was on the operating table, undergoing surgery for the pituitary tumour that had been pumping growth hormone into his circulation. He was lucky. If the surge of growth hormone had occurred earlier, he would have become a 7 foot weakling. If it had happened after the growth spurt, he would have had nothing but grief from a slow-growing pituitary tumour. Looking back, Bob Sharp, who went on to become an orthopaedic surgeon in Oxford, had absolutely no regrets.

'Growth hormone is a fantastic drug if you want to get big for sport,' he wrote.

> My life, my career, my mates and my outlook on life have all been entirely shaped during this period of my life, and I have loved the opportunities this extra drug gave me, although I will probably have to pay the consequences later in life. If I was a 15-year-old non-academic schoolboy who was quite good at sport and my future lay in flipping burgers or taking growth hormone and having a short but glittering career as an international athlete . . . I would do it in the blink of an eye.[3]

Our phenotype is the one thing we can truly call our own, and we contemplate it with feelings ranging from complacency to despair. Few people are entirely satisfied with their bodies, and you probably wouldn't want to meet them. Most of us would like to be younger or thinner or fitter, and we make sporadic efforts to eat less or to attend a gym. If things go well, we watch with pride as our muscles get firmer and our waist more trim. But suppose that a pill could do this? Wouldn't it be good to watch your fat stores dissolve while your muscles swell? This is the siren song of designer phenotypes. Genetic engineering may feature in the news, but phenotypic engineering is already here.

The growth and maintenance of our bodies is supervised by a complex network of signalling molecules. These include hormones, growth factors and a variety of other chemical signals. Minor variations in the pattern they weave make it possible for the same genotype to express different phenotypes. Changes in early development have a more lasting effect, but our bodies constantly remodel themselves as we go along, and chemical agents can have dramatic effects upon this.

Synthetic steroids have long been administered to beef animals in the USA for their muscle-bulking effect, and athletes have used them since the 1950s. The quest to shed fat or to build muscle is a professional necessity in fashion models and sportsmen and has become an obsession for many other members of the population. Since the people these seek to resemble are extreme phenotypic outliers or the product of pharmacological manipulation, traditional approaches to diet and exercise no longer suffice. This, despite endless mumbled denials, is why drugs are almost mandatory in some sports, as recent revelations about the Olympic Games have shown. As I write, chemical analysis of a London 'fatberg' (a monstrous chunk of fat blocking a sewer) shows that more Londoners are using illegal drugs to reshape their bodies than to blow their minds.[4] Of greater concern, a range of chemical pollutants have hormone-like actions and the potential to induce lasting change in the human phenotype. Substances such as these reshape our bodies, and this chapter will look at some of the ways in which they might do so.

RESHAPING THE BODY

The drugs in your bathroom cupboard – beta-blockers, statins, ACE inhibitors and so forth – are inhibitors or antagonists: they work by switching things off. Like magic bullets they are designed (with varying success) to strike only where needed. Hormones, in contrast, are agonists; they switch genes on and make things happen; their effects radiate outward like ripples on a pond. Hormones produce their effects by docking with receptors on their target tissues. Receptors for insulin have a very narrow bandwidth; only one key will fit the lock that switches on their effects. The receptors for steroid hormones are at the other extreme. Steroids are fat-soluble molecules which slip through the outer membranes of cells to reach receptors located in the membrane surrounding the nucleus. The feet of these receptors are resting, so to speak, upon genes which influence the composition of our bodies. Steroid receptors are open to a wide variety of signals and are, in the jargon, highly promiscuous. As an old textbook phrased it, 'one of the outstanding characteristics of these compounds is the extraordinary differences in physiological activity produced by minute structural distinctions'. This characteristic has permitted extensive engineering of the steroid molecule.

Our acquaintance with the sex steroids began with castration, for the male sex glands need to keep cool and are temptingly exposed to view. Aristotle, who wrote in the fourth century BC, was familiar with its effects. 'If you mutilate [males] in boyhood,' he said 'the later-growing hair never comes, and the voice never changes but remains high-pitched . . . a eunuch never grows bald . . . all animals, if operated upon when they are young, become bigger and better-looking than their unmutilated fellows.'

Eunuchs were employed in royal courts from the Middle East to South-East Asia. Their infertility made them suitable custodians for a seraglio, and a lack of dynastic ambition ensured their loyalty; some achieved high rank in court circles. Topkapı Palace in Istanbul housed around 200 in the early 1920s, and the Chinese imperial court then had around 2,000, although these were expelled in 1923 by Pu Yi, the last emperor. Chinese eunuchs underwent amputation of both penis and testicles and were noted for their pervasive aroma of urine; their missing parts were preserved in glass jars and buried with them in the hope that they might be reunited in some future life. More bizarre still were the Skoptzy, an eighteenth-century Russian sect which took its cue from the biblical comment that 'there be eunuchs, which have made themselves eunuchs for the kingdom of heaven's sake' (Matthew 19:12). Their founder, Kondraty Selivanov, performed the operation on himself, and his followers believed that the Kingdom of Heaven would be delayed until 144,000 others had followed his example. No one knows how close they came to this target, but an estimated 1–2,000 survived to see Stalin's Russia.

More sinister was the practice of medical castration for the mentally impaired, performed for eugenic reasons or to render them more tractable. Sex offenders can still opt for chemical castration in return for lighter sentences in many parts of the world, including the USA, Australia and South Korea.[5] A study of individuals born between 1890 and 1931 and housed in a US institution compared 297 surgical eunuchs with 735 intact males and 883 females. It found that the castrates lived significantly longer than intact males (69.3 vs 55.7 years) and that castration before puberty was associated with longer survival. A study of the records of eighty-one eunuchs at the Imperial Court of the Korean Chosun Dynasty (1392–1910) reported an average lifespan of seventy years, as against fifty-one to fifty-six years for a comparison group. Three eunuchs survived for a century, an astronomically unlikely outcome for such a small sample. Neutered cats live longer than intact animals, and even salmon live longer without their sex glands.[6]

Those castrated before puberty have longer legs because the growth plates in their bones do not receive the expected hormonal 'stop' signal, and they lay down more fat and less muscle in the absence of male hormones. Elderly eunuchs were described as long in the leg with small heads and smooth, hairless faces. Their bones thinned with age, resulting in the characteristic spinal curvature of osteoporosis. Many were obese, with pendulous cheeks, breasts and enlarged pelvises, and they looked like old women – a resemblance enhanced by their characteristic high-pitched voices.

Castrated animals grow bigger and more tractable, and this procedure was a major step towards domestication. They also lay down more fat, greatly valued by past generations for its high energy content. Castrated cattle are known as oxen or bullocks when used for draft purposes, or as steers if raised for meat. Pigs are routinely castrated in many parts of the world, for the meat of intact males has a 'boar taint' which some find distasteful. Removal of the ovaries is more heroic, for it involves opening the abdomen. Amazingly enough, this operation was performed on sows in the days of Aristotle and continues to this day in the dry-cured industry. Sows performed a useful function in seventeenth-century London by eating garbage from the streets and, since gelded sows grew fatter for the winter, professional sow gelders were a familiar sight on the streets of the city (figure 30).

On 22 August 1730 the Assizes in Bridgwater indicted a man for attempting to geld his wife. 'The sow-gelder being in company with several other married men over a pot of ale, they all join'd in complaint of the fruitfulness of their wives, because of the charges brought upon them thereby; and asking him, whether he could not do

Figure 30: A sow gelder. From *The Cryes of London Drawne after the Life* (1688).

by their wives as by other animals, he said he could.' Swearing a great oath, he rushed home, gagged his wife, tied her to a table and opened her abdomen,

> but after much puzzling, and putting the poor woman to great tor-
> ment, he found there was some difference between the situation of
> the parts in the rational and irrational animals, and so, sewing up the
> wound, he was forced to give up the experiment. The woman in her
> first agonies appeared strenuously against him, but being recovered by
> the time of the trial, was so generous as to forgive him, and plead for
> his pardon.[7]

DESIGNER PHENOTYPES

Drugs that affect the relative proportion of muscle and fat are known in the food industry as partitioning agents, and their potential was soon explored by people who wanted to modify their bodies. Male steroids are collectively known as the anabolic-androgenic steroids because their effects range from androgens, which act mainly upon secondary sexual characteristics, to anabolic steroids, which promote muscle bulk. Testosterone was first isolated and characterized in Germany in the 1930s. It may or may not be true that Hitler wanted to use it to make his soldiers more aggressive – troops on both sides certainly went into battle hyped up on amphetamines – but drugs in this class are routinely used by the human attack dogs of modern society, including members of the New York Police Department and private security contractors in Iraq.

Engineered variants of the steroid molecule soon became available. Modern consumers have a strong preference for lean meat, and drugs that increase the efficiency of food conversion to protein were thus of great interest to the farming community. Stilboestrol, a synthetic oestrogen first produced in 1938, promotes lean meat production when given to cattle in combination with a high-protein diet. A pellet containing the hormone is inserted in the cow's ear, and the ear is cut off at slaughter to avoid contaminating the carcass. Although banned in Europe, stilboestrol has been used in the USA for decades, and it was estimated in 1974 that this drug yielded an extra 135 million kg of animal protein for the same intake of protein.

Russian weightlifters were taking anabolic steroids by 1954 and were not banned from doing so until the 1960s. More recently, the US Olympic Committee conducted unannounced blood tests without punitive sanctions and found that 50 per cent of their athletes were taking anabolic steroids; it is indeed virtually impossible to perform at the highest level in power-to-weight sports without using them. To take one example, the women's shot-put record was established in the 1980s, before effective screening for steroids was possible. The distances achieved by female shot-putters have fallen steadily since then, and the winning throw in the Beijing Olympics of 2008 would not have qualified for a place in the final in the 1980s.[8]

No surprise that many top sportspeople now depend upon skilled pharmacological manipulation of their phenotype: the rewards are too great and the alternative too bleak for them to do otherwise. Russian athletes have been heavily penalized in recent times, but this may reflect a deficit of pharmaceutical expertise rather than one of sporting ethics. Effective regulation is impossible and is only half-heartedly attempted by professional bodies. They are only too well aware of the real situation, which is that only hypocrisy ('the tribute that vice pays to virtue') prevents formal recognition and acceptance of drug use in sport.

Sport apart, anabolic steroids are big business. At least 1 million Americans have used them, and the global market reaches into billions of US dollars. They are readily accessible online. When I consulted Buysteroidsuk.com some years ago it offered a 1 ml ampoule containing 250 mg of testosterone enanthate for €8. Once weekly injections were recommended, but the site did not fail to point out that some users take 500–1,000 mg daily, at a cost of up to €1,000 per month – doses astronomically greater than nature intended. The website mentions side effects such as severe acne and premature closure of the growth points in bones: adolescents who take steroids in the hope of accelerating manhood can be permanently stunted.

The website mentions that steroids are effective male contraceptives (they suppress production of testosterone), but it does not mention heart problems, aggressive or criminal behaviour, murder and suicide, all well documented in the literature. 'Roid rage' is a particular problem at the extreme doses used in some sports. In the 2014 off-season, twenty-eight NFL players had criminal charges brought against them, including one murder, one attempted murder and six violent assaults, with girlfriends at particular risk.[9] Although the US Anabolic Control Act of 1990 redefined anabolic-androgenic steroids (AAS) as Schedule III controlled substances (Class C in the UK), they can be legally purchased, pursuit of offenders is notably lacklustre, and the margin between lucrative misdemeanour and political acceptance grows ever narrower.

Fat, expensively acquired and more expensively shed, is the curse of the consumer phenotype. Bodybuilders face the two-fold challenge of acquiring muscle – which obliges them to eat – while avoiding the subcutaneous fat which would mask their muscles from view. The Holy Grail of pharmaceutical research, therefore, is to develop an agent that will melt fat. Nature's way of doing so is to release adrenal hormones which mobilize fat in order to release energy, and synthetic variants of adrenaline have similar effects. Since activation of fat cells generates enough energy to raise local temperature, drugs which do so are appropriately known as fat burners. Ephedrine, long used in Chinese medicine, has weak fat-burning properties, and so too does caffeine: both are used in the legal cocktails of fat-burning drugs you can buy on the internet. More potent adrenaline-like compounds with fat-burning properties include amphetamine (approved by the FDA for weight reduction in 1947 but later banned) and a range of related compounds. In general, however, and despite enormous pharmaceutical interest, the history of weight-loss medication has been uniformly disastrous. The drugs that work are poisonous, and the ones that aren't poisonous don't work.

Illegal fat-burning chemicals are far more potent, but also far more dangerous. The most notorious of these is dinitrophenol (DNP), an uncoupling agent which has an effect on fat cells like racing the engine of a stationary car. Since fat breakdown generates heat, fever is a characteristic symptom of overdose, and victims may die of hyperpyrexia despite all attempts to cool them down.

This came to attention in the munitions industry during the First World War, at a time when explosives were mass produced with few

Figure 31: Bodybuilders take DNP to improve the definition of their muscles.

safety precautions. Explosives contain nitrates, as we saw earlier. The British used TNT, and the women who handled it in Britain's munitions factories were known as canaries because they turned a bright yellow. The French made their explosives from nitrate-containing picric acid and employed men from their colonies, particularly Senegal, to handle it. It soon became apparent that these workers had a high death rate, although no one will ever know how high, since the immigrant workers were known by number rather than name, and each number was passed to another person when someone died.[10] In 1933, DNP was recommended as a safe weight-loss drug in the USA and could be bought over the counter until the FDA declared it 'not fit for human consumption' in 1938. The craze for bodybuilding produced another spate of deaths later in the century. DNP is still freely available on the internet, and tragedies still happen.

HOW TALL IS ENOUGH?

Hormones drive growth before puberty and tell the body when growth should end. The height of a healthy population has a bell-shaped distribution, which means that 95 per cent of people fall within a range of about 25 cm; those outside this range are investigated for possible endocrine or genetic abnormalities. Very short children fall into two main groups: statistical outliers from the healthy population, and those who have a deficiency of growth hormone. Growth hormone injection can overcome this deficiency, and has been routine for several decades: but should children who are short but normal in all other respects also be given growth hormone? European regulators rule this out, but one child in a hundred in the USA is treated on this basis.

The debate about giving hormone treatment to healthy but undersized children crosses a lot of ethical territory. The child cannot give informed consent, and the treatment is therefore directed to the parents. Some see short stature as a serious disadvantage, others offer unconditional acceptance to the child they have been given. This can be troubling for paediatricians, who do not like to act as 'cosmetic pharmacologists'. Should the likelihood of future social discrimination be treated as a disease? If so, what are the risks and benefits? One review concluded that a healthy short child gained 3–5 cm from 2,500 injections, at a cost of $18,000 (1999 values) per centimetre. There was little or no evidence that treatment offered psychological benefit. All that can be said is that some children are very unhappy about being short, others are less concerned. Some may benefit, others will not, and treatment should as far as possible be focused on the child rather than the parents.

Short stature is deemed a greater disadvantage for boys, whereas it was formerly assumed that very tall girls would find it hard to marry. Growth ends in response to the hormonal signals of puberty, and diethylstilboestrol (DES), which mimics these 'stop' signals, was used in Australia and elsewhere in the 1960s to limit the growth of tall girls. This involved many uncertainties, for it is not at all easy to predict the end of natural puberty, and the average reduction in height was only about 3.8 cm. One poor girl discovered that this had destroyed her chances of being a model. And then, in 1971, the thunderbolt fell: cases of vaginal adenocarcinoma – an exceptionally uncommon cancer – appeared in women whose mothers had been prescribed DES in pregnancy. Since this had been given to up to 5 million pregnant women in the hope of preventing spontaneous abortion, the realization that treatment of one generation might cause cancer in the next caused major concern. The history of phenotypic engineering in childhood has not been a happy one and is thoughtfully and sympathetically discussed in *Normal at Any Cost* by Susan Cohen and Christine Cosgrove (2009).

Drugs acting on the phenotype are here to stay, and the limits of social acceptability will continue to be challenged. Anabolic steroids have been used in most contact or power-to-weight ratio sports since the 1950s and will continue to be used while gym rats admire their torsos and competitive sport remains an extension of the entertainments industry. Athletes and bodybuilders accept the risks involved, and some have become expert pharmacologists who are in a position to make informed choices. Less so are the overweight, driven by desperation to seek desperate remedies. Modified hormones are widely available for use in the treatment of obesity, and even more powerful (and potentially lethal) alternatives can be obtained over the internet. Once again, the distinction between medically approved and illegal agents is moot; potent muscle-building drugs are illegal, whereas equally dangerous drugs are prescribed for obesity because this is deemed a medical condition. Meanwhile Black Pharma – a totally unregulated industry that markets its products with impunity over the internet – continues to grow and flourish. It has been estimated that the illegal market in growth hormone for bodybuilding or supposed anti-ageing properties is worth around $2 billion each year.[11]

WILL WE BECOME EXTINCT?

On 25 July 2017, a BBC headline warned that 'Sperm count drop "could make humans extinct"'. Apocalyptic pronouncements are routine media events, and this one attracted no more than passing notice. The reference was to a comprehensive meta-analysis which suggested that the sperm counts in Europe, Australasia and North America had fallen by an average of 52 per cent between 1973 and 2011. No such decline was seen in Africa, Asia or South America.[12] This trend, as the authors noted, was associated with an increase in other markers of compromised male reproductive development.

Before looking further, it must be pointed out that we are entering an academic minefield. Sperm come in their millions, the range of the normal is enormous (from 9 million/ml at the 5th percentile to 192 million at the 95th percentile), techniques for counting them have changed, and men who take part in surveys may not be representative of the general population. Sperm counts vary according to the age of the donor, the preceding period of abstinence, and from sample to sample.[13] Despite these qualifications, there is general agreement that sperm counts are falling in many populations.

What does this mean? Here again we must tread carefully. To begin with, fertility cannot be estimated with any confidence from a sperm count, although it is reduced at concentrations below 40 million/ml, reported in 20–30 per cent of healthy young men in several recent studies.[14] Sperm quality also matters, however, and a lower count is associated with a rising proportion of non-motile sperm and of abnormal forms. Pregnancy is the ultimate test of fertility, however, and sperm quality is only one among many factors involved. We saw that total fertility spiked after the Second World War but fell back to below replacement level by the end of the century in many affluent countries. Contraception was the major reason, although increasing maternal age also reduces fertility. Against this background, it is hard to determine whether male fertility is actually declining. Prospective studies of couples who want to have children report that some 12–18 per cent experience problems with infertility for at least one year. In Denmark, which exports human sperm to fifty other countries, assisted reproduction now plays a part in some 8 per cent of successful pregnancies.

Which brings us to the most intangible, technically challenging, emotionally charged, politically sensitive and ultimately terrifying question of all: can chemicals unwittingly released into the environment produce lasting effects upon the human reproductive system? To begin with, there is not the slightest doubt that a host of pesticides, plastics and other chemical by-products are lodged in our bodies, or that these have the potential to cause harm. Many have the undoubted potential to mimic or block hormonal signals, and the suggested effects upon male reproductive health are among the more plausible. Maleness might be thought of as a 'canary in the coal mine' when it comes to creeping threats to the human phenotype.

Men are modified women from an embryo's point of view, and a complex sequence of chemical events is required to make the transition. This occurs between seven and fifteen weeks of foetal life, which is therefore the time of greatest threat to maleness. An authoritative expert statement released thirty years ago detailed effects of chemical pollution such as 'decreased fertility in birds, fish, shellfish and mammals; decreased hatching success . . . gross birth deformities in birds, fish and turtles . . . defeminization and masculinization of female fish and birds; and compromised immune systems in birds and mammals'.[15] These and similar findings were endorsed by the American Endocrine Society in 2015. In the interim, numerous experimental studies had shown that endocrine disruptors, as they are called, can have devastating effects upon animal reproduction and growth, including the potential to induce permanent changes in our genes that can be passed on to future generations.[16]

All that is lacking, therefore, is conclusive evidence of direct effects on the human population. Despite many pointers, the evidence remains patchy and inconsistent. The reasons are not far to seek, for hormonally active substances can have an impact at almost undetectable concentrations and potentially harmful effects will vary according to dose, the stage of development and the presence or absence of other hormonally active substances. Standard methods of epidemiological or toxicological investigation are simply not designed to evaluate possible effects produced by complex interactions between multiple agents. Animal studies of endocrine disruptors are almost certainly of human relevance, even though this cannot be proved directly. The resulting impasse is familiar to environmentalists, for evidence of an intangible threat may not become conclusive until it is too late to do anything about it. The threat is undeniable.

II

The Fat of the Land

THE FIRST VENUS

Female obesity is frequently depicted in European statuettes dating back 20–30,000 years to the golden age of Palaeolithic hunters. Those who have never seen gross obesity could scarcely imagine it, yet the people who carved these images were evidently familiar with the condition (figure 32). The significance of these figurines is unknown, although food and fertility probably came into it. One clue may lie in the once widespread custom of fattening young women before marriage. In the first half of the twentieth century, for example, the Annang of Nigeria sent nubile girls to the fattening room in preparation for wedlock. The fattening room 'was simply for fattening – to make a girl fat and beautiful, to make her desirable as a choice of wife, to show all the villagers how wealthy her family was in being able to produce such a fine fat girl'. The girl lived in seclusion, stuffed herself with food and underwent instruction in the mysteries of womanhood. Months later, she was adorned with beads, feathers and bells, and – otherwise nude – was paraded through the village.[1] Similar customs have been described in Malawi and on the Pacific island of Nauru. An overweight bride has banked her assets, for the energy costs of pregnancy are equivalent to perhaps 10 kg of fat, and a year's exclusive breastfeeding requires twice that amount. The girls who came out of the fattening room would probably not stay fat for long.

Long-term obesity must have been exceptional in hunter-gatherer communities, but short-term accumulation of fat can be very useful in seasonal conditions. European farmers killed the animals they were unable to feed over the winter period, and the traditional orgy

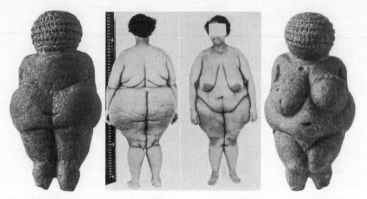

Figure 32: The artist who carved the Venus of Willendorf knew what gross obesity looked like, although his model was evidently younger than the textbook example.

of over-eating at Christmas was succeeded by an obligatory fast during the spring festival of Lent. Those who could pack on the fat when food was plentiful undoubtedly did better when food was scarce, and farmers in premodern times knew that plumpness in a prospective wife was an insurance policy for the winter, a marker of child-bearing capacity and an indication that she did not have tuberculosis. More recently, it implied freedom from HIV in parts of sub-Saharan Africa.

Weight is the archetypal marker of conspicuous consumption. Armour made for Henry VIII of England had a 137 cm waistline, his appetite was legendary, and a rope and tackle were needed to hoist him upstairs in later life. His obesity was complicated by a chronic leg ulcer. In the eighteenth century, the philosopher David Hume and the historian Edward Gibbon were notably overweight, and so too were many gouty aristocrats. Their gout was precipitated by lead poisoning and was due to their fondness for wines that tasted sweet because they were stored in lead-lined containers. Lord Byron weighed 88 kg when he was an eighteen-year-old undergraduate at Cambridge in 1806. His BMI of 29 was so unsuited to the fashionable tubercular look of a Romantic poet that he became the first celebrity dieter, soaked his food in vinegar and brought his weight down to 57 kg within five years. We know this because overweight aristocrats weighed themselves on the scales of Berry Bros and Rudd, a fashionable wine merchant in London. Politicians were less concerned about their appearance, but even the irascible Otto von Bismarck (111 kg, BMI 30.9) felt obliged to diet in 1883, losing 27 kg in the process. William Howard Taft, twenty-seventh president of the United States, turned the scales at 161 kg when he took office in 1909 and reputedly got stuck in the White House bath. The nineteenth-century French bourgeoisie used the term *embonpoint* approvingly to signify prominence of the female bosom or male belly.

Chronic obesity was relatively rare outside the ranks of the well-to-do.[2] Hunters and foragers attained something close to their maximum weight in their twenties, remained at this plateau level until their fifties and shed weight in later life. Adolphe Quetelet found this pattern in Belgians in the first half of the nineteenth century, and it also characterized Japanese men in the first half of the twentieth century,[3] suggesting that this may have been the norm in premodern societies.

Deviation from this traditional pattern characterizes the privileged phenotype in the past and today's consumer phenotype. The first evidence of the modern trend came from the life insurance industry. The *Medico-Actuarial Mortality Investigation*, published in 1912, was based on analysis of 221,819 insurance policies issued to American men from 1885 to 1900 and policies for 136,504 women over a longer period.[4] Insured Americans were then almost exclusively white, above average in income and taller than the background population. Figure 33 compares the male age and weight in Quetelet's Belgians of the 1830s, Americans insured between 1885 and 1900, as reported in 1912, and a survey sample of US men at the start of the twenty-first century.

The figure shows that Quetelet's males were 27 kg lighter than twenty-first-century Americans at fifteen years of age, partly because they had yet to experience their pubertal growth spurt, and that they gained no further weight after the age of thirty. Young insured Americans at the end of the nineteenth century were remarkably slim by our standards (male and female BMIs were 23.2 and 22.7 respectively) but were set to gain another 6 kg by middle age – an increase of 0.65 g per day when averaged over the intervening thirty years.

Hillel Schwartz, a social historian of obesity, notes that physicians

Age and weight, 1835, 1885–1900, 2007

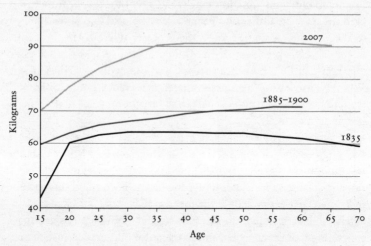

Figure 33: The trajectory of age and weight in Belgian men (1835), insured American men (1885–1900) and men participating in a US health survey (2007–10). Data from Quetelet (1835), the *Medico-Actuarial Mortality Investigation* (1912) and NHANES.

who prescribed diets in the early years of the twentieth century generally did so in order to assist weight gain after illness.[5] By the 1920s, however, overweight was a consistent topic of magazines aimed at women, and it features in every issue today. Even so, the condition did not become really common until later in the century.

Figure 34 compares the BMI of American women in their twenties and fifties at different time points over the past century; the most striking development is the rapid increase in the 20–29-year age group from 1980 on. Although the difference in BMI between women in their twenties and in their fifties might appear unchanged, do not be deceived: the women sampled in their twenties in 1976–8 come from the same age cohort as those sampled in their fifties in 2007–10. This implies that they gained 16.7 kg in weight (as against 15.2 kg in men) between their twenties and their fifties, an average gain of roughly 1.5 g per day.

Weight gain in the young was the first sign of the impending

BMI difference between 20–29 age group and 50–59 age group (female)

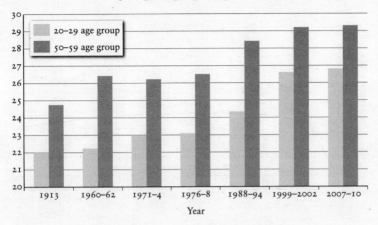

Figure 34: Body Mass Index comparison between American women in their twenties and fifties, 1913–2010. Bear in mind that the young adults of 1976–8 are sampled from the same age cohort as the middle-aged women of 2007–10.

obesity epidemic. Three long-term prospective studies of American children were launched in the 1930s, motivated in part by concerns about the impact of the Great Depression upon future generations. The Fels Study, based in Ohio, continues today, and showed a steady upward trend in BMI in children born after 1960. In girls, this was almost entirely due to increasing fat mass, whereas boys additionally showed decreasing muscle, presumably due to inactivity.[6] The Fels children were almost exclusively of European descent, but black and Hispanic children appear to have been gaining weight even more rapidly.

This increase in childhood obesity was ushered in on a tide of cheap calories, for Americans increased their per capita food consumption by 20 per cent between 1980 and 2000 (figure 35). This was associated with a greater intake of processed foods with high energy density and a less active lifestyle. The young got fatter, and obesity spread around the world.

US per capita calorie consumption, 1970–2010

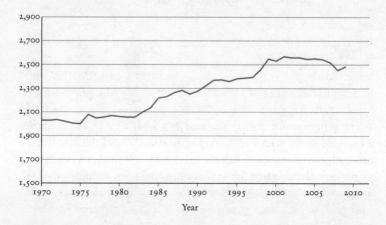

Figure 35: US per capita food availability, adjusted for spoilage and waste. Availability of food calories increased by 500 calories per head per day between 1980 and 2000. Source: USDA

THE GLOBALIZATION OF OBESITY

The obesity epidemic was the legacy of unprecedented prosperity in post-war America. Fossil energy was poured into food production, and farmers invested more calories than they obtained as food.[7] For all their negative connotations, fossil energy, machinery, fertilizers, hybrid crops and insecticides were able to feed 3 billion more people by the end of the twentieth century, and global food production stayed abreast of population growth. Multinational corporations took over America's role as suppliers of raw farm produce, and foreign direct investment made them stakeholders in enterprises that produced and processed food around the world. This was backed by immense wealth, sometimes rivalling that of the countries they invested in, and the ability to jump tariff barriers. Aggressive free trade policies were a hallmark of coca-colonization.[8]

Some forms of food processing remove almost everything but calories, generating energy-rich foods and drinks which are effortlessly
absorbed into the bloodstream and fat cells. Their products are
attractively packaged, travel and store well, and are addictively tasty
and cheap. Adult baby-food has largely supplanted traditional and
more nutritionally balanced diets. A rise in global BMI was the
result. Analysis of 127 countries showed that mean BMI increased
from 23 in 1980 to 25 in 2008.[9] This represents a 6 kg gain for a man
170 cm tall.

The geography of obesity (defined as a BMI >30) in 191 countries
is outlined in the CIA Factbook. Pacific islands head the list, and the
first full-size countries to register are Egypt and the USA, both with
33 per cent obesity rates. Some European countries, including the UK,
Spain and Russia, register 33–26 per cent, whereas others – Italy, the
Netherlands, Sweden, France, Denmark and Switzerland – come in
below 20 per cent. Other affluent societies, South Korea, Singapore
and Japan for example, have rates well below 10 per cent. As this
league table indicates, obesity is by no means an inevitable consequence of wealth. Even so, it generally affects the poor in rich
countries and the rich in poor ones. WHO found that higher levels of
education are associated with lower BMI, especially in women, and
that the obesity rate moves down the social scale as incomes rise,
with the tipping point at a per capita GDP of around $2,500.[10] Excess
weight has become a stigma in wealthier societies; a potent marker of
low social standing, poor marital prospects, lower chances of employment and reduced earning capacity.[11] Social exclusion has become
associated with obesity: the rich get richer, and the poor get fatter.

THE RISE OF THE CONSUMER
PHENOTYPE

There are times, as the author who wrote under the pen-name of Saki
once said, when an ounce of imprecision can be worth a ton of fact.
The argument that follows is offered in the same spirit and consists
in this: we are all overweight. This point requires some emphasis,
for we are often told that obesity is someone else's problem, and that

overconsumption only harms those who overconsume more than the rest. Not so. The internal affairs of the body are controlled by an intricate network of self-regulating systems which only come to notice when something goes wrong. Weight, blood pressure, blood glucose and circulating lipids are elements of this network and remained in stable balance across the human lifespan in traditional societies. The first signs of a large-scale disturbance to this equilibrium came when people began to gain weight in adult life. Markers of internal regulation such as blood pressure and glucose then began to creep upwards, more so as people became heavier and lived longer. A loss of internal regulation signals a phenotype under stress, and a phenotype which struggles to regulate its internal affairs is clearly not in good shape.

Obesity, especially when located around the midriff, is strongly associated with hypertension, diabetes and hyperlipidaemia. The resulting phenotype (which comes in various shapes, sizes and definitions) is known as the metabolic syndrome. Around half of us will qualify for inclusion at some stage in our lives. The metabolic syndrome carries an increased risk of vascular disease and increases your chances of weight-associated cancer. Each one of its features is associated with overconsumption of food, every feature responds to a reduced food intake, and every associated risk is reduced by eating less. As such, it represents an extreme form of the consumer phenotype (figure 36).

When everyone overconsumes, it seems unfair to blame those who consume more than the rest, for the consequences affect us all. This shows up most clearly when a whole population is obliged to limit its food intake. Germany starved in the First World War, for example, and the recorded mortality from diabetes – a sensitive marker of calorie intake – fell by 50 per cent in Berlin. Equally dramatic reductions in deaths from diabetes and heart disease occurred in occupied Norway during the Second World War.[12] The population of the UK went on an enforced diet in wartime: mortality from diabetes halved and stayed low for a decade after the war had ended.[13]

Cuba provided a more recent demonstration. The island survived a prolonged US trade embargo during the Castro regime by exchanging sugar for gasoline from the USSR. When the Russian economy crashed in 1990, Cuba suffered: food calories fell from 2,900 to 1,860

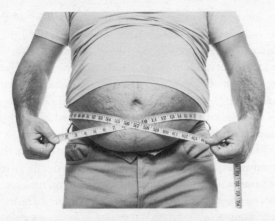

Figure 36: Overconsumption is associated with varying combinations of central obesity, hypertension, high levels of cholesterol and glucose, arterial disease and weight-associated cancer.

per day, and adult weight dropped by 4–5 kg (5–6 per cent). Overall mortality fell by 18 per cent between 1997 and 2002, with a 51 per cent reduction in deaths from diabetes, 35 per cent fewer deaths from coronary heart disease and a 20 per cent reduction in death by stroke.[14] As this shows, calorie restriction improves the health of a whole population, even when few of its members are actually obese.

Chronic overconsumption is a novel phenomenon. Its hallmarks are progressive weight gain in adult life and mounting evidence of a phenotype under stress. We define obesity and its complications as diseases – thus establishing a convenient psychological distance from the rest of the population – but the problem lies in the lifestyle, not in our response to it. This having been said, why *do* we respond to it in different ways?

OBESITY IN EVOLUTIONARY PERSPECTIVE

Nothing in our evolutionary history prepared us to eat so much, which might explain why our responses to it are so diverse. Hundreds

of genes are implicated in obesity, but we should avoid the tempt-
ation to call them 'obesity genes' – they were passed on to us by
ancestors who were rarely if ever obese. These genes are there for
good reasons, but making us fat was not among them. One striking
observation (which confirms what everyone knows) is that some
people gain weight far more easily than others. To take one example,
an African-American woman who was 162.6 cm tall and on the 10th
percentile for BMI would, at the end of the twentieth century, be
expected to gain 5 kg between her mid-twenties and her mid-fifties.
A matched woman on the 90th percentile would have gained 58 kg
over the same period.[15] We vary considerably in our propensity to lay
down fat.

Which brings us to a related question: how does our body know
how heavy it wants to be? Most of us have unrestricted access to
food, but we match our intake to our needs with remarkable accuracy. A typical thirty-six-year-old white American man weighs 86 kg
and consumes ten times his body weight – 907 kg – of food in the
course of a year. His calorie intake is around 2,700 calories per day,
or just under a million calories per year.[16] With little or no conscious
effort, he will balance his annual energy inventory (calories in/cal-
ories out) to within 0.63 per cent of its starting point over the course
of the year. Ask an obesity expert how this is done, and you will learn
a great deal apart from the answer.

The key point to note is that he will retain a small positive weight
balance. Unlike a thermostat, which returns room temperature to the
same starting point, Mr Average is programmed to reset his weight to
a slightly higher level. The increment translates to around 550 grams
per year, or a gain of 10 kg by the age of fifty-four. His weight regulation is forward-feeding and creeps upwards, year after year. This is
an example of *allostasis*, a characteristic feature of the phenotypic
transition.

Genes influence your weight, but food is the overriding factor.
Overweight dogs have overweight owners, and there is no genetic
explanation for this.

THRIFTY GENES

The geneticist James V. ('Jim') Neel (1915–2000) suggested in 1962 that obesity is driven by genes that evolved in response to starvation. Geneticists thought at the time that there was a 'diabetes gene': one copy gave you late onset diabetes and two copies caused early onset diabetes. Since the latter was invariably fatal in the days before insulin, a 'diabetes gene' should theoretically be eliminated in the course of time, despite which diabetes is remarkably common. This reminded Neel of sickle cell disease, in which one copy of the abnormal gene confers resistance to malaria, but two cause lethal disease. Malaria would rage unchecked if no one had the gene, but one child in four would die of sickle cell disease if everyone had it. The optimal outcome is thus an equilibrium between carriers and non-carriers which geneticists call a *balanced polymorphism*. Neel speculated that one copy of the hypothetical gene for diabetes might help you to survive starvation, and that the counterbalancing risk of diabetes would be negligible in people living at the margins of subsistence. The boot would be on the other foot in times of plenty, however, for the gene which helped you when starving would now give you diabetes; it would be 'A "thrifty" genotype rendered detrimental by "progress".'[17]

The great tragedy of science, according to biologist T. H. Huxley, is the 'slaying of a beautiful hypothesis by an ugly fact', and Neel's beautiful hypothesis was soon put to the sword. There is no single diabetes gene, and its proposed mechanism of action was discredited. The emphasis shifted from diabetes to obesity, however, and the idea lived on as 'one of the most influential hypotheses in genetic epidemiology'. Neel himself had no more than a passing interest in thrifty genes, and devotes less than a paragraph in his lengthy autobiography to the idea for which he is best remembered.[18]

How might a 'thrifty gene' help you to survive starvation? There are two main possibilities. One is that the gene would make your energy metabolism more efficient, thus enabling you to survive on less. The other is that it would encourage you to eat more and store fat. The hypothesis that some people have a more efficient metabolism than others can be tested by starving them under experimental conditions.

PLASTICITY

Let's imagine that you have just stopped eating. Nothing but water will pass your lips for two months. You won't notice much to begin with, just the familiar pangs when your next meal is due. These are conditioned responses. Drink some water, go to bed, and the discomfort will probably ease. Twenty-four hours later, the pangs become more insistent; you are distinctly uncomfortable and will begin to feel weak and tired. You are 170 cm tall and you weighed 75 kg when the fast began. Your weight has already fallen by just under a kilo, mainly because water is lost when carbohydrate is broken down. Your brain, which weighs in at around 1.5 kg, or 2 per cent of your total weight, is now responsible for nearly a quarter of your energy consumption. The rest of your body has switched to energy-saving mode, and your liver is racing to produce the glucose needed by a hungry brain. Other tissues, meanwhile, are burning fat to economize on glucose, while ketones (the breakdown products of fat metabolism) accumulate in the circulation. By forty-eight hours or so your brain has switched to ketones, and your breath has a distinctive smell akin to that of stored apples. The switch to ketones is faster in women than in men, and in lean people as against the overweight. You are increasingly disinclined to engage in unnecessary effort and you feel faint if you try. Your interest in sex has faded, and you feel detached from practical concerns other than food. You may experience the mild euphoria which accompanies religious fasts, possibly related to the surge of ketones or to the release of endogenous opioids.

Your fast has now lasted a week. Your weight has dropped more than 6 kg, although much of this is due to fluid loss and would soon be regained if you started to eat. By three weeks you will have lost 18 kg, after which the rate of loss will slow to one-third of a kilo per day. Your intestine no longer wastes energy by making digestive juices. Your muscle mass is shrinking, and you are getting weaker. You are still alert, but your resting pulse has fallen to below 40 beats per minute, and your blood pressure falls when you stand, forcing some volunteers to withdraw from prolonged fasts. Your core temperature has fallen, encouraging your body to consume less oxygen. The situation is serious but not yet desperate, for you were well-nourished when your fast began, with access to around 15 kg of reserve fat and 6 kg of protein. This equates to more than 160,000 calories, enough to keep you going for more than two months. But time is running out.

Starvation has been studied intensively in the laboratory, and the fact is that we all respond to it in much the same way. This implies that natural selection has hardwired efficient genes into us all and that we vary little in terms of metabolic efficiency. We must therefore look elsewhere for the origins of obesity.

An observer of the Great Irish Famine of 1849 noted that 'no one has yet ... been able to explain why it is that men and boys sink sooner under famine than the other sex; still, so it is; go where you will, every officer will tell you it is so'.[19] The explanation is simple: women have a higher proportion of fat, and each kilo contains enough energy to support several days of life. This might explain why (regardless of gender) the important obesity-associated genes are expressed in our brain. One such is FTO, so named because it was originally linked to fused toes in inbred mice, no other effect being known at the time. It was later identified in the course of a search for genetic loci associated with diabetes; FTO affects this indirectly by encouraging people to store fat, and increased fat predisposes to diabetes. Those with one copy of the risk-associated variant – a billion people worldwide – are 1.5 kg heavier than those without, and two copies make you 3 kg heavier. In blinded tests, carriers of the gene eat more, select more calorie-rich food and do not experience the same feeling of satiety as those with the neutral variant. The gene is present in around 50 per cent of the European population, suggesting that it may be particularly useful in conditions of seasonal hunger.[20] Its effects are relatively modest, yet they are three to six times greater than those of any other obesity-related gene. As with other complex traits, obesity is determined by the mass action of many genes with tiny effects.

THRIFTY PHENOTYPES

We met Anders Forsdahl and David Barker earlier. Barker showed that low birth weight predisposes to the later development of high blood pressure, diabetes and high circulating levels of fat – particularly if an underweight child goes on to gain excess weight in later life.

Barker joined forces with the biochemist Nick Hales to stress the key role of insulin, for this, with other insulin-like molecules, is an essential factor in foetal development. Modulation of these signals in foetal life can have lasting effects upon the composition of the baby, and Hales and Barker suggested that underfeeding channels scarce resources towards vital organs such as the brain by making other tissues less sensitive to insulin. As a result, undernourished babies may be programmed in ways that are dysfunctional in an affluent environment. This, in deference to Neel, they called the thrifty phenotype hypothesis.[21] As the name implies, this represents a shared pattern of response to a frequently encountered environmental challenge, and is largely unrelated to variation in individual genes.

If undernutrition predisposes to small babies, overnutrition predisposes to big ones. This happens if a mother has diabetes. Her glucose moves freely across the placenta, but her insulin (or the insulin that she injects) does not. The foetus has an overdose of glucose, which sends its own insulin-producing cells into overdrive. The resulting baby is born with a florid countenance, weighs up to a kilo more than expected and resembles a small alderman who has dined too well. It is more likely to gain weight in later life than the offspring of non-diabetic mothers. Diabetes is exceptionally common in the Pima Indians of Arizona, and babies born before the mother develops diabetes are smaller than those born after its onset, indicating that the difference is driven by the increased glucose supply from the mother rather than by her genes. Overweight mothers (including those who gain excessively during pregnancy) also have big babies who are predisposed to weight gain in later life. Since babies can be programmed for weight gain before birth, it is logical to suppose that such programming can be reversed, and a clinical trial was performed in Edinburgh in which overweight mothers were invited to take metformin (a diabetes treatment known to be safe in pregnancy) or a placebo in double-blind fashion. It was hoped that the active tablet would modulate the flow of fuel to the foetus, and that this would result in a thinner adult. In the event, birth weight was unaffected, but the trial was remarkable in its attempt to modify the phenotype of an unborn generation.[22]

How then do we link thrifty genes to thrifty phenotypes? Genetic variation explains around 65 per cent of the variation in obesity within (not between) populations, but the individual genes predisposing to obesity so far identified actually explain little more than 7 per cent of that variation. Why so little? One possibility is that the interaction between these genes has unpredictable consequences (often referred to as 'emergent properties') which go well beyond their individual effects.

OBESITY: DISEASE OR PHENOTYPE?

The US authorities first became concerned with the health aspects of obesity around the middle of the twentieth century, and their initial estimates of its risks were based upon weight-for-height tables provided by the insurance companies. 'Desirable' weight conferred the lowest mortality in those who purchased life insurance between 1935 and 1954. BMI is a cruder measure but easier to use and went on to become the standard. A consensus panel of the National Institutes of Health was given the task of deciding how much weight was 'too much' in 1985. They set the limit at a BMI of 27.3 for men and 27.8 for women, this being equivalent to the 85th percentile of the 20–29 age group in their latest survey. Little did they appreciate the storm that was heading their way, for within a decade 33.3 per cent of men and 36.4 per cent of women had already surpassed this threshold.[23]

Inevitable though it might seem in retrospect, the obesity epidemic of the late twentieth century took even the experts by surprise.[24] Put bluntly, they failed to predict that a massive increase in food intake would make people fat. Clothes got bigger, airline seats got wider, but demographers and epidemiologists were slow to spot the trend. The idea that there *was* an obesity epidemic did not really penetrate the public consciousness until the 1990s, when it came with a drumbeat of doom-laden predictions. Epidemiologist Paul Zimmet said in 2008 that obesity was the greatest public health challenge of the twenty-first century and 'as big a threat as global warming or bird flu' – an interesting juxtaposition. British health minister Alan Johnson borrowed the comparison with climate change. The experts who had failed to predict the obesity epidemic then went on to overstate its consequences and to garnish superlatives with unreliable facts. America, we were told, is the most obese nation (not true). Obesity kills 400,000 Americans every year (debatable). Obesity will cause a secondary epidemic of heart disease (heart disease fell rapidly). Increasing obesity will send life expectancy into reverse (still rising until recently). Over-eating is more of a threat to global health than starvation (which would *you* prefer?). The doomsayers of the obesity epidemic confidently predicted a massive increase in heart disease and declining life expectancy. Nothing, as Macaulay might have said, is quite so ridiculous as the public health lobby in full cry.

An international panel of experts sat down a few years ago to decide whether obesity should be classed as a disease. After weighty discussion and mentioning some well-known philosophers, they based their conclusion upon a simple syllogism: a disease makes you ill, obesity makes you ill, ergo obesity is a disease. No one could deny that massive obesity is a dreadful affliction, and those affected deserve all our understanding and support. It is nonetheless counterproductive to define it as a disease. A disease is (by definition) abnormal, and to apply this name to obesity is to imply that everyone above an arbitrary cut-off point is diseased and in need of specific treatment. Conversely, it implies that those below the cut-off are healthy, thus placing the blame squarely upon the shoulders of the victim. Nor will this change. Since consumer society is based upon the premise of ever-increasing consumption, we need not anticipate a meaningful political response. Nor should we look for help from the people who gave us cigarettes and alcohol, and who measure responses to advertising by scanning people's brains. They know that excessive calorie intake stokes the demand for weight loss, and that a demand that can never be satisfied is the marketer's dream. Diet books and diet pills offer hope, but little more, and the cultural stigmata of obesity are so potent that those affected submit meekly to their plight. Treating obesity as a medical condition has the effect of disowning it, for 'medical problems' are assumed to have medical causes and medical solutions. Obesity surgery offers undoubted benefits for severely overweight people but – while hailed as a success – it is also the ultimate admission of failure.

Obesity is a phenotype, and this phenotype is a direct consequence of our way of life. Even our cats and dogs suffer from it.[25] Ever-increasing production driven by ever-increasing consumption is scarcely a rational or achievable goal, yet we all participate to a greater or lesser extent. The message is reinforced every time we watch television or fill our cars with packaged food at the supermarket. You can treat a disease, but you can't treat a phenotype.

It is hopelessly simplistic to think of obesity as a medical condition rather than as a phenotype. There are many obesity phenotypes, and BMI is a very inadequate way of defining them. Tell that to Jermane Mayberry, in 2001 a twenty-seven-year-old with a BMI of 39.6, just short of 'extreme' obesity. Should he have been offered remedial surgery? Mayberry was 193 cm tall, weighed 148 kg and played football for the Philadelphia Eagles.[26] Fat he wasn't.

We use BMI to assess health risks, yet women with the same BMI have more adipose tissue than men but only half the health risk, and this applies at any level from skinny to grossly overweight. Women store it in the hips and thighs, and men around the middle. The feminine pattern is controlled by oestrogens, which is why fat migrates to

Body mass index

22.3   22.3

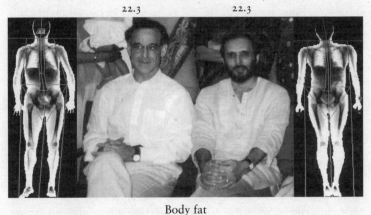

Body fat

9.1   21.2

Figure 37: Two friends of the author, John Yudkin and Ranjan Yajnik, had the identical BMI but John (an ex-marathon runner) had 9.1 per cent fat, and Ranjan (whose 'main exercise is running for the lift') had 21.2 per cent.

the female midriff after the menopause. There are also major differences between ethnic groups. Indian populations carry more fat than Europeans for any given level of BMI (figure 37), whereas Europeans carry more fat than Africans or Polynesians.

When does fat become a health hazard? The epidemiological approach is to measure a risk factor in a population and then to monitor its long-term health outcomes. This allows you to decide (for example) the level of blood pressure that translates into a meaningful risk of stroke, or the level of blood glucose associated with diabetic eye disease. This is not so easy for obesity, however, mainly because it has multiple outcomes. Faced with this limitation, WHO opted for an operational criterion in 1997, albeit with a strong hint of digit preference. The upper limit of normal BMI was set at 25, with 30 for overweight, 35 for class I obesity, 40 for class II ('very severe') and >40 for Class III 'extreme' obesity. Arbitrary, but easy to remember. As one expert commented, 'over the past 3 or 4 decades in the United States we have come almost full circle in the arena of weight criteria and definitions'.[27]

Sex and ethnicity apart, the amount of fat in your body varies with age and exercise. Muscle replaces fat if we train hard, which is why people who haunt the gym lose less weight than they hoped. Conversely, fat takes over from muscle as we grow older. From a health perspective, the total amount of fat is less important than where it is, how long it has been there and what it is doing.

The health consequences of obesity are classed as mechanical or metabolic. Extreme obesity causes mechanical problems such as worn-out joints, breathing difficulty and problems getting around. These are collectively known as 'fat mass disease'. Lesser degrees of adiposity – now the norm in western societies – are potentially harmful because of their association with diabetes, hypertension, high levels of circulating fat and heart disease. Associated risks include fatty infiltration of liver and muscle and an increased risk of some common cancers. There is, however, no simple association between obesity and its metabolic complications, for many of the people who have these complications are not particularly overweight. Conversely, those with so-called 'metabolically benign' obesity (perhaps 10–30 per cent of the total) have a lower risk of coronary heart disease and derive less benefit from weight loss.[28] All this nuanced complexity is lost when we think of excessive

weight as a single medical condition with a highly inadequate definition. We muddle health risk with social obsession.

A disease is an outcome, but a phenotype is a process, and a
process that is both flexible and interactive, for our phenotype is
changing. The people affected by obesity are getting younger, and
their proportion of abdominal fat is increasing relative to BMI. Earlier fat deposition means that people are exposed to its potentially
harmful effects for longer. Despite this, the life expectancy of the
overweight is increasing, largely because the obesity epidemic has
coincided with a surprising and massive decline in death from coronary heart disease. In the USA this decline amounted to a 73 per cent
reduction in men and a 75 per cent reduction in women between
1973 and 2008. Since heart disease is the leading cause of death in
both obesity and diabetes, these too have become safer (figure 38).

A WHO survey conducted in thirty-eight countries found, contrary to expectation, that the coronary risk associated with an
increased BMI was falling.[30] In line with this, analysis of US national
surveys over a forty-year period documented fewer people with high

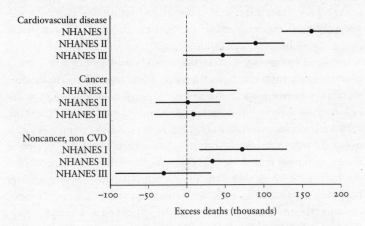

Figure 38: Excess deaths related to obesity in three US national surveys:
NHANES I (1971–5), NHANES II (1976–80) and NHANES III
(1988–94). This was associated with a major fall in death from
cardiovascular disease, a smaller fall in excess deaths from cancer
and an overall reduction in other causes of death.[29]

cholesterol or high blood pressure, and fewer smokers (reductions of 12 per cent, 18 per cent and 12 per cent respectively). The extent to which this is due to medical intervention remains uncertain, and the authors comment that 'the net result of these phenomena may be a population that is, paradoxically, more obese, diabetic, arthritic, disabled and medicated, but with lower overall cardiovascular risk'.[31]

Forty years ago, fat was considered an inert cupboard for the storage of calories. It has since come to life, and fat cells are now pictured as a buzzing hive of metabolic activity. Excessive fat has become a major health problem for the first time in our evolutionary history, although not to the extent that some people have claimed. There is a thriving and profitable trade in the creation of fat, and an equally thriving trade in expensive means of trying to remove it. Skinniness, expensively achieved, is the new form of conspicuous consumption, and excess weight is only one strand in a complex web of disability which extends to social denial, damaging behaviour, depression and all the miseries of poverty. It cannot and should not be considered in isolation. Natural selection did not equip us to cope with chronic overconsumption, and we vary in our ability to handle it. Additional influences – prenatal, familial, social and cultural – influence our progression along the fat escalator. Obesity may not be destiny, but it all too easily becomes our fate.

Increasing adiposity is a culture embodied in a phenotype, but a phenotype that is interactive. As a result, we appear to have become more fat-adapted than in the past. It is often said that 'sixty is the new fifty' when it comes to age, and 80 kg seems to have become the 'new 70' in terms of weight. This might explain why the obesity epidemic did not culminate in the predicted health apocalypse. How else do we explain the astonishing decline in arterial disease, the changing burden of obesity and the expanding frontiers of old age? Any upturn in our health prospects is generally attributed to better medical care: the possibility that we ourselves might be changing scarcely features in our thinking. But we are.

PART 3

Life's Journey

12

At Home in the Multiverse

The size, shape and content of our bodies has changed in the course of the phenotypic transition, and so too has our relationship with the teeming life-forms that share the life of our bodies. Our immune system senses their presence while formulating its response, and the interaction constitutes our immune phenotype.

The true masters of the earth are too small or too inconspicuous to be seen. Some harvest the sun, others extract key minerals from inorganic matter, and all other life is parasitic upon them. The first person to guess the existence of this unseen multiverse was Antony van Leeuwenhoek (1632–1723), an amateur scientist who ran a dry goods store in the Netherlands. He used his spare moments to make microscope lenses from beads of glass, lenses so good that they enabled him to see what no one had ever seen before. He scraped some of the white matter from between his teeth and then 'to my great surprize perceived that the aforesaid matter contained very many small living animals, which moved themselves very extravagantly . . . their motion was strong and nimble, and they darted themselves thro' the water or spittle, as a Jack or Pike does through the water'.[1]

When Leeuwenhoek rinsed his mouth with vinegar, he found that he could kill the small animals on the surface of the white matter between his teeth, but not those deep within. A first sight of this unseen world can be disconcerting, as the bacteriologist Theodor Rosebury discovered. He was in the habit of starting his course for medical students by repeating Leeuwenhoek's demonstration of the life between our teeth, and he generally picked on the least salubrious mouth in the vicinity for maximal effect. On one occasion he recruited a passing cleaning lady and invited her to look down the microscope.

She was so impressed by what she saw that she arranged for a dentist to remove all her teeth.[2]

Our understanding of the body is filtered through many academic specialities, each jealous of its territory. Evolution is less discriminating, however, and its solutions cross disciplinary boundaries. Our brains, our guts, our hormones and our immune cells interact seamlessly in the process of growth, for example, and animals raised in germ-free conditions do not develop normal brains, guts or immune responses.[3] Bacterial colonization of the large intestine is such a routine feature of our entry into the world that other aspects of our growth have adjusted around it. Some life-forms have been routine passengers in our bodies for so long that our immune system has learned to anticipate their presence, so much so that things can go wrong in their absence. Microbiologist Graham Rook has called them the 'old friends' for this reason.[4] Since they are not always friendly, however, I shall refer to them as our *fellow travellers*.

We evolved to co-exist with other life-forms, and they evolved to co-exist with us. Every creature in the multiverse uses the same nucleic acids as we do, possesses similar genes and manufactures its proteins from the same amino acids: there are no tidy boundaries between us. This unstable interface is regulated by our immune system, and this chapter is about the way in which this system has adjusted to a changing environment.

THREE AGES OF IMMUNITY

The changing balance between life and death was famously described by epidemiologist Abdel Omran. Our birth rate is limited by the number of fertile women, and he noted that this ran close to full throttle in premodern times, while the death rate – which knows no limits – determined the size of past populations. Our numbers fluctuated at the mercy of plague or famine, and Omran called this the *Age of Pestilence and Famine*. Early modern times then became the *Age of Receding Pandemics*, followed by the *Age of Degenerative and Man-made Diseases*. Collectively, these three 'ages' make up what he called the epidemiologic transition.[5]

Useful though it is, Omran's scheme overlooks the fact that we existed as scattered groups of hunter-gatherers for 95 per cent of our time on earth, and that his Age of Pestilence and Famine only really applies to the agrarian phase of our career. Our relationship with the lives in and on our bodies has varied considerably over this time, and our changing pattern of immunity is more logically described in terms of the Palaeolithic, agrarian and consumer phenotypes. We will track this progression by following the careers of some well-known fellow travellers.

Our ancestors typically lived at a density of about one per square kilometre in pre-agrarian times. Epidemic disease would not have been able to spread under such conditions, whereas infections or parasites which passed vertically from one generation to the next would be more likely to survive. This pattern is seen in other widely dispersed species. Given the long-term nature of this relationship, and the fact that fellow travellers that cause serious harm to their hosts will die with them, a modus vivendi emerged. A state of equilibrium between passenger and host thus characterized the Palaeolithic phase of our immune phenotype, only to be transformed when we began to live in settled communities amid our own waste products, vermin and domestic animals. Molecular dating techniques show that many new infections entered the human population around this time, often jumping species in order to do so. Since these newer infections passed easily from one person to another, they were unaffected by the survival of their host. Virulent forms spread rapidly, and the first major epidemics appeared.

Omran seems to have assumed that his Age of Pestilence and Famine represented the natural condition of mankind, but the agrarian phase of our existence was in fact a relatively brief interlude of little more than 10,000 years. Changes in the man-made environment invited new infections into the human population, and further changes were sufficient to banish them – which is why many infectious diseases were already in full retreat before antibiotics were available. Paradoxically, some of our oldest fellow travellers have proved surprisingly resistant to a changing environment, and worms, malaria and tuberculosis remain global scourges today. Other fellow travellers disappeared from the immune radar with unexpected consequences.

Campaigns to eradicate parasites have been complicated by outbreaks of asthma and allergy, for example, and their absence may predispose to some of the immune-mediated diseases of modern life. The consumer phase of our immune phenotype is therefore characterized by the retreat of horizontal infections, by the persistence of some of our older fellow travellers, and by the rise of new medical conditions related to the loss of co-evolutionary partners.

THE PREHISTORY OF IMMUNITY

The word 'parasite' (literally, 'beside food') was once a derisive Greek term for an impecunious guest who paid for his meal by flattering his host: 'whose bread I eat, his praise I sing'. In medical usage, a parasite is an organism that lives in or on other organisms and harms its host. Since the distinction between organisms that harm and those that don't is somewhat elastic, two experts recently concluded 'that the only unambiguous definition is that parasites are those organisms studied by people who call themselves parasitologists'.[6] Parasitologists, so defined, generally focus upon larger multicellular organisms ranging up to worms and biting insects. There are plenty of these. As one textbook points out, 'few people realize there are far more kinds of parasitic than non-parasitic organisms in the world' and that 'more than a hundred kinds of flagellates, amebas, ciliates, worms, lice, fleas, ticks and mites have evolved to feed upon us'.[7] A recent catalogue of human parasites listed 437 species. Non-human primates generally carry fewer than eight types of parasitic worm in the wild, although some have more than forty; those with more parasites tend to be bigger and longer-lived and to exist in denser populations.[8]

Worms might seem of remote concern to many readers, but they were ubiquitous in the past. Modern hunter-gatherers are not a reliable guide to our primal condition, but a review of parasite loads in fifteen groups of forest-dwelling hunter-gatherers found a median infestation rate of 74 per cent for hookworm and of 57 per cent for roundworm, albeit with wide variation between groups.[9] The parasitologist Norman Stoll estimated that 31 per cent of North Americans and 36 per cent of Europeans hosted helminths in 1947 and claimed that few would escape contact at some stage in their lives.[10] Some 40–60 per cent of children in Europe and North America were infested with pinworm (also known as threadworm), and even this was a possible underestimate. Fifty years later, a billion people carried parasites, and the proportion of the world's population affected was said to be unchanged.[11]

Pinworms are harmless enough, for they feed on intestinal bacteria, but blood offers a much richer harvest. Hookworms are stout comma-shaped creatures around 1 cm long, and two varieties have played an important part in history. Both originated in the Old World, and *Necator americanus* is thought to have crossed the Atlantic inside African slaves. *Necator* has a preference for sultry climates with alternating wet and dry intervals and does best near the Equator. Its sister species *Ancylostoma duodenale* is mainly concentrated in a strip running from southern Europe and north Africa through the Middle East to India and China. Hookworms mature and mate in the small intestine and burrow into its wall to feed on our blood. A female lays 4–10 billion eggs each year, and these hatch into microscopic larvae which feed on contaminated soil. If conditions are favourable, they migrate to the surface. Should they encounter a naked foot, they slip between the scales of the skin, burrow into a blood or lymph vessel and travel in the bloodstream to the capillaries of the lung. Once there they break into the airways and are wafted upwards by a Mexican wave of respiratory cilia until they reach the gullet, descending from there to celebrate their nuptials in the gut.

Despite this highly invasive behaviour, hookworms generally pass unnoticed. If you have fewer than 25 *Necator*, you feel fine; 25–100 cause mild symptoms; 100–500 and you are unwell; more than 500 means trouble, and your end is nigh when they approach 1,000. *Ancylostoma* is thirstier; each worm sucks 0.26 ml of blood per day, and 100 can remove half a litre every nineteen days. Even healthy adults soon develop iron-deficiency anaemia, let alone those who are malnourished or suffer from malaria. Hookworms are the commonest cause of iron-deficiency anaemia in the world today, and chronic anaemia causes characteristic skeletal changes which appeared for the first time in settled communities.

Those with experience of African hospitals will know that people can survive the loss of up to 90 per cent of the iron in their blood – and will not have forgotten the expression in the eyes of those affected. Huckleberry Finn went barefoot and was undoubtedly infested with parasites, as were almost all poor people in the southern states at the start of the twentieth century. Mark Twain himself commented that 'hookworm . . . was never suspected to be a disease at all. The people who had it were merely supposed to be lazy, and were therefore despised and made fun of, when they should have been pitied.'[12] The best way to acquire a massive dose of hookworm is to walk barefoot on soil contaminated with faeces, and more than 500 million people suffer today from a condition that could be prevented by wearing shoes.

Few parasites have exerted as much evolutionary pressure as malaria, and four varieties have co-evolved with us. Studies of wild species combined with molecular dating techniques show that all four originated in Africa. Of these, *Plasmodium malariae* seems best adapted for life in small bands of wandering people, for it survives in the body for years and is relatively benign; its main feature is a fever which recurs at seventy-two-hour intervals and gave it the name of quartan malaria. It was once widespread in north-western Europe and was known as the ague; British fen farmers were known for their habit of marrying fresh young brides from the uplands who sickened and died in their new environment. Another variant was *Plasmodium vivax*. Although this originated in Africa, almost everyone in sub-Saharan Africa is now immune because the parasite can only invade blood cells with the Duffy blood type, and natural selection appears to have eliminated this from Africa. *Plasmodium falciparum* is closely related to a species that preys on gorillas and appears not to have established a stable reservoir in humans until Neolithic times. It would become the greatest killer in human experience.[13]

Other parasites live on the surface of our bodies. On the night of 29 December 1170, the body of Archbishop Thomas à Becket lay on a bier in Canterbury Cathedral awaiting burial. He had been murdered earlier in the day, and the cooling flesh of the future saint created such panic among his surface-dwelling fellow travellers that 'vermin boiled over like water in a simmering cauldron, and the onlookers burst into alternate weeping and laughter'.[14]

The skin of a newborn child is rapidly colonized by micro-organisms which live on its oils, secretions and dying cells; dead skin feeds the dust mites in our carpets. Fleas, lice, bed-bugs, ticks and many others prefer blood. Pubic lice, known as *Pthirus pubis* or crabs, favour thick bushy hair; their nearest relatives live on gorillas, which are densely covered except (oddly enough) in their pubic regions. Crabs flourish in beards, but the groin is their natural habitat, and their spread was guaranteed by the frequency with which groins come into contact.

As our ancestors shed body hair, another louse retreated to the thicket on our heads. According to a recent estimate from the US Centers for Disease Control (CDC), these currently live on the heads

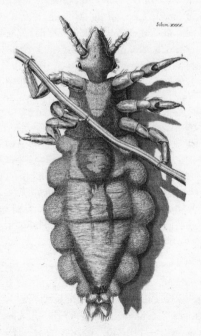

Figure 39: Louse clinging to a strand of hair. From Robert Hooke, *Micrographia* (1665).

of 6–12 million Americans. Head lice move through a family or classroom like 'an actively intermingling community inhabiting an archipelago', and thrive on children; adult hair is too widely spaced (especially in men) to provide an optimal environment. They attach their eggs to the base of a hair, and a few millimetres from the scalp offers the optimal incubation temperature. Seven days later, the nymph pops a lid on the egg casing and ejects itself by pumping air into the cavity. The empty container turns white, the telltale hallmark of nits. Aristotle was fooled into the belief that lice eggs never hatch, and generations of mothers have wasted their energies on the empty containers; fertile eggs are darker and better concealed.

Head lice feed on our blood five times a day. 'The newly-hatched louse is a pale, almost transparent, helpless little creature,' said one investigator.

> Place one on the back of the hand and observe it with a good lens. For a moment it merely basks in the warmth, then its head is firmly lowered. Although nothing is felt at the time, its fangs have shot into the skin! A faint heaving commences at the front of the body, showing that the massive salivary glands, housed in the thorax, have begun pumping saliva into the wound ... Then, gradually, the gut fills and swells, and as the light shines through it, the little louse comes to resemble a ruby on legs.[15]

Body lice did not appear until we started to wear clothes. This, if bone needles are anything to go by, happened 50,000 years ago. Eighteenth-century sailors knew that body lice perished when they 'crossed the line' of the Equator, whereas head lice lived on.[16] This was because they shed their clothing in the tropical heat, leaving the newly hatched nymphs nothing to feed on. 'The clothing louse', says the medical historian J. W. Maunder,

> is the louse of abject poverty. This louse is particularly characteristic of people who only possess one set of clothes, and [is] also most prevalent in cold lands where that one set might be but rarely removed. It is the louse of refugees, of the inadequate, of the wretched and despairing people of the world, of those affected by war, by famine or by natural disasters.[17]

Dr Samuel Johnson maintained that 'there is no settling the point of precedency between a louse and a flea', and taxonomists lump *Pediculus capitis* and *Pediculus corporis* together as *Pediculus humanus*. There is, however, one important difference, for the CDC consider head lice to be innocuous, whereas body lice have killed more people than every battle in history.

The body louse was harmless enough until it acquired a disease of its own, most probably in the course of the agrarian transition. Typhus is an infection of lice, and the human body is just a convenient way of ferrying it from one louse to the next. When the French bacteriologist Charles Nicolle (1866–1936) became head of the Pasteur Institute in Tunisia in 1903, outbreaks of typhus were an annual occurrence and killed one in three of his doctors. During major outbreaks the street in front of the hospital filled with patients waiting to be processed, and Nicolle noticed that those involved in the admission process regularly went down with the disease, whereas staff who received patients on the wards after they had been washed and dressed did not. He guessed that lice were the missing link. Later research showed that they too suffer from typhus; the gut of the moribund louse fills with bacteria and turns red with undigested blood; infected louse faeces are then smeared on the skin and obligingly scratched under the surface by the human victim. Nicolle also showed that people who survive the condition or develop it in a sub-clinical form can pass it on to others, and he considered this his most important observation. Humans were the reservoir of a louse infection.

Lice were ubiquitous in the trenches of the First World War and could be scraped off the clothing with the blade of a knife. Lieutenant Robert Sherriff, future author of the play *Journey's End*, assembled his men before leading them into attack. 'Some of the men looked terribly ill,' he recorded: 'grey, worn faces in the dawn, unshaved and dirty because there was no clean water. I saw the characteristic shrugging of their shoulders that I knew so well. They hadn't had their clothes off for weeks, and their shirts were full of lice.'[18] You could kill lice by running a lighted candle along the seams of your shirt, and troops coming out of the line routinely went to delousing stations to take a bath and have their clothes steam-heated.

Figure 40: Soldiers delousing in the First World War.

'If in 1914', said Charles Nicolle in his 1928 Nobel lecture,

> we had been unaware of the mode of transmission of typhus, and if
> infected lice had been imported into Europe, the war would not have
> ended by a bloody victory. It would have ended in an unparalleled
> catastrophe, the most terrible in human history. Soldiers at the front,
> reserves, prisoners, civilians, neutrals even, the whole of humanity
> would have collapsed. Men would have perished in millions, as un-
> fortunately occurred in Russia.

Up to 30 million people were infected in eastern Europe and perhaps 3 million died – no one really knows. Typhus never reached the
Western Front. If it had, the medical capabilities of the time might
well have collapsed. Lice on the Western Front did, however, carry a
milder infection known as trench fever. Without trench fever, which
caused Lieutenant J. R. R. Tolkien to be invalided home in 1917, *Lord
of the Rings* might never have been written, a small reminder of the
crippling loss of human potential that took place. Nicolle concluded
his Nobel lecture by saying that 'Man carries on his skin a parasite,

the louse. Civilization rids him of it. Should man regress, should he allow himself to resemble a primitive beast, the louse begins to multiply again and treats man as he deserves, as a brute beast.' Epidemic typhus, long considered extinct, broke out in Burundi in 1996. Trench fever, its milder cousin, is due to an organism called *Bartonella quintana*, which shadowed typhus in Napoleon's Grande Armée, and infected perhaps one soldier in five on the Western Front in the First World War. Health inspection of 138 homeless people in San Francisco recently found lice on thirty-three (24 per cent); one body louse in three carried *Bartonella*, as did one head louse in four.[19] Make no mistake: the louse is somewhere near you, just biding its time.

Tuberculosis has been an unexpected addition to the list of ancestral infections, for it was long believed to have jumped from cows to humans in Neolithic times. Molecular dating techniques now suggest that it may have co-existed with hominids for 2.6–2.8 million years. Bony evidence (albeit disputed) suggests its presence in *Homo erectus* 500,000 years ago. *Mycobacterium tuberculosis* comes in variant forms, and Africa was its ancestral domain. Two 'ancient' variants linger on in west Africa, and have shown little inclination to spread; another ancient lineage is found in the Philippines and around the fringes of the Indian Ocean. Three 'modern' variants seem to have left Africa with the human exodus about 80,000 years ago, heading respectively for India (with a foothold in east Africa), east Asia and Europe. These are more contagious and progress more rapidly to overt disease, aggressive features that favoured their subsequent spread and produced a backwash into Africa in modern times. Europeans took TB to the Americas, where it devastated Pre-Columbian populations, although a less virulent form may already have been there.[20]

There are two stages in the natural history of TB. The initial infection, known as primary TB, occurs when someone (usually a child) inhales the bacillus. This is promptly engulfed by an immune cell and triggers an alarm that brings more immune cells to the spot. By the time they arrive, however, *M. tuberculosis* is safely tucked inside the cell that discovered it. Frustrated in their attack, the latecomers form a defensive wall around the infected cell, producing the tiny lumps – tubercles – which give the condition its name. The infection may escape into the bloodstream in younger children, but is usually sealed into a primary focus in the upper part of the lung.

TB is a sleeper. It tucks itself away, signals its presence to the immune system, gets walled in and hangs around for a lifetime. It may die with us, but the sleeper will arise from its tomb and multiply if host resistance weakens. Other immune cells then flock to the scene, only to die after gorging on bacilli; cheesy ('caseous') pus accumulates and ruptures into the lungs. This produces the bloodstained sputum which enabled the poet Keats to diagnose his own condition and signals secondary or pulmonary TB. The victims live long enough to cough TB bacilli into the surrounding atmosphere, thus ensuring their spread to other people.

The co-evolutionary explanation is that tuberculosis gained access to our remote ancestors. Aggressive variants of the disease killed their hosts and died with them, and genetically susceptible hosts were replaced with more resistant ones. People who carried the bacillus often remained reasonably healthy. Should the immune system falter, however, the prisoner will break out and proliferate. This helped to eliminate unfit members of the host population – the old, the malnourished, those weakened by other diseases – while spreading the infection to healthy young people who would carry it into the future.

Our co-existence with tuberculosis closely reflected our living conditions. TB flourishes on poverty, ill-health, poor nutrition, alcohol abuse, old age and the co-existence of other diseases, HIV being a recent example. The two conditions for its spread – rampant exposure and a diminished host response – are fulfilled in poverty, and poverty is the child of civilization. Cities allowed pulmonary tuberculosis to enter upon a new phase of its existence because horizontal transmission favoured its more contagious variants. Hippocrates noted that it affected thin people, thus confusing cause with consequence, for wasting of the flesh – consumption – was its cardinal symptom. He knew it as a common and invariably fatal condition that ran in families. It was equally widespread in seventeenth-century England, when John Bunyan called it the 'captain of all these men of death'. It ran riot in the crowded slums of the new industrial cities in the nineteenth century due to the conjunction of poverty, malnutrition, overcrowding, heavy exposure and the influx of susceptible people from the countryside. It also cut a swathe through the middle and upper classes, who could not avoid contact with the rest. Exposure and genetic susceptibility worked hand in hand, which may explain why it tended to run in families and was considered hereditary.

Consumption set its mark upon the Romantic movement. A sensible farmer might opt for a plump bride with pink cheeks, but fashionable ladies starved themselves to resemble the heroines of fiction, who were invariably thin, languid and noted for their pallor and translucent skin. Their eyes were preternaturally brilliant and intense, even their happiest moments were tinged with sadness, and these ethereal beauties invariably expired in the most heartbreaking of circumstances. So too did a roll call of famous poets, writers and musicians, so much so that it has been suggested that tuberculosis promoted genius. More realistically, awareness of impending death may have spurred them to express the transience and fatal beauty of life. Romanticism and tuberculosis went hand in hand.

It had less glamour in other walks of life. In Victorian Britain, 100 per cent of the population was exposed, at least 80 per cent were infected and up to 20 per cent of those affected died. From 1851 to 1901, TB killed 4 million people in England and Wales, and accounted for a third of deaths in those aged fifteen to thirty-four. And then the tide began to turn. In the US, its annual mortality was around 400 per 100,000 in New York, Boston and Philadelphia in 1830, but had fallen to 26 by 1950 – long before effective therapy was available.[21] Better living conditions and better nutrition were largely responsible, and the introduction of the antibiotic streptomycin in the late 1940s appeared to have given the quietus to a moribund disease. This, alas, would prove to be an illusion.

13

The Retreat of Infectious Disease

In central London, just opposite the former main post office, there is a tiny garden known as Postman's Park. Here you will find a touching memorial to the heroism of ordinary people, a wall of tiles honouring men who dived into icy rivers in the attempt to save a drowning child, or women who dragged unconscious victims from a house on fire. Dr Samuel Rabbeth died because he tried to save a child from diphtheria. The diphtheria bacillus produces a toxin that leads to the formation of a membrane in the throat which resembles the white of an egg and causes suffocation. Few could bear to witness such a death and, in an agony of despair, some tried to suck the membrane away with a glass tube. Samuel Rabbeth shared the fate of the child he tried to save, as did one of Chekhov's characters.

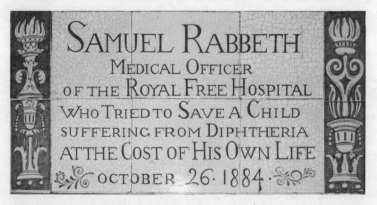

Figure 41: Plaque commemorating Dr Samuel Rabbeth, Postman's Park, London.

Doctors of the nineteenth century had few effective remedies at their disposal, but they were willing to put their own lives on the line. The American surgeon John Finney pioneered tracheostomy for diphtheria, frequently operating alone upon a desperately struggling child by flickering lamplight. 'Many were the times', he reflected 'when I began the operation not knowing whether or not I should have a living patient at the end of it.'[1] Diphtheria swept through the childhood population in waves, killing about 50,000 children each year in Germany alone in the latter part of that century. All this is long forgotten, as are the physicians who tried to fight it.

For the most part, they were helpless. In 1897, a Baptist minister called Frederick Gates read Osler's magisterial *Principles and Practice of Medicine*, published in 1892, and was appalled. Modern medicine, he learned, did not pretend to be able to cure more than four or five diseases; 'it was nature, and not the doctor, and in most cases nature practically unassisted, that performed the cures ... about all that medicine up to 1897 could do was to nurse the patients and alleviate in some degree the suffering'.[2] When John D. Rockefeller's first grandchild died of scarlet fever in 1901, he was horrified to learn that his doctors had no idea what caused the condition, let alone how to treat it. He turned to Gates, his adviser on philanthropic activities, and the Rockefeller Institute for Medical Research was founded in that same year.

This was the heroic age of investigative medicine. One by one, deadly infections were tracked down and isolated in the laboratory. Meanwhile deaths from infection in the UK fell from 24.6 per cent in 1911 to 0.6 per cent in 1991.[3] How much of this was due to medical intervention? Thomas McKeown (1912–88), professor of social medicine at the University of Birmingham, showed that TB, typhus, typhoid, diphtheria, scarlet fever, pneumonia and other infections were all in full retreat before effective remedies were available. This became known as the Social Theory, and Thomas McKeown was its apostle.[4]

McKeown pointed out with some glee that modern medical treatment was largely irrelevant to the decline of TB (figure 42). He went on to argue that the retreat of infectious disease was due to better nutrition and living conditions, that glamorous advances in high-tech medicine were of marginal importance, and that the future health of mankind would depend upon effective manipulation of the

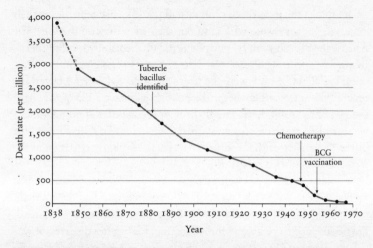

Figure 42: Death rate from tuberculosis in the UK, 1838–1970. Source: T. McKeown, *The Role of Medicine: Dream, Mirage or Nemesis* (Blackwell, 1979).

environment. His work was bitterly resented, partly because he was largely correct – not easy to forgive – but also because he did not always appreciate the difference between burying an opponent and jumping up and down on the grave. In effect, he compared medical science to the fly in Aesop's fable which sat on a fast-moving chariot and congratulated itself on the amount of dust it had raised. The fly was not amused.

Infectious disease was already in retreat before antibiotics were discovered. When they were, it seemed for one glorious moment as if total victory lay within reach. In 1962, the great Australian immunologist Macfarlane Burnet sat down with some satisfaction to write the Preface to the third edition of his *Natural History of Infectious Disease*. 'At times', he reflected, 'one feels that to write about infectious disease is almost to write of something that has passed into history.' In 1971, J. R. Bignall was so impressed by the falling notification rate that he predicted that by 2010 tuberculosis 'should be of interest to the medical historian only'.[5] The Law of Complacency ruled, and many institutes began to close down research into tuberculosis in the 1970s – although not for long. A rebound came when the AIDS epidemic spread TB among otherwise healthy members of the population; the number of patients with clinical TB trebled between 1980 and 1990, but only 20 per cent of these had HIV.

Why is contact with TB so common but open infection so rare? Since there is no evidence that the bacillus has become more benign, the answer must be that well-nourished bodies are more effective at containing it. As Joshua Lederberg said in relation to the risk of new or re-emerging diseases, we are 'a very different species from what we were 100 years ago'. TB is a barometer of living conditions, and runs riot whenever people are herded together in jails, prison camps or army barracks: more people were discharged from the US armed services in both world wars because of tuberculosis than for any other medical reason. Of those who survived Belsen concentration camp, 88 per cent had active TB.[6] Both world wars brought a surge in its prevalence, and this was repeated when Cuba and eastern Europe experienced the collapse of the communist system in the 1990s.

The western world now pays little attention to tuberculosis, but there is a fissure beneath its feet. This is the Fourth World of the deviant, disturbed, criminal, alcoholic, feckless or simply unfortunate, those for whom, in Robert Malthus's words, 'there is no place at life's feast'. Prison is one of the places where they congregate. A survey of 90,000 inmates in New York State showed that 30 per cent of those with no evidence of previous exposure developed a positive skin test within two years of incarceration. At least twenty-three prisons had inmates whose tuberculosis was resistant to up to seven standard drug therapies. TB, including multi-drug-resistant forms, may be active in 5 per cent of those sleeping rough on the streets of London.[7] Our main hope for the future is not to eliminate TB, but to contain it, and few seem to appreciate that we are sleeping on a volcano.

It is no coincidence that malaria and tuberculosis have evolved resistance to our most effective chemical weapons, for the attempt to combat evolution with pharmaceuticals easily becomes a losing battle. Containment is more effective in this war than pharmacology and this – alas for our chances – means winning the war against poverty and ignorance. The coronavirus epidemic of 2020 has mainly proved lethal to the old and the vulnerable. Should it be followed by widespread economic disruption, as seems likely, the diseases that found us first are likely to take over. They know us too well.

GHOSTS OF EVOLUTION

Some ancestral fellow travellers cause problems by not being there. Physicians of the nineteenth century were familiar with stomach (gastric) ulcers, but duodenal ulcers were virtually unknown. These first appeared among the affluent in the early years of the twentieth century and migrated down the social scale. Unlike gastric ulcers, which are associated with low acid secretion and high cancer risk, duodenal ulcers are related to high acid secretion and have a low cancer risk. Recurrent pain and misery apart, both types of ulcer may cause fatal bleeding or perforate into the abdominal cavity. These were bread-and-butter surgical emergencies for much of the twentieth century but are rarely encountered today. Epidemiologists noted that people born in the UK between 1870 and 1900 bore the brunt of the duodenal ulcer epidemic, regardless of the age at which they came to medical attention. The same pattern was seen in other countries, with a tendency for stomach ulcers to peak ten to twenty years before duodenal ones. Investigators wrestled to explain why this might be. They showed, for example, that cigarette smoking and stress stimulate acid production and make duodenal ulcers worse, and some of them composed lengthy dissertations about ulcers and personality.

The answer came from an unexpected direction. Robin Warren, an Australian pathologist, saw bacteria when he looked at stomach biopsies in the 1970s. Other pathologists had described the presence of bacilli like these in the stomach lining – the earliest report dated back more than a century – but medical dogma asserted that microorganisms could not survive in stomach acid. Warren's clinical colleagues discounted his reports for precisely the same reason. Undeterred, he paired up with a clinical trainee looking for a research project in 1981. As biopsy after biopsy was examined, they saw with mounting excitement that people with conditions ranging from gastritis (inflammation of the stomach lining) to ulcers all seemed to be infected. Might they respond to antibiotics?

In the heroic tradition of medical research, Barry Marshall, Warren's trainee, tested this hypothesis by swallowing infected fluid from a patient's stomach. Nausea and vomiting set in after seven days, and on the tenth day he finished his own gastroscopy list before resubmitting to the procedure himself. The lining of his stomach, previously normal, now proved to be swollen, inflamed and fringed with bacteria; antibiotics resolved the situation. The demonstration that generations of distinguished physicians had been barking up the wrong tree was not exactly welcome, but these findings were repeatedly confirmed before the mysterious spiral bacillus was renamed *Helicobacter pylori* in 1987.[8]

One characteristic of a successful parasite is that no one knows it is there. *Helicobacter* is far and away the most successful chronic infection of mankind and currently inhabits every second person on the planet. It thrives on poverty, and transmission by close personal contact is almost inevitable in overcrowded dwellings. As living conditions improved towards the end of the nineteenth century, however, people began to escape infection, or to acquire it later in life. It seems likely that early infection is associated with gastric complications, whereas later infection predisposes to duodenal ulcer. Improved hygiene might well explain why the well-to-do were the first to develop duodenal ulcers, why the incidence increased so rapidly in people born between 1870 and 1900, and why gastric ulcers still predominate in poorer parts of the world.

The *Helicobacter* story shows that the timing of our first contact with fellow travellers can be important. Another example is polio. The polio virus is a normal faecal contaminant, routinely and harmlessly encountered early in life by previous generations. Late contact is however associated with paralytic nerve damage; improvements in basic hygiene are thought to have been responsible for the outbreaks of paralytic polio which first appeared in the twentieth century.

What happens when an accustomed evolutionary partner does not arrive on time, or goes missing altogether? An interesting parallel comes from Central America. Fruit invites eating because birds and animals spread its seeds around. But what could possibly eat an avocado, a fruit with a tough outer rind, rich creamy contents and a seed so large that the Aztecs compared it to a testicle? Only an animal that no longer exists. Several of them in fact, for megatherium, toxodon, glyptodon and the gomphotheres were giant mammals to whom an avocado seed would be no more of a challenge than an apple pip. These giants vanished from the face of the earth – quite possibly with human assistance – before the last ice age. Thus deprived of its customary means of dispersal, the avocado became a 'ghost of evolution', and only survived because we became its new co-evolutionary partner.[9]

Why might this story be relevant? In the first half of the twentieth century it was rank heresy to believe that our immune systems could harm our own bodies. By the 1950s, however, it became clear that we can and do make antibodies against our own cells and may then go on and reject those cells as if they belonged to another person. Both type 1 diabetes and multiple sclerosis are caused by invading immune cells, a phenomenon known as *autoimmunity*.

Autoimmune diseases appear to have been rare before the twentieth century. Type 1 diabetes, for example, is a highly distinctive condition that comes out of the blue accompanied by raging thirst and weight loss; affected children died within two or three years before insulin became available. It was relatively rare before the second half of the twentieth century (figure 43). Multiple sclerosis became more common around the same time. In Norway, for example, the increase in the incidence of type 1 diabetes was matched by a four-fold increase in new cases of multiple sclerosis between

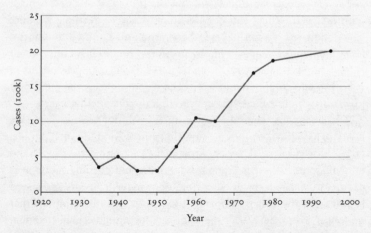

Figure 43: The rise of childhood-onset diabetes in Norway. Its incidence began to rise around the mid-century in populations of European descent.

1961 and 2014.[10] Multiple sclerosis is rare in immigrants to western countries from poorer parts of the world, but children born in those countries acquire the same risk as its inhabitants. This prompted an extensive search for new trigger factors in the environment, a search that has largely been unsuccessful. The alternative possibility, only recently considered, is that the rise of immune disorders relates to the loss of something that *had always previously been there*.

Graham Rook has argued persuasively that co-evolutionary partners play an important role in programming our developing immune system. He has proposed that a co-evolutionary partner should satisfy two criteria: it should have been present over the long haul of mammalian evolution, and it should have departed from the industrialized world over the past few decades. *Helicobacter* is an example of how such ghosts of evolution might operate, and there are other candidates to consider. If this view is correct, safe and simple manipulation of our developing immune phenotype could make it possible to prevent dysfunctional patterns of immunity.

In sum, our immune system has encountered three very different environments over the course of human existence, corresponding to the Palaeolithic, agrarian and consumer phenotypes. In the long term – which predates the first humans by millions of years – our fellow travellers were passed on by one generation to the next. Omran's Age of Pestilence and Famine really applies only to the subsequent, agrarian phase of our existence. Changes in the man-made environment invited new types of infection into our population, and further changes made it possible to exclude them once again.

Our escape from natural selection, as reflected in the consumer phenotype, took less than the wink of an evolutionary eye. For a time, it seemed possible that complete victory over transmissible disease might be achieved by a combination of better living conditions, public health measures, vaccination and antibiotics. This dream soon faded, for you cannot suppress infectious disease without suppressing poverty. Malaria, tuberculosis and worms still dominate the global health scene, and linger on in the Fourth World of destitution that underlies our prosperity. We have created the environment in which both new and old variants of infectious disease can flourish, and these seem set to outpace our attempts to fight them with drugs.

14

The Final Frontier

Achilles traded a long and undistinguished existence for a brief and glorious one – he was young – but found little solace in being first among the dead when Odysseus visited him in the Underworld. Life is the sum of all meanings. The modern extension of life into old age was thus of seismic significance. No one predicted it, the experts miscalled it, and old age is as much of a challenge to the wealthy nations as population growth is to the poor. It is nonetheless a wonderful gift. Just imagine, for example, that a scientist had discovered an elixir which added thirty years to human life: her statue would be seen in every city. This gift is ours, and we didn't even ask for it.

'Nothing in biology makes sense except in the light of evolution,' as Theodosius Dobzhansky famously said, and extreme old age makes little sense. 'It is evident', said Darwin's rival Alfred Russel Wallace, 'tha[t] when one or more individuals have provided a sufficient number of successors, they themselves, as consumers of nourishment in a constantly increasing degree, are an injury to those successors. Natural selection therefore weeds them out, and in many cases favours such races as die almost immediately after they have left successors.'[1] Active grandparents help to support their grandchildren, but evolutionary explanations falter once people outlive their usefulness. Our ancestors cared for their elderly when they could but, from an evolutionary point of view, they had already ceased to exist. Extreme old age is seen only in humans, domestic animals and species such as Galapagos tortoises that have no natural predators.

The first indication of our potential for longevity came when life expectancy began to rise in the last quarter of the nineteenth century. The life insurance companies were quick to spot this. In 1909, the economist Irving Fisher told the assembled presidents of US insurance companies that life expectancy had increased at a rate of nine years per century over the first three quarters of the nineteenth century. The rate of increase then accelerated to seventeen years per century in parts of Europe, and to twenty-seven years per century in Prussia, the 'home of preventive medicine'. Longer life, as he pointed out, could only be good news for the insurance business, and companies should try to promote it. Factory fires became less common when insurers refused to provide cover for buildings which lacked adequate fire safety precautions, and health should be no different.[2] As Theodore Roosevelt put it, 'we [ought] no longer to ignore the reproach that this government takes more pains to protect the lives of hogs and cattle than of human beings'. Fisher chaired a Committee of One Hundred dedicated to health improvement and health education, and the FDA and the US public health movement got going at around the same time.

Fisher estimated that one life in three could be prolonged. In 1915, he sent the list of ninety medical conditions under which deaths in the USA were classified to leading medical authorities, asking them to rate the likelihood that each could be prevented. He then subtracted the possibility of prevention from the overall frequency of each cause of death. On this basis, he calculated that the life expectancy of a newborn child might potentially be extended from 49.4 to 62.1 years, and the life of a sixty-year-old from 74.6 to 77.9 years.[3]

Although death from disease is potentially avoidable, biologists took it for granted that natural death is non-negotiable. The geneticist J. B. S. Haldane made this assumption in 1923, when he said that 'the abolition of disease will make death a physiological event like sleep. A generation that has lived together will die together.'[4] Our lives would run down together like clockwork in the absence of disease. There is indeed a form of successful ageing in which the major organs enter a more or less synchronous decline. Such people fade gently into the grave. Their flesh melts away, they retreat into a quiet place of their own and they slip peacefully away. Their passing creates a brief existential hush on the busiest hospital ward, a momentary sense of shared destiny. Someone will then write 'heart failure' (the heart did stop, after all) or 'pneumonia' ('the old man's friend') upon the death certificate. I have filled in sufficient of these to know that most certificates for the aged contain an element of fiction: successful ageing is when the doctor doesn't know what to write on your death certificate.

Louis Dublin, chief statistician for the Metropolitan Life Insurance Company, assumed a natural term to life when he estimated in 1928 that 'in the light of present knowledge and without intervention of radical innovations or fantastic evolutionary change in our physiological make-up, such as we have no reason to assume', the average lifespan would peak at 64.75 years for both men and women, as against the contemporary expectation of 57 years.[5] The assumption of a fixed limit to human life was endorsed by gerontologist James Fries in a thoughtful and influential review from 1980. He noted that the lifespan of Americans had risen from forty-seven to seventy-three years over an eighty-year period, at a rate equivalent to four months of extra life for each calendar year of birth. The increase at age sixty-five seemed to be slowing, however, and he saw no evidence that maximal lifespan had increased. On this basis he concluded that biology and statistics would converge on an average lifespan of eighty-five years by the year 2045. This final cliff, he argued, is consistent with progressive attrition of the functional reserve that our organs possess in youth.

To set against this, he noted that the victory over acute non-accidental disease had virtually been won, and that the campaign against chronic disease was making steady progress. 'Clearly', as he remarked, 'the medical and social task of eliminating premature death is largely accomplished.' The duration of life may be set in stone, but the duration of health can be extended, resulting in a 'compression' of morbidity in later life. The medical task, therefore, was to shift disease and disability into the final years of life, and to cushion the inevitable when it arrived – although 'high-level medical technology applied at the end of a natural life span epitomizes the absurd'.[6]

His hope that disability and disease might be compressed into a brief agonal period at the end of life has not been fully realized. An estimate for the period 2013–15 gave sixty-five-year-old men and women in England an added life expectancy of 18.7 and 21.1 years, but 43 per cent and 47 per cent of these years would be spent in (self-rated) poor health. Furthermore, unhealthy years were accumulating

THE FINAL FRONTIER

more rapidly than healthy ones.[7] Fries had argued that the rate of increase in life expectancy in later life was slowing, but table 3 shows that life expectancy has in fact stretched like a piece of elastic in all age groups, more so in the old than in the young, and his 'final frontier' of 85 years seems set to be breached. Not until 1998 did anyone dare to suggest that no such limit might exist.[8]

Where biologists had assumed a fixed term to life, statisticians simply extrapolated from the data – as when the UK Office of National Statistics issued its forward projections in 2010 (figure 44).

Table 3: Life expectancy in England and Wales, 1891–2012 (OPCS data)

Mean life expectancy (years)						Overall increase (%)
Base age	1891–1900	1950–52	1970–72	1990–92	2012	
Males						
E^0	44.1	66.4	69.0	73.2	78.9	(79)
E^{65}	10.3	11.7	12.2	14.2	18.4	(79)
E^{80}	4.2	4.7	5.7	6.4	8.2	(95)
Females						
E^0	47.8	71.5	75.2	78.7	82.7	(73)
E^{65}	11.3	14.3	16.1	17.9	20.9	(85)
E^{80}	4.6	5.0	7.3	8.4	9.5	(107)

E^0, E^{65}, E^{80}: life expectancies at birth, 65 years and 80 years
Table from Tallis (ed.) (1998), p. 2, with addition of UK data for 2012: source OPCS

These projections made no assumptions as to a natural term to life, and suggested that one girl in three and one boy in four born in 2010 would live for 100 years. Sadly, the increase in life expectancy began to slow in Britain and the USA very soon after. Failing social welfare provision was blamed, given that the life expectancy of people in Japan (where people live five years longer) continued to rise. The key question thus remains unanswered: how long might we live under optimal conditions?

Actual and projected period expectation of life at birth according to mortality rates for given year, 1981–2085, United Kingdom

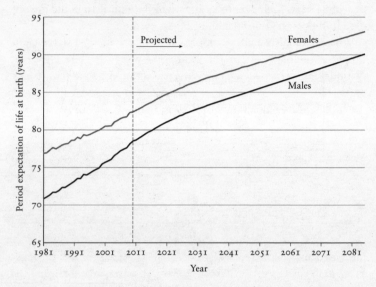

Figure 44: Actual and projected expectation of life at birth in the UK, as estimated in 2010.

THE AGE EPIDEMIC

Two developments combined to roll back the age frontier. The first was the virtual elimination of avoidable death in childhood. In 1901, 37 per cent of deaths in the UK were under the age of four, with 12 per cent over the age of seventy-five. By 1994, these proportions were 1 per cent and 58 per cent. Only 10 per cent or so of people in the UK currently die before the age of fifty, and average life expectancy would increase by no more than 3.5 years if all these deaths were eliminated.[9] Since premature mortality – largely due to infectious disease – was already low by the mid-century, the steady increase in

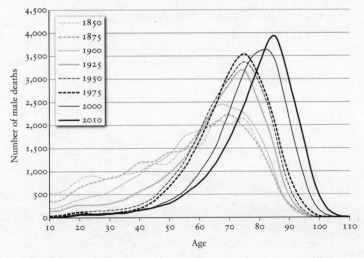

Figure 45: Age at death of males in the UK, 1850–2010 (ONS data). Note the emerging bell curve of death in old age.

life expectancy in the second half of the century must be due to longer survival in later life. A bell-shaped distribution has emerged from the clutter of earlier times, even as our age at death has shifted to the right (figure 45).

If we omit the skew to the left produced by those who die early, what remains would resemble a normal distribution with its lower and upper limits at around sixty-five and 105 years. Otherwise said, and as has often been pointed out, most people now die of age-related conditions arising within their own bodies. Are these 'diseases', or manifestations of an underlying ageing process? This is a question for the next chapter. For the moment, however, we must consider that there is a pattern to our dying.

THE ARROW STORM OF AGE

As one medieval army moved forwards to attack another, it was met by a storm of arrows. The arrows did little harm at first, picking off

Mortality in England and Wales, 2016 vs 1847

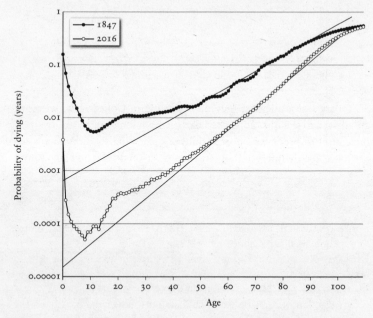

Figure 46: The probability of dying at a given age in England and Wales in 1847 and 2016. The difference between the curves is due to high premature mortality in 1847. Source: www.mortality.org.

a few unlucky victims here and there, but the carnage mounted rapidly as the attackers entered what military historians call the 'killing zone'. If the army kept marching forwards to the point of destruction the number of fallen would rise to a peak in the killing zone, only to fall again as fewer and fewer survivors remained, thus generating a bell-shaped curve.

Contrariwise, if you were one of the soldiers, your likelihood of encountering an arrow would increase as you approached the archers. This was given statistical expression by Benjamin Gompertz. A self-made mathematician who worked for an insurance company, he noted in 1825 that the death rate increases logarithmically over the age of thirty, doubling every 8.5 years (figure 46). The graph might create the alarming impression that we are accelerating towards death, but this is not what it shows. The rate at which the amount of water in your bath halves increases logarithmically when you pull the plug, but the water itself is travelling no faster. The bell curve and the Gompertz function simply express the same thing in different ways, and they tell us that there is a pattern to our dying, regardless of the reason for our death.

Statistics describe, but they do not explain. Collectively, we want an answer to the question asked earlier: how long might we live if all the causes of premature death could be removed? As individuals, we are more keenly interested in our own position on the bell curve, and why we age at different rates.

ARE WE AGEING MORE SLOWLY?

Everyday observation tells us that some people age faster than others. If the pace of ageing reflects our living conditions, it might explain why most of us are living longer, and why some populations are ageing more rapidly than others.[10]

In October 1998, a retiring US senator called John Glenn was blasted into space for a nine-day mission inside the *Discovery* shuttle. He was seventy-seven years old. Glenn (1921–2016) was an all-American hero who flew 149 combat missions as a fighter pilot in the Second World War and the Korean War and had been the first American to orbit the Earth, in 1962. Many felt that sending an old man into space was merely a stunt, but his ability to survive the rigours of space flight made a powerful statement. Journalists duly noted that old people seemed to be getting younger. Space flight for the elderly would have come as no surprise for Hardin B. Jones (1914–78), a professor of physics and physiology at Berkeley; he predicted in 1955 that a seventy-five-year-old man would have a physiological age of sixty by 1999. John Glenn's career suggests that he was not far wrong.

Jones noted that adults who live in areas of high infant mortality die younger than those who live in areas of low infant mortality. Americans were at that time more likely to die at any given age than

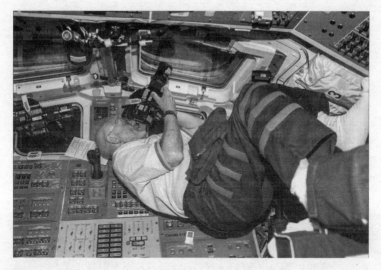

Figure 47: John Glenn aboard the Space Shuttle *Discovery* (1998).

people in long-lived countries such as Sweden, Norway or the Netherlands: statistically speaking, they were five years older. He deduced from this that we live at different rates, and that this is determined very early in life. He expressed this in a simple metaphor: we start life with a certain amount of vital capital, and our length of life depends upon the rate at which we spend it. Let's say that we start life with a million credits. An expenditure of 10,000 a year will keep us going for a century, whereas we will expire at sixty-seven if we spend 15,000. Simplistic, no doubt, but a useful way to start thinking about the problem.[11]

His central contention was that your biological rate of ageing cannot be estimated from your date of birth, and insurance companies do indeed make their money by betting on the difference between the two. Blood pressure, cholesterol and glucose can be used as markers of the ageing process, for example, and your doctor is assessing your biological age when she performs a routine health check. Researchers supplement these time-honoured indices with more sophisticated measures of ageing; these include markers of inflammation, a well-described but poorly understood process which plunges cells into a low-grade but toxic brew of chemicals. Inflammatory markers are a useful measure of accelerated ageing because they increase in tandem with many of the degenerative conditions of later life. The more age-related markers you have, the greater your biological age, and the cumulative tally predicts your life expectancy far better than your chronological age.[12]

A study from Dunedin, New Zealand, analysed markers of age in 1,000 people followed from birth to thirty-eight years and went on to estimate what they called the 'pace of ageing'. The investigators found that biological age conforms to a bell curve, and varies from chrono-logical age by up to seven years in thirty-eight-year-old people. Those with higher scores felt less healthy, performed less well on tests of balance, had a declining IQ and were at greater risk of future stroke or dementia. And yes: they also looked older.[13] The Dunedin study supported Jones's belief that ageing is a life-long process which affects multiple biological pathways and progresses at different rates.

The Pace of Ageing

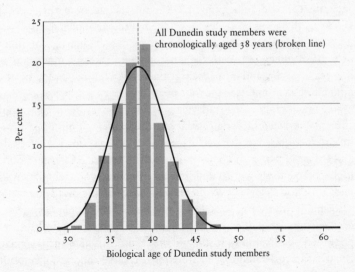

Figure 48: The biological age of thirty-eight-year-olds varies widely and is normally distributed.

Other studies confirm this. Two US National Health Surveys (NHANES III and NHANES IV) were conducted in 1988–94 and 2007–10 respectively. These measured blood pressure, cholesterol, glucose status, kidney and liver function, the ability to breathe out forcefully and C-reactive protein, a marker of generalized inflammation. Analysis of these markers confirmed that women are biologically younger than men, but showed that biological age had fallen faster in men between the studies. In biological terms, men of 20–39, 40–59 and 60–79 years of age were 1, 2.5 and 4 years younger respectively in the second survey.[14] As in other studies, higher educational attainment was associated with lower biological age, and a separate study from NHANES III showed that black Americans are biologically three years older for any given chronological age.[15]

It should, however, be borne in mind that the health behaviour of the US population was changing rapidly when these reductions occurred; Americans were smoking less but gaining weight, and the number on medication for blood pressure or cholesterol was increasing rapidly. All this undoubtedly contributed to (but does not necessarily account for) a falling biological age. Newer and more accurate 'biological clocks' are based upon the rate of methylation of DNA: methylation produces tags – the molecular equivalent of Post-it notes – on our genetic material, and these tags are markers of direct or indirect interaction with the environment. The tags mount up as the years go by and provide a remarkably accurate index of the amount of wear and tear on your phenotype.[16]

Age implies increasing frailty: loss of muscle mass, reduced arterial elasticity, reduced filtering capacity by the kidneys, diminished insulin production, cognitive decline, reduced capacity for tissue repair and so on. Not a great combination but, as Maurice Chevalier said, it beats the alternative. A 'multiple hit' hypothesis of ageing fits well with this, and helps to explain why socio-economic disadvantage is associated with shorter lives. Poverty comes with psychological stress, accidents, violence, harmful behaviour, lack of access to health care, poor diet, obesity and so forth, and the accumulation of such damage equates to accelerated loss of functional reserve capacity. The poor pass the same landmarks on their journey through life, but they are travelling faster.

The observation that people who live in an unhealthy environment do not live so long is scarcely novel. Conventional explanations attribute this to environmental pollution or blame the victims for poor diet and unhealthy habits. There is something unappealing about the suggestion that people who live miserable and frustrated lives could extend them by drinking less or smoking fewer cigarettes, although these undoubtedly come into the equation. Research into markers of ageing does, however, suggest something more fundamental, which is that an adverse environment can affect the whole process of growth and development and thus the whole trajectory of life. Otherwise said, poverty and deprivation can generate a distinctive phenotype of their own. This being the case – and we will see more evidence in a moment – we should focus upon the environment as a whole rather than upon individual risk factors.

IS THERE A PACEMAKER OF AGEING?

Some people grow old too fast, and few medical conditions are more horrifying than progeria, in which a child passes from birth to old age and death within fourteen years. It is mercifully rare, with some 130 reports since it was first described in 1886. The child is hairless and has a rounded head with a disproportionately small face, prominent eyes, beaky nose, receding chin and a high-pitched voice. Those affected do not grow properly and soon develop tightness and thickening of the skin, loss of subcutaneous fat, fragile bones and dislocation of the joints. The skin ages with disconcerting speed, and progressive arterial disease produces coronary heart attacks and stroke. Progeria is not inherited, but is due to a spontaneous mutation which occurs early in embryonic development. It does not explain ageing, but it does show that a single defect can trigger a generalized ageing process.

Werner syndrome is another form of accelerated ageing, and first becomes apparent in adolescence. Those affected are small and light with a beaky nose, are hairless or prematurely grey and have pigmented skin, a hoarse voice, diffuse arterial disease, cataracts and osteoporosis. The skin thickens and ulcerates as calcium is deposited beneath it and within the Achilles tendon. Victims are prone to diabetes and other endocrine conditions, their brains begin to shrink, and they are at greatly increased risk of cancer. Few survive beyond their fifties. Werner syndrome is an autosomal recessive disorder which affects coiling of DNA; many variants have been reported, but the most common mutation is found in Japan and accounts for 1,128 of 1,487 cases in the medical literature. Japanese people with Werner syndrome grow bigger and live longer today than in the past, suggesting that they too have responded to a changing environment.[17]

These unpleasant conditions fascinate investigators because they suggest that a single genetic defect can trigger the entire spectrum of ageing. This establishes two principles. The first is that, despite its many and varied manifestations, age is somehow a unitary process. The second is that a process that can be accelerated might also be delayed.

One persistent mystery is why women live longer than men. The *Almanach de Gotha*, first published in 1763, is a guide to the social empyrean of Teutonic Europe. In essence, it is a stud book for aristocrats and provides information as to the lesser blood lines into which they are permitted to marry. When Princess Victoria Louise of Prussia married Prince Ernst August of Hanover in 1913, the band played a waltz which could only be danced by those who featured in volume 1 of the *Almanach*. At a later date, when aristocratic families were stranded on the beach of time with little more than debts and pretensions, its pages became a happy hunting ground for husband-hunters, fortune-seekers, pedants and pretenders. The unexpected reappearance of the *Almanach* in 1998 after a lapse of fifty-three years unmasked quite a few fake pedigrees,[18] but its detailed record of some 200,000 births, marriages and deaths makes it an incomparable source of data.[19]

As expected, the *Almanach* showed that the upper echelons live longer, and that women live longer than men. Sons averaged 64.6 years at death, and daughters averaged 73.5 years – an unusually wide gap that might reflect the feckless behaviour of male aristocrats. Squalid male habits are frequently invoked to explain why women live longer but cannot explain why females of other species also do well. One possible reason is the 'mother's curse', a hypothesis based on the fact that mitochondrial DNA is inherited exclusively from the mother. Sex-selective mutations that harm women will be weeded out by natural selection, whereas those harmful to men – for example a mitochondrial mutation that affects sperm motility – will accumulate.[20]

In 1899, Mary Beeton and Karl Pearson attempted to see if longevity is inherited, but the haphazard way in which death operates greatly complicated their task. My mother and two of her four siblings survived past the age of eighty-five, as did her own mother, but my maternal grandfather died early of cancer of the jaw, probably (as with Sigmund Freud) related to heavy smoking. My remaining uncle was killed by a German sniper in 1944. Death, as Beeton said, is a marksman whose bullets strike at random. She turned to the pages of *Foster's Peerage* and *Burke's Landed Gentry* as reliable sources of family records, although by no means free of bias. Death in childhood rarely rates a mention, for example, nor does the age at which women died. Beeton did, however, show that longer-lived fathers have longer-lived sons. Subsequent studies confirmed that longevity runs in families, leading Raymond Pearl to conclude in 1920 that the best way to assure oneself of a long life is to choose long-lived parents. Later observations showed that the age of a son is influenced more by the age of the mother than by that of the father, once again raising the possibility that mitochondrial genes (always transmitted by the mother) might be of particular importance.

The place to look for an explanation of longevity is in those who live longest. The number of centenarians in the UK has been recorded since 1837, and the 1911 Census identified a total of 110, or 3.6 per million of the population. The achievement was so remarkable as to merit a telegram from Buckingham Palace. The message to Reverend Thomas Lord in 1908 read 'I am commanded by the King to congratulate you on the attainment of your hundredth year, after a most useful life.' Telegrams were sent regularly after 1917, later to be replaced by personal messages. Lucky centenarians currently receive a photograph of the Queen in a lime-green dress, wearing the brooch she gave her own mother on her 100th birthday. There were 4.5 centenarians per million in the UK in 2015, but the number in Japan has risen from 153 in 1963 (when records began) to almost 70,000 in 2018.[21]

Figure 49: In this celebration of ten centenarians at Clarewood House Senior Community, Houston, only two are male: women are four times as likely to reach 100.

Why some people live to extreme old age – and whether it is worth it – are secrets that belong to the very old. Some features are consistent, for example that 85 per cent of centenarians are women, but others are surprisingly varied. Furthermore, centenarians appear to be getting younger, and the genes that characterized centenarians in previous generations now cluster in 'super-centenarians' of 110, just as Hardin Jones would have predicted. Those who live for a hundred years are vividly described as falling into three categories: *survivors*, who develop health problems before the age of eighty but soldier on, *delayers*, whose problems develop late in life, and *escapers*, who have no clinically evident disease. Some 15 per cent are lucky enough to be escapers, with an equal split between survivors and delayers.[22] The general rule, however, is that longer health translates into longer life, and that men who reach extreme old age are healthier than women of the same age, presumably because they have been through a tougher selection process.

Centenarians are diverse in terms of education, wealth, background, religion, ethnicity and lifestyle. Unsurprisingly, few have smoked heavily or been obese, and they score well on personality tests in terms of personal relationships and general resilience. A sense of humour also seems to help, as in the woman of 104 who cited lack of peer pressure as one of the benefits of ageing. About 50 per cent of centenarians have a family history of extreme old age, and their children appear to be heading the same way. The down side to longevity is that our brains may not age as well as the rest of the body. One survey of centenarians found that about half had signs of dementia, not necessarily due to Alzheimer's disease. The more common form was characterized by 'a constricted universe with limited awareness of events outside their personal sphere; they repeated themes and topics endlessly'.[23]

ADVENTISTS LIVE LONGER

If you want to live longer, should you change your genes or your environment? The Seventh Day Adventists speak for the environment. Their beliefs stem from the teachings of William Miller (1782–1849), a Baptist minister who predicted that the Second Coming would occur in the year following 21 March 1843. His followers are known as Adventists because of their belief in the imminent arrival of Jesus; the 'Seventh Day' component derives from their assertion that the Sabbath falls on a Saturday (the seventh day of the week) rather than the first, which is Sunday. The Second Coming did not arrive on schedule, but this did not dampen the enthusiasm of Miller's followers. There is a fascinating account of the psychology involved in a book called *When Prophecy Fails*, which relates the experience of a modern cult whose members believed they would be airlifted from global apocalypse by a flying saucer. When this failed to happen, they descended from their mountain in a crisis of doubt. Some lost faith, but the remainder – people who had previously contemplated the destruction of the entire human race with equanimity – now set out to convert others to their belief.[24]

The Advent was redefined as a spiritual event – it did happen, but on a spiritual plane – and Seventh Day Adventists went on to become the twelfth most widely subscribed-to religious belief in the world, with 18 million believers and missionaries. They are noted for their conservative social habits and for a diet which avoids pork and shellfish because these are prohibited in the Bible. Vegetarianism is advocated, although no more than 35 per cent are totally observant in this respect. Tobacco and alcohol are banned, and other stimulants are frowned upon. Take your pick as to which helps most, but the package is effective: the life expectancy of Adventist men and women in California was 81.2 and 83.9 years as compared with 73.9 and 79.5 years respectively for other Californians.[25]

If a favourable environment extends your life, an adverse environment will shorten it. A black man living in Harlem in the 1950s had the same life expectancy as a man in Bangladesh. Overall, black men and women in the US lived 11.5 (men) and 13.2 (women) years fewer than whites in 1929–31, as against 6.3 and 4.5 years in 2003. Subsequent analysis showed that black Americans presented more signs of ageing at all ages. Poverty alone did not account for the divergence, and the authors conclude that the stress and frustration of life in a prejudiced society is likely to account for the 'weathering' effect seen in disadvantaged peoples.[26]

Ecological comparisons confirm the importance of social disadvantage. Life expectancy is rising around the world, and the combined score of the ten leading countries is referred to as the international age frontier. On this scale, the USA comes thirty-seventh for both men and women. The United States is divided into more than 3,000 counties, and county-level data from 2000–2007 showed that some counties were fifteen calendar years ahead of the international age frontier, and that others were fifty years behind. When restricted to black Americans, the analysis showed that 65 per cent of counties were fifty years or more behind for men, against 22 per cent for women. The longest-lived communities were on the East and West Coasts and to the north, whereas the worst performers were in Appalachia and the Deep South.[27] A glance at the map shows that those with the lowest life expectancy vote Republican.

If America had a good twentieth century, Russia had a disastrously bad one. At its start, life expectancy was thirty-one years for males and thirty-three years for females, and an early upswing was cancelled out by the famines of the 1930s and the slaughter of the Second

World War. Rapid recovery followed, with a gain in life expectancy of more than twenty years from 1945 to 1965, but the proportion of those living at or below the $4 a day standard of poverty soared from 2 per cent to 50 per cent when communism collapsed.[28] Male life expectancy was thirteen years behind female in 1995, largely because of heart disease, alcohol and accidents. Income inequality can be more harmful than the size of your pay packet, and heartbreak and hopelessness bring their own health dividend.

DOES WEALTH MEAN HEALTH?

It is not surprising that the safest people who ever lived should be so obsessed with their safety, that the healthiest should be so obsessed with their health, or that the longest lived should be possessed by the desire to live longer. It was not always that way. As a young doctor I worked on the wards of a public hospital in a fading industrial city in the English midlands. There I encountered a dying generation of men and women whose working lives had unrolled from the 1920s through to the 1950s. As they passed the age of seventy – an age beyond which they did not expect to live – they could look back at a lifetime of exhausting work, at relationships of the 'for better or worse' variety and at the families they had raised. They did not see health as a commodity. Worn out but undefeated, they showed me how to die.

A retiring director from the National Institutes of Health (NIH) noted in 2003 that life expectancy in the US had increased by six years between 1970 and 2000 and claimed that physicians should be credited with three of these (public health was credited with one). He failed to mention that life expectancy had been rising even faster before NIH got going. The sour note in his account was that life expectancy in the US trailed that in twenty-two other countries despite a massive investment in health care. Some might believe that this was due to social inequality, he noted, but he himself believed that it was because existing medical knowledge was not being translated into practice.[29]

Retiring directors are not under oath, and we may question this. Figure 50 shows the relationship between wealth and life expectancy in countries around the world, a comparison which suggests that a threshold GDP of around $10,000 per capita (2005 values) confers a life expectancy not far behind that of the world's most affluent countries.

People in the United States do not live longer than the people of Chile or Costa Rica, for example, despite four times the average income and access to the most sophisticated medical facilities in the world. Modern medicine does many wonderful things, and thank goodness for it, but increasing the average lifespan is not necessarily among them. As gerontologist Caleb Finch phrases it, 'the similar age-related mortality rates throughout all human populations despite their wide differences in the incidence of specific diseases suggests the unexpected possibility that certain processes

Life expectancy at birth vs average annual income

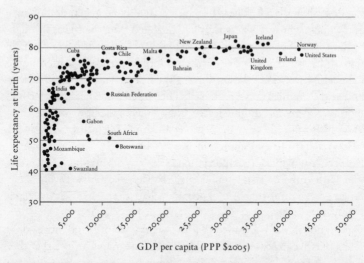

Figure 50: Life expectancy at birth vs annual average income. South Africa and the Russian Federation fall well below the curve, whereas Norway and the USA have no added benefit from their high per capita GDP.
Source: https://underpoint05.wordpress.com/2011/10/03/inequality-first-world-problems/

related to mortality risk are not closely linked to specific age-related diseases'.[30]

Income inequality may well be more important than average income. It might for example explain why the most favoured US counties top the range for life expectancy, whereas other counties compare to sub-Saharan Africa. It might also explain why average life expectancy in the UK is now falling back after a century of growth.

In sum, people are living longer than ever before. This was largely due to the elimination of premature death in the first half of the twentieth century, whereas lifespan increased in the second half because older people were living longer. This development was unanticipated, and no one knows where it will end. The two main explanations are that our lives have been prolonged by medical science and that we are ageing more slowly. Both are involved, but advances in medical care are not necessarily more important. In all events, long life beckons – provided you choose your parents, your nationality, your social position and your way of life with some care. Slower ageing has emerged as a feature of the phenotypic transition, but there are still many loose ends. Are we approaching a natural term to life, or will privileged populations keep getting older? If so, this raises the spectre of Jonathan Swift's Struldbruggs: people gifted with immortality who suffer the miseries of old age in full. Unlike Achilles, most of us would prefer a longer life to a glorious death, but what we really want is longer youth.

15

Fastened to a Dying Animal

'All living things are subject to decay,' as the Buddha said on his death-bed, and our ageing bodies tell the story of a future that was prefigured by the past. Most people now die from age-related conditions that arise within their own bodies, develop over the course of many years and progress at a rate influenced by the interplay between genes, the outside world and our own behaviour. Nothing in the history of our species could have prepared us for this, for post-reproductive life is not subject to natural selection. There are no genes 'for' longevity, only genes that evolved for other reasons and just happen to predis-pose to longer life in a modern environment. Our journey into old age is determined by the interaction between genes that evolved for other reasons and an environment that never previously existed. Should we then think of the afflictions of later life as diseases – or as the endgame of a phenotype?

A body is a commonwealth of mutually dependent cells whose integrity depends upon a host of regulatory or 'housekeeping' func-tions. Since many of these deteriorate over time, old age entails a progressive failure of self-regulation, a failure that has accumulating consequences for the cells whose function is being regulated. Two types of regulatory failure concern us here: a failure to maintain the internal environment upon which our cells depend, and a failure to service the cells themselves.

A thermostat which returns a room to the same temperature is a standard example of a process called homeostasis. Our ability to regulate the temperature of our own bodies generally works well enough for a lifetime (although it becomes less efficient in old age) and it maintains the same set point. Other homeostats are less robust in modern conditions, as can be seen by a comparison with twentieth-century hunter-gatherers. Their lives were shorter, but their weight remained constant in adult life, and their blood pressure and blood glucose did not increase with age. Obesity, hypertension and diabetes soon swept through their ranks when they abandoned their traditional way of life and drifted to the margins of industrial society.

Those of us who grow up in affluent societies acquire weight, hypertension and diabetes in a slower and more insidious fashion. We consume the best part of a ton of food each year, yet our weight is almost the same. Almost, but not quite: for we retain a small positive balance, and our year-on-year weight creeps steadily upward. As every dieter knows, the body soon adopts each increment in weight as the 'new normal' and resists our efforts to lower it back again. Blood pressure and blood glucose also creep upward with age and resist our efforts to treat them. We saw earlier that this forward-feeding type of adjustment is known as allostasis. This affects all members of a consumer society, but we travel at different speeds. We have much the same access to food, for example, but some people gain weight faster than others. Increasing weight predisposes to hypertension and diabetes, but some are fast-tracked to these and others are not. Despite these individual differences, however, allostasis is a leading hallmark of our phenotype.

Similar environments produce similar 'rising tide' effects, and the consumer phenotype converges towards a 'metabolic syndrome' in which central (male-pattern) obesity is associated with high blood pressure, arterial disease and disturbed metabolism of lipids and glucose. This syndrome (literally, a 'running together') has given rise to much controversy – partly because there are many competing definitions – all somewhat arbitrary – and partly because ownership of the concept has been vested in a medical profession that does not distinguish clearly between a phenotype and a disease.

THE RISE OF THE RISK FACTOR

Aldous Huxley remarked that fortune tellers never make a fortune and that insurance companies don't go bankrupt. Life insurance is a bet on how long someone will live, a bet based on statistical techniques which correct your chronological age for your biological age. Empirical though they are, these statistical techniques are tried and tested, and they adjust your biological age for variables such as gender, ethnicity, occupation and socio-economic status. Height and weight provide an indication of growth and lifestyle; blood pressure, glucose and cholesterol indicate internal wear and tear, and smoking and drinking tell of the stress you have superimposed upon this. Life is uncertain, which is why people take out insurance, but the casino always wins.

The life insurance companies generated the most reliable statistics concerning population health in the first part of the twentieth century, and they introduced the concept of risk – *their* risk, not yours! They viewed risk as a fixed attribute, rather than as something that could be altered by your own actions. Epidemiology then emerged as a full-fledged academic discipline and came of age with the Framingham Heart Study, launched in 1948. This was a long-term follow-up study of 5,000 people from a small town in Massachusetts, and (as the name indicates) the investigators were primarily concerned with the epidemic of coronary heart disease that was sweeping the country. The study showed that (age apart) the risk of progression to heart disease directly relates to a person's blood pressure, cholesterol and glucose, and introduced the term 'risk factor' into the clinical lexicon.

It changed the face of medicine, for the notion of treating risk rather than disease was almost unknown until then. Franklin D. Roosevelt had dangerously high blood pressure (200/100) when re-elected president of the USA in 1944. Six months later, he clutched his head and died of a massive brain haemorrhage. Meticulous records show that no attempt had been made to treat his blood pressure; the drugs available had too many side effects, and it was not yet clear that lowering blood pressure protects against stroke. People only went to a doctor when they thought they had a problem, and medicine was a purely reactive speciality. Identification of risk factors meant that doctors could now diagnose medical conditions in people without symptoms, and treat conditions that had yet to develop. Medicine became proactive rather than reactive, and more and more people came within its scope.

This was a major step towards the medicalization of modern life, and it required powerful justification. It is one thing to point out that a risk factor is *associated* with heart disease, but quite another to show that it *causes* it. You can only test this by adjusting the risk factor in question and watching what happens. Huge prospective clinical trials got underway in the US in the 1960s, with mixed results. Blood pressure treatment was so effective against stroke that the trial had to be stopped, but the effect on heart disease was more modest. Lowering blood glucose in diabetes initially suggested that the treatment actually increases your chances of heart disease. Further trials were needed to show that this is not the case, and that blood glucose reduction protects against diabetic eye and kidney disease. Trials of cholesterol-lowering therapy were limited by the lack of really effective therapy until the introduction of statins in the 1990s.[1]

MICROCOSM

We are what our cells make us, but we are also what we make of our cells. Life begins with a single cell which then diversifies into more than 200 specialized variants. These daughter cells respond to cues from their environment, and they too grow old and die. Some cells – those that form our skin and line our intestine, for example – go through regular cycles of death and rebirth. Although the copying mechanism is almost infallible, errors inevitably arise when billions of cells are replicated and – unless detected and eliminated – some of these errors will progress to cancer. Since cancer risk is directly related to the rate of replication, tissues that turn over frequently give rise to the greatest number, and anything that promotes replication – inflammation, for example – will increase this risk. Our likelihood of cancer is thus related to the presence or absence of genetic variants that might influence the risk of a copying error, the rate at which the cells in question turn over, external factors which might provoke inflammation, and the ability of the body to detect and eliminate copying errors. Cancer risk increases in the older age groups because copying errors accumulate with time and because surveillance mechanisms become less efficient.

To complicate matters, different cells grow old in different ways. Cells that turn over regularly commit suicide when their cell-cycle is completed, but this orderly sequence is disrupted in later life by cells that grow old but refuse to die. These senescent cells accumulate in the tissues and send harmful signals to the cells in their vicinity. A failure of surveillance and elimination of these dysfunctional cells may be a feature of normal ageing and might point the way to future interventions in the ageing process itself.

Some cells do not replace themselves in adult life, however, and nerve cells are a prime example. These replicate with burgeoning frequency as the brain is growing, and die in swathes as the brain reshapes itself. A sea change sets in as the brain approaches its adult configuration, however, for established cells no longer replicate and must then serve us for a lifetime.[2] Other long-lived cells are found in muscle (heart muscle included), the nephrons that serve as the functional units of the kidneys, and the pancreatic beta cells that produce insulin. These cells are at risk from any stress that might threaten their survival, and they all experience slow, age-associated attrition. The cumulative effect adds up to the failure of a body system or organ that we refer to as disease. Why then do common diseases ebb and flow?

AS OLD AS YOUR ARTERIES

Heart disease has long been with us, but its expression has changed. Ötzi, a forty- to fifty-year-old man frozen into an alpine glacier 5,300 years ago, was found to have chalk deposits in his major arteries 'indicating an already advanced coronary disease state'. Long-standing cholesterol deposits produce little flecks of calcium, and X-rays have demonstrated these in the coronary arteries of ancient mummies from different societies around the world. Arterial disease is a feature of the ageing process, but progressive coronary disease was rare before modern times.

The coronary arteries 'crown' the heart they nourish, and their narrowing produces the characteristic symptom of *angina pectoris* – chest pain on exercise which radiates to the throat and arms and stops when you rest. These symptoms were clearly described in the seventeenth century but were deemed so unusual that an unnamed eighteenth-century physician who experienced them offered his own body for autopsy in the hope of solving the problem. William Heberden (1710–1801) performed this last service for him but neglected to look at the coronary arteries. Further cases came his way, usually men in their fifties, 'most of them with a short neck and inclining to be fat'. Since the pulse is steady during an episode of angina, he doubted that the heart was involved, and he bemoaned the fact that the sudden and unexpected deaths of his patients rarely gave him the opportunity to 'open' them. In 1772, however, a colleague sent him a report which allowed him to glimpse the role of the coronary circulation, and the link was finally established.

Feel your pulse. An artery has an outer protective jacket called the adventitia, a middle layer called the media and a silky inner lining known as the intima. The media is elastic in the larger arteries and turns to muscle further down the arterial tree; these muscles contract to stop us from blacking out when we stand up. Arteries are subject to different forms of damage. In the early part of the twentieth century pathologists emphasized *arteriosclerosis*, or hardening of the arteries due to a damaged media. In the second half of the century the focus switched to *atherosclerosis*, or infiltration of the intima by cholesterol-rich plaque. Atheroma (the word comes from the Greek for 'gruel') is a nondescript cholesterol-rich infiltrate within the intima which may swell, blocking the passage of blood; alternatively, the lining of the artery may strip away over the deposit, leaving a raw patch on which a clot can form.

The phrase 'as old as your arteries' was coined by the physician William Osler in 1900. He noted that his private practice had filled with cases of angina in middle-aged men who ate too much, smoked too much and worked too much. His advice was to 'go slowly and attend to your work, live a godly life and avoid mining shares'. He was among the first to recognize 'that the early degenerations, particularly of the arteries and the kidneys, [are] due to too much food'. 'It is an old story,' he said, 'this association of a long life with a small intake [of food].' He did not necessarily practise what he preached, however, for he once caught a patient smoking in the park and advised him to stop. When the man threw the pack away, Osler grabbed it, lit a cigarette and strolled off.[3]

It is hard to know exactly when the twentieth-century epidemic of coronary heart disease began, for doctors were unfamiliar with the condition in the early part of the century and had no access to diagnostic methods such as the electrocardiogram. Deaths were not recorded as due to 'disease of the coronary arteries' until 1930; the terminology changed to 'arteriosclerotic heart disease' in 1949 and to 'ischaemic heart disease' in 1965, by which time around 90 per cent of heart deaths were given this label. It is therefore uncertain when the coronary epidemic began; all we really know is that its mortality reached a peak in the years from 1950 to 1970 and that it has fallen steadily ever since.

Stark evidence of this retreating epidemic came from autopsies of US servicemen killed in action. Fatty streaks were found in the coronary arteries of 77 per cent of healthy young men who died in the Korean War, as against 45 per cent of those who died in the Vietnam War and only 8.3 per cent of those who died in Iraq.[4] Hospitalization for coronary heart attacks in people under the age of sixty-five halved

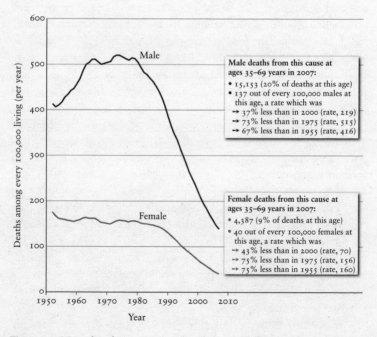

Figure 51: Mortality from coronary heart disease fell by 70–80 per cent between 1980 and 2007 in men and women in the UK aged 35–69.

over the same period, and the rate of decline was greatest from 2000 to 2010, despite the introduction of more sensitive diagnostic tests, which should have boosted numbers. The same effect was seen across the whole of the western world (figure 51), and death from strokes (other than those caused by haemorrhage) fell sharply and to a similar extent over the same period.[5]

Arterial disease declined so rapidly that deaths from cancer came to outnumber deaths from coronaries and strokes in people under the age of sixty-five. France reached this tipping point in 1988, the US in 2002 (figure 52) and Italy and the UK in 2011–12.[6] Likely contributors to this decline include a marked reduction in cigarette smoking and increasing use of drugs to control coronary risk factors, but vascular mortality was already in full retreat before such strategies were in place. Sherlock Holmes commented on the strange case of the dog that did not bark in the night, and the health watchdogs are strangely subdued when it comes to celebrating what might be considered the greatest public health triumph of the twentieth century – if they

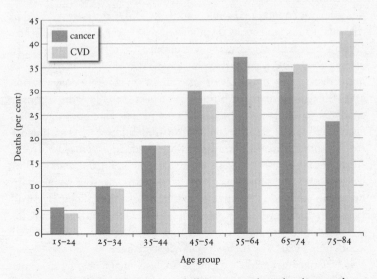

Figure 52: The tipping point: cancer kills more people under the age of sixty-five than cardiovascular disease (CVD) in the USA, as reported in 2002.

could just explain it. Instead, they bang the drum for prevention of a rapidly retreating condition.

Smoking is a major risk factor for coronary disease, probably because it promotes inflammation. Inflammation is a programmed response to tissue damage. Celsus, a Roman physician of the first century AD, reported its four cardinal signs: *calor*, *dolor*, *tumor* and *rubor* – heat, pain, swelling and redness. This creates a war zone in the affected tissue, bathes cells in chemical alarm signals and summons immune cells to the vicinity. Recent reviews of vascular disease recognize that immune cells and the chemicals they produce (known as cytokines) play an active part in arterial damage. Since coronary artery disease is retreating so rapidly, this raises the previously heretical possibility that a changing immune system might somehow be implicated. It is conceivable, for example, that changing exposure to infection could influence the intensity of the immune response, and hence the severity of arterial disease.[7] This links back to the observation that obesity itself appears to have become less damaging in a modern environment.

A changing pattern of disease demands an explanation, especially when it runs counter to dogma, and we should therefore take heed of the only person who correctly predicted the retreat of arterial disease. Anders Forsdahl, the general practitioner from north Norway we encountered earlier, suggested that the epidemic of coronary disease in his district was due to a *mismatch* between childhood deprivation and affluence in later life. If this was correct, he noted, the coronary epidemic should go into reverse as more people were born into affluence. By the same token coronary disease should soar when affluence reached other parts of the world. Both predictions proved correct.[8] Coronary heart disease had its greatest impact in Europe and the USA between the 1950s and the 1980s, principally affecting people born between 1900 and 1930, often in conditions of material poverty. In all events, and whatever the explanation, the fact remains that we are far less susceptible to vascular disease than we were two or three generations ago. Heart disease hasn't changed: we have.

It was once believed that genetic analysis might help us to distinguish between health and complex disease, but we have learned that all it can ever do is to provide an estimate of probability within a given setting. A nineteenth-century lesson had to be learned all over again. Experts of the time were awed by the power of statistical description. It could, for example, predict the number of people who would commit suicide in Paris in a given year, right down to age, sex and method. Such regularity, as they reasoned, must reflect an underlying law, as indeed it does – but the law relates to probability rather than biology. Statistics describe but they don't explain. They can identify some of the characteristics of those who commit suicide, but they can never tell us who will do it, or when. Likewise, genome scans can offer very precise estimates of the risk of complex disease in large populations but are of little predictive value at the individual level. Nor should genetic risk be considered outside the environment in which it was assessed.

THE CLAWS OF THE CRAB

We may think of cancer as a single entity, but experts see each type of cancer as a disease in its own right, complete with its own history, epidemiology and predisposing factors. It is now the leading cause of death in men under the age of sixty-five in more affluent parts of the world, not because the risk of cancer is increasing – in most cases it isn't – but because deaths from heart disease are falling, and you have to die of something.

We see cancer as binary: you either have it or you don't. This may be true to everyday experience, but the seeds of cancer are sown all the time and are frequently detected on careful post-mortem search in old people. Since cancer arises as a copying error in cells that are turning over rapidly, anything that increases cell turnover will also increase cancer risk. Cigarettes are the world's leading carcinogen. The US population consumed an average of 54 cigarettes per head in 1900, rising to 4,345 in 1963, and lung cancer mortality rose fifteen-fold between 1930 and 1990.[9] Lung cancer is responsible for 22 per cent of cancers in the UK, but its incidence has halved in men since the 1970s; women have been slower to kick the habit. As smoking declines in younger people, the age at which lung cancer is diagnosed has moved upwards; peak incidence in men is currently in those aged 85–89.

It may come as no surprise to learn that 20 per cent of global cancer is associated with smoking, but it is less often appreciated that 16 per cent of cancers are related to infection. Liver cancer was the second commonest cancer in men in 2012, and China accounted for half of the total; 90 per cent of cases were due to sub-clinical infection with hepatitis virus. Stomach cancer, strongly associated with *Helicobacter*, is almost equally common in lower-income countries, and cervical cancer, associated with human papillomavirus, is the second most common cancer in women in poorer parts of the world. Other cancers are associated with lifestyle – smoking, alcohol or food. Obesity increases your risk of eleven types of cancer, and height (a proxy for growth and food intake) is an additional risk factor in six.

Although cancers have a genetic component, the environment matters. There is for example a strong genetic contribution to breast cancer, especially in those who carry the notorious *BRCA* genes. Historical analysis shows that women in Iceland with these mutations are four times as likely to develop breast cancer today as they were in 1920, but this was accompanied by a four-fold increase in other types of breast cancer. As with diabetes and heart disease – and for reasons that are largely unknown – genes determine relative risk, but absolute risk is related to lifestyle and environment.[10] Yet another 'rising tide' effect.

THE WORLD IS UNHEALTHY: PLEASE ADJUST YOUR PHENOTYPE

Our society has chosen to draw the boundary between health and disease by measuring everyone against the yardstick of youth. The range of 'normal' for weight, blood pressure and so forth is defined as the range in healthy young adults, for example, and any upward shift in older people is considered unhealthy. Since these measures increase with age, the distinction between old age and disease has become hopelessly blurred. To take one example, the metabolic syndrome was estimated to affect fewer than 10 per cent of young adult

Americans in 2007–12, but around 60 per cent of men and women in their seventies.[11] And here's another: 77 per cent of European women and 56 per cent of European men over the age of eighty were shown to have a defect in glucose handling or frank diabetes.[12] The effect of choosing youth as the yardstick for disease is to convert old age into a morbid condition. Since those who survive into old age might reasonably be considered the healthiest members of any population, it takes a society that equates youth with health to label them as sick.

The same cultural attitude is reflected in our attempt to counteract an unhealthy environment by modifying the people who inhabit it, which is why pills have become part of everyday life. In 2014, 50 per cent of women and 43 per cent of men in the UK were taking regular prescription drugs, rising to 70 per cent in those over seventy-five. By 2018, nearly half of those over the age of sixty-five were taking five drugs or more. Meanwhile, the boundaries of ill-health have been extended by reducing the threshold of healthy blood glucose, blood pressure and cholesterol, a process that currently identifies 56 million Americans (one in three of an adult population of 187 million) as in need of treatment. More recent international guidelines for hypertension imply that almost everyone over the age of forty-five is in need of medication.[13] This is the pursuit of therapeutic futility.

Pills are now a routine feature of later life. There is nothing intrinsically wrong in this, for pharmaceuticals are no more unnatural than spectacles or shoe leather, but we should consider the Law of Inverse Benefit. Those at greatest risk of heart disease, for example, will develop it younger and will benefit most from intervention, whereas those at lower risk will be affected later or not at all. The effect of applying the same criteria to all age groups is to define the majority of the over-seventy age group as in need of treatment for high blood pressure, cholesterol or glucose, although they are far less likely to derive individual benefit than younger age groups. Furthermore, since drug metabolism slows with age, they are also far more likely to experience side effects. This is the Law of Inverse Benefit.

Much of this, as I believe, is simply due to muddled thinking about age and disease. Old people can and must be offered all the medical help they need, but only when there is reasonable evidence of direct

Figure 53: *Cradle to Grave* (2003), an installation at the British Museum, features 14,000 pills: the number estimated to have been consumed by the average British woman by the time she reaches her early eighties.

benefit. The common age-related disorders arise inside our own bodies, their causes are indeterminate, multiple genes and environmental factors influence their development, and all older people experience them to some extent. They can and should be managed effectively, but we should treat individual people rather than our own sense of inadequacy. Old age is not a disease; it is the endgame of a phenotype and it should be played out with humour and dignity.

PART 4

Changing Our Minds

16

The Milk of Human Kindness

Homer pauses amid the carnage of the *Iliad* to capture the moment when Hector strides into Troy, battered and bloody from the latest skirmish. His wife Andromache awaits him, and a maid holds their son Astyanax in her arms. When Hector reaches out to him, the boy squeals in fear of the nodding horsehair plume on his father's helmet. His parents laugh indulgently; Hector doffs his helmet, hugs his son and says that he will be a greater warrior than his father. Only we, the invisible onlookers, know what fate has in store for this contented trio.*

The indefinable something that grips us in Homer's description relates to a common humanity that has never changed, and probably never will. Even so, our ancestors evidently thought and behaved in ways that were very different from ours. Homer's heroes are vain, petulant, irrational and murderously violent, and their gods are no better. The pre-literate heroes of Homer or the Norse sagas act on the spur of the moment and display remarkable lack of empathy; only a few old men (Homer's Nestor, or the protagonist of *Njal's Saga*) show signs of a wider perspective.

How different are we? We undoubtedly grow and develop differently. We differ in our experience of life and death. We differ from previous generations in the way we interact, express our thoughts and emotions but – since we have no objective means of comparison – we are left with differences that are intuitively obvious yet impossible to measure. Even so, it is important to try, and I will seek to

---

* Hector is killed in battle, Andromache becomes a slave, Astyanax is thrown to his death from the towers of Troy for fear that he might live to avenge his father.

demonstrate that our bandwidth of self-awareness and empathy has both shifted and become wider than in the past.

We reflect the society in which we live. Since the face is our primal means of interaction, I will begin by looking at the way faces display our feelings, how we read them and how this display has been changing. We will move from there to our temperaments, our emotions, our capacity for empathy, the impact of literacy and – in more existential terms – the ways in which we locate ourselves within our society and universe.

JUDGING BY APPEARANCES

'My face is my fortune,' says the girl in the English folk song, and we are so deeply imbued with cues for social acceptance, dominance and hierarchy that a face or posture on an advertising hoarding triggers an instant response. A face is the focus of intense personal interest and gives rise to emotions ranging from complacency to despair when viewed in a mirror. Its signals range from physical attraction to fashion, gender, social class and ethnicity, and the disproportionately vast array of nerve cells devoted to the face in the motor and sensory areas of the brain suggests that we are more expert than we know at reading them. Para-verbal communication is the medium for much of our social interaction, and we are practised at reading its signals – or trying to conceal the signals we ourselves transmit. Despite the overwhelming dominance of the face in social communication, its subtlety and complexity resist translation into the numerology of science.

How, then, do we judge one another? Many would agree that a few minutes (or even seconds) of conversation are sufficient to sound out the background, education and disposition of the person we have just encountered. Physical charm and markers of social standing are readily established, after which we generally value people for their personality and entertainment value. Where more serious choices are involved – is this the person you want beside you in battle, business or bed? – trust becomes paramount. Shakespeare's tragedies almost all revolve around trust and betrayal: think *Julius Caesar* ('a lean and hungry look'), *Macbeth* ('a gentleman on whom I built an absolute trust'), *King Lear* ('those pelican daughters'), *Hamlet* ('one may smile and smile and be a villain') and *Othello* ('yet she must die, else she'll betray more men'). Ironically, only Antony and Cleopatra, his two least reliable characters, remain true to each other until death.

'There's no art to find the mind's construction in the face,' said King Duncan in *Macbeth*, and he was right. We are unreliable when it comes to detecting trustworthiness in others, or even – truth to tell – in ourselves. Participants who rated faces for trustworthiness in a recent study were unable to distinguish between convicted and unconvicted corporate executives, between military criminals and decorated veterans, or between students who cheated on tests and those who didn't. There was substantial agreement between the ratings, but it bore little relation to reality, merely confirming that those who look trustworthy get trusted.[1] Some try to live up to their appearance, and others prey upon the trust they inspire. Not for nothing are they called confidence tricksters.

Stronger guarantees are needed by those who must depend upon the loyalty of strangers. Early business networks worked through bonds of family, community or religion. Legal sanctions have superseded personal values in business, but trust remains paramount in social life. Eighteenth-century people thought in terms of virtue and vice rather than salvation and damnation, and saw virtue as the best guarantee of trust. The marriage market is the core business of Jane Austen's novels, and her heroines must distinguish between the honest yet uninspiring safe bets as against the trifling charmers whose affections lack a sound financial basis. Outside her drawing room, people increasingly encountered strangers who played by unfamiliar rules, which might explain why people of the nineteenth century placed greater reliance upon external markers of character than most cultures before or since. One celebrated instance came when Captain FitzRoy of the *Beagle* met Charles Darwin for the first time and worried that Darwin's large and spatulate nose might denote a lack of the energy and determination needed for the voyage.[2] Physiognomy, the belief that you can judge character from the face, still influences us more than we realize, for attractive people are more successful at securing jobs, and those who look the part do better at interview. Men in the military whose faces express dominance are more likely

to achieve high rank, irrespective of other qualifications. More striking still, judgements of competence made on a one-second exposure
to photographs predicted the outcome of elections to the US Senate
or Congress on around 70 per cent of occasions.[3]

The art of reading the face was practised in ancient Greece, and no
doubt long before that. Socrates was noted for his ugliness, and his
disciples protested when a physiognomist declared that he was 'given
to intemperance, sensuality and violent bursts of passion'. They were
silenced when Socrates admitted that such was his nature, although
held tightly in check.[4] In the 1770s, pioneer physiognomist and Swiss
pastor Johann Caspar Lavater published a weighty and influential
tome on the subject which remained a firm favourite with readers
for more than a century and informed the portrayal of character in
Victorian novels ranging from Dickens and Charlotte Brontë to the
penny dreadfuls. The murder victim in the first adventure of Dr Watson and Sherlock Holmes, *A Study in Scarlet*, had a 'low forehead,
blunt nose and prognathous jaw' which 'gave the dead man a singu-
larly simous and ape-like appearance'.

Lavater distinguished between physiognomy, 'the observation of
character in a state of tranquillity, or rest', and pathognomy, 'the study
of the character in action', meaning the play of expression.[5] His belief
was that 'the countenance is the theatre on which the soul exhibits
itself'. Counterfeits abound, since all men seek the approbation of
others, but he argued that no amount of dissimulation can change the
structure of the face, and that this can be deciphered by those with the
necessary skills. He came from Zurich, the home of Calvinism, a doctrine which drew the sharpest of dividing lines between those destined
for everlasting felicity and those condemned to eternal punishment. It
was therefore of the utmost importance to choose your partners in
business or marriage from among the elect. Lavater argued that piety
could be counterfeit, but that the face could not. Physiognomists could
tell the difference and should themselves have a pleasing appearance,
with (among other features) a well-developed nose, an organ with
which he himself happened to be well endowed.

Lavater had a ready hand at sketching faces backed by a flowery
prose style – his sermons were probably not short – but his interpretation was unashamedly aesthetic. The great naturalist Georges-Louis

Figure 54: Lavater's nose.

Leclerc, Comte de Buffon, was prepared to give some credence to the idea that personality is reflected in the expression of emotion, but he derided those who thought that a man might have a better character because (as he rather spitefully remarked) he had 'a better-shaped nose'. 'Nothing can be more chimerical', he concluded of the physiognomists, 'than their pretended observations.'[6]

Sculpture is frozen physiognomy. Accurate depictions of the human face and body tend to disappoint, and the great sculptors introduced subtle distortions of perspective that haunt us to this day. Sir Charles Bell (1774–1842), a pioneer neurologist, pointed out that 'the forms which we regard as models of perfection are unlike what has existed in nature . . . no living head ever had the facial line of the Jupiter, the Apollo, the Mercury, or the Venus'.[7] Realistic portrayal was in vogue by Roman times, partly driven by the creation of funeral masks, and the stone faces you confront in museums are those of real people, world-weary, shrewd, tough, competent yet wistful. Such at least is my own characterization of Pompey's face (figure 55), in which histor-ian Peter Green sees a 'weak chin, piggy eyes and self-satisfied smirk',

Figure 55: Pompey the Great, *c.* AD 30–50. Ny Carlsberg Glyptotek, Copenhagen.

evidence of subtle denigration by a presumed Grecian artist.[8] No matter which of us is right: the real point is that we are both prepared to rest an enormous weight of inference upon a chunk of carved stone.

Artists depict the face along a spectrum in which realism is flanked by idealized portrayal on the one side and distortion or caricature on the other. Sacred art presents an ageless face floating in repose, with symmetrical features, a gentle mouth and lowered eyes which avoid those of the beholder. Distracting detail is avoided, for the saint or Madonna is poised at the juncture of two worlds and merely human characteristics have been leached away. Computer-generated composite faces have a curious resemblance to sacred art in their beauty and impersonality, whereas more realistic depiction provides the context and idiosyncrasy that sacred art avoids. Dutch portraits of the seventeenth century, for example, show the person depicted in terms of their stage of life, social status, demeanour and business setting. Formal portraits generally show the face at a slight angle, two-thirds of them from the left, reflecting the unconscious preference of right-handed painters. Clues as to character are provided; a square male face with narrowed eyes suggests power and competence, but too broad a face or eyes that are too narrow send a different message. And so it goes, on through a whole range of stereotypes reinforced by soap operas and advertising hoardings.

Balance between the features has always been highly appreciated. This might explain the odd attraction of composite photographs, a technique used by Francis Galton in pursuit of the elusive family face. Superimposition of photographs of family members tended towards a generic and more balanced facial outline with no idiosyncratic features. Those concerned felt robbed of their individuality. Superimposed photographs of criminals also revert towards the mean, and the merged face looks decidedly more prepossessing than the ravaged individuals who went into its making. Galton's overlay technique inevitably resulted in some fuzziness of outline, which he attempted to reduce by equalizing the distance between the eyes, but computers can now merge faces without loss of sharpness, producing an oddly ethereal appearance which observers rate as more attractive than most of the faces that went into it.

The perception of beauty might simply be due to enhanced symmetry but agrees well with the hypothesis of painter Sir Joshua Reynolds 'that beauty is the medium, or centre, of the various forms of individuals . . . towards which nature is continually inclining, like lines terminating in a centre'.[9] Modern observers have wondered if beauty might have evolutionary significance by stabilizing characteristics within a population, and the idea of beauty as a regression towards the mean was tested by adding a composite to a line-up of sixty female faces, each scored for attractiveness by both men and women. When merged, the fifteen most highly rated faces were considered more attractive than the overall composite, disproving the notion that beauty resides in the average. The authors then identified the features that distinguished the high average group from the rest and enhanced them by 50 per cent (such differences are almost imperceptible to an observer): this composite was rated higher still. We respond to imperceptible cues when we rate facial beauty, and since the experiment produced the same result in Japanese women as in westerners, the effect is not restricted to one culture or ethnicity.[10]

The difference between past and modern faces is easier to sense than to define. A photographic studio near Cardiff specializes in the transposition of the faces of its clients into old photographs but, despite the skill with which this is done, the faces just look wrong. Art forgers find it more difficult to reproduce faces from previous centuries than to replicate the technical mastery of the great painters.[11] Francis Galton studied English portraits from several centuries and claimed to see 'indisputable signs of one predominant type of face supplanting another', but this might relate to artistic style rather than anatomy. An alternative possibility is that the habitual play of our facial muscles might change the resting configuration of our face in ways that escape conscious detection. Arthur Koestler commented that Jewish friends who had settled in the USA soon began to look like Americans, and this finds support in a study which showed that students could identify wealthy individuals with better-than-chance accuracy from greyscale photographs showing neutral expressions.[12]

The attempt to infer character from external cues will always limp behind the truth. Eighteenth-century thinkers believed that godliness and virtue were inherent qualities, and that the character of an individual must fall to one side or the other of the line between vice and virtue. Sadly enough, virtue is not particularly interesting, whereas vice holds endless fascination. Early novelists got round this by keeping the reader guessing as to which side of the line a character would fall until everyone's true colours were revealed at the end of the story. The *Bildungsroman* was a step forward: character was no longer portrayed as a fixed attribute, but as an outcome to be achieved by a testing rite of passage. Nineteenth-century novelists located the struggle between vice and virtue within its heroes and heroines, and religious thought and biography went through a similar transition. Piety and the exercise of virtue no longer guaranteed salvation; only when purged in the fires of anguished self-examination could the soul aspire to rise towards the light.

The notion of Hell faded away in the nineteenth century; so too did the concept of character as unitary and fixed. Psychologist William James wrote in 1890 that the newborn baby is plunged into a 'blooming buzzing confusion' of sensation, and the characters portrayed by today's novelists are swamped by insurmountable opportunities for self-expression. Despite tantalizing insights into their behaviour, the central core of their being remains as elusive as our own. Character has gone, and we are left clutching at personality, attributes and habitual behaviour, things that cannot be inferred from the nose.

EXPRESSING THE EMOTIONS

Although there is no reason to suspect that our feelings of joy or pain have changed over time, our way of expressing them undoubtedly has. Theatre reflects this, for the face had a limited role when the actors were at some distance from the audience, and the players of ancient Greece performed in masks. Those who perform on a stage must project their voices and feelings to the back rows of a theatre, thus favouring the histrionic style of performance so evident in early film productions. Close-up cinematography was a revelation, for it permitted a whole world of feeling to be transmitted by almost imperceptible shifts in the play of the facial muscles. Our faces are rarely, if ever, entirely at rest when we interact together, and the famous beauties of earlier times would not have made good pin-ups, for their beauty lay in their charm, vivacity and range of facial expression.

Speech and expression go hand in hand, for the muscles of the face shape the words that issue from the mouth and provide an animated commentary on what is said, reinforced by movements of the hands, shoulders and body. Darwin noted that 'the force of language is much aided by the expressive movements of the face and body. We perceive this at once when we converse on an important subject with any person whose face is concealed.' He never had to struggle with a telephone or an email, but we know how easily serious misunderstanding can arise: the face-to-face meeting is never likely to be superseded.

Although Lavater-style physiognomy has no credibility today, it seems reasonable to believe that the conformation of the facial muscles is affected by the habitual play of expression. These muscles form a complex meshwork underlying the mask of the face, and they respond in complex and infinitely nuanced synchrony to messages passing down our nerves. In contrast to the facial muscles of primates, which are largely composed of fast-twitch muscle fibres for rapid movements, ours are slow-twitch and better suited to slower shifts of mood and expression.[13] The facial muscles differ from muscles elsewhere in that they terminate on skin rather than bone. This means that the face literally hangs off the skull. Place a mirror on your bed, look vertically down into it, relax your facial muscles, and prepare for an unpleasant experience.

Charles Bell noted that nerve and muscles are engaged in ceaseless readjustment of the facial mask by altering the play of the eyes and mouth and the contour of cheeks and forehead, and the importance of the facial nerve that controls these movements is clearly evident in the temporary paralysis known as Bell's palsy, when personality is erased by a drooping mask that covers half of the face.

Bell inspired Darwin to study the emotions, and he concluded that the range of human facial expression could be derived from a few primary emotions, albeit subtly interwoven. Primary emotions such as fear and anger are easily understood across species barriers, and

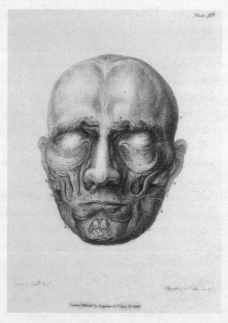

Figure 56: Charles Bell's depiction of the facial muscles.

the same basic range of expression could be observed in different racial groups, children and the blind, suggesting a common origin in natural selection. He pointed out that 'so many shades of expression are instantly recognized without any conscious process of analysis on our part', which implies that we are preprogrammed to send and receive non-verbal signals.[14]

Given the close working partnership of face and voice, it is no surprise that both language and face recognition are innate. Babies respond to human faces – or even drawings of a face – almost immediately after birth and can smile back at you within a few weeks; the habit of reading faces into clouds or other random shapes stays with us throughout our lives. Conversely, most adults respond with a rush of affection towards anything resembling a baby's face. Konrad Lorenz argued that we possess innate releasing mechanisms which are triggered by cues such as this, as can be seen in the helpless idolatry displayed in the stunned expressions of new parents.

Emotions differ from other thought processes in that they generate a physical response, and one that can be astonishingly powerful. In the words of the psychologist William James, 'every one of the bodily changes, whatsoever it be, is FELT, acutely or obscurely, the moment it occurs', further, 'each morsel of it contributes its pulsations of feeling, dim or sharp, pleasant, painful, or dubious, to that sense of personality that every one of us unfailingly carries with him'.[15] The way in which we express our emotions and thus – to some extent – the way we experience them, changed markedly in the early modern period.

Tears were a routine part of emotional expression in Britain in the eighteenth and first half of the nineteenth century, but male tears became strictly taboo towards the end of the nineteenth century.[16] A stiff upper lip was considered necessary for the hauteur of an imperial race, although some might argue that the public school system produced generations of emotional eunuchs. E. M. Forster recalled that the bravest thing he ever saw was when a boy at his school openly acknowledged his parents and sister at Open Day and went so far as to walk with them across a playing field.

Expressions follow social convention. The cinema replaced telegraphed histrionics with close-up images of facial expressions, but soap operas or game shows on television require emotions of joy or despair to be exaggerated in a way that has percolated through to the gestures of everyday life. Cricketers leap around gesticulating with joy when a batsman is dismissed rather than applauding respectfully as he leaves. Another innovation is the toothy smile. Thousands of older portraits can be seen in art galleries, yet the modern smile through parted lips dates from the 1780s and was considered obscene at the time.[17] Animals show their teeth only in menace, which is why pets may recoil when you flash a smile at them. There could be other reasons, bad teeth among them, why our ancestors kept their lips together, but our modern greeting owes a lot to Hollywood, tooth-paste advertisements and orthodontics.

Artist John Singer Sargent, in his 1890 study for *Miss Eleanor Brooks*, drew his subject with a warm and civilized smile. He was clearly not satisfied with the result, and replaced it with a more

Figure 57: Detail from a self-portrait by Madame Vigée Le Brun, who introduced the half-smile into portraiture in the late eighteenth century and caused scandal by doing so. Her wayward hair, parted lips and dilated pupils add an erotic flavour to this picture of freshness and innocence.

composed expression in the final work. One reason why smiles are absent from portraits and old photographs is that it is impossible to sustain a natural one for more than an instant. Men aimed to look severe or commanding rather than cheerful, and women were told to say 'prunes' to give their mouths the desired rosebud appearance. A study of US student yearbook photographs over a century showed that both the frequency and the intensity of smiles increased steadily with time, and that women smile more readily than men.[18]

Much of the brain's motor and sensory cortex is dedicated to facial movement and sensation, but an area in the fusiform gyrus is dedicated to telling faces apart – no mean feat, if you consider the endless minor variation of eyes, nose and mouth to be witnessed in any city street. We live and move in a sea of faces, so nearly alike and yet so different. Our ability to tell one from another is truly remarkable and allows us to store a database of around 5,000 faces, until recently well in advance of computer software. Face recognition involves interaction between different regions of the brain, and failure within this system results in a condition known as prosopagnosia. This is quite unrelated to intellectual function, and people with extreme forms of the condition may be unable to recognize their own children or identify the gender of the face they are addressing. It seems that faces are taken in holistically at a glance, just as a practised reader swallows a sentence, whereas a person with face blindness struggles to piece it together. As one victim put it, 'I can see the eyes, nose, and mouth quite clearly but they just don't add up. They all seem chalked in, like on a blackboard.' Although the condition was once seen as a neurological oddity resulting from brain injury or stroke, it is now appreciated that about one person in fifty has real difficulty in face recognition; one such being the neurologist Oliver Sacks, who diagnosed himself after researching *The Man Who Mistook His Wife for a Hat*.[19]

It is not surprising that many of us struggle with face recognition, for our brains grew to their current size while our ancestors lived in small groups as hunters and foragers. When confronted with thousands of faces, we must rely on other cues to identity, and most of us have been embarrassed by a failure to recognize an old acquaintance in an unfamiliar context. Not to recognize or name someone you are supposed to know is at best a discourtesy, at worst an insult. I have frequently struggled to identify people at medical meetings – my trick is to enquire after 'that person who works with you – can't remember the name'. Like a foreign language, the ability to name faces can be switched on and off. I struggle to speak French if addressed unexpectedly, for example, but can converse more fluently within a few hours; something comparable happens to my facial recognition system as a meeting goes on.

In evolutionary terms, a failure to recognize the face of an enemy can be fatal, but a failure to read the faces of those around you can also wreak havoc. Psychopaths often lack this ability. When shown photographs expressing fear, for example, one responded that this was how people looked before he killed them. At the other end of the spectrum, some people – psychopaths included – are almost preternaturally adept at reading the expressions of others. The need to interpret, influence and deceive others is a likely reason for our large and expensive brains. Given that we now encounter other people by the thousand, snap judgement is necessary, just as 'fast thinking' takes care of routine decisions. Snap judgement generally serves us well, for most people try to live up to the expectations they create, but over-reliance on first impressions provides social predators with their natural habitat.

People like me bumble around in a contented haze, but complicated situations created by misinterpretation of social cues provide much of the pleasure we derive from reading Jane Austen, and indeed fiction in general. Practised observers can derive considerably more information from a casual encounter. Sherlock Holmes claimed that 'deceit . . . was an impossibility in the case of one trained to observation and analysis', and Sigmund Freud commented that 'he that has eyes to see and ears to hear may convince himself that no mortal can keep a secret. If his lips are silent, he chatters with his fingertips; betrayal oozes out of him at every pore.' We only have his word as to how often he got it right.

THE TEMPERAMENTS

The original meaning of 'to temper' is to mix or balance, as when we temper justice with mercy or lose our temper. Temperament is the mix of personality traits in your character. The Greeks believed that your disposition came from the mixture of four bodily fluids, or humours. These were blood, yellow bile, black bile and phlegm (watery fluid), and the predominance of one or the other made you sanguine, choleric, melancholic or phlegmatic. The doctrine proved tenacious. By the late nineteenth century, for example, a popular outline by the surgeon Alexander Stewart offered the same four-fold classification, now described as sanguine, lymphatic, bilious and nervous, 'nervous' having supplanted melancholy.[20]

Francis Galton, as might be expected, despised those who were satisfied with mere description. 'It is an easy vice to generalize,' he

Figure 58: Detail from Dürer's *Four Apostles* (1526), painted after his conversion to Protestantism. Each apostle represents one of the temperaments. On the left, a calm and melancholy John shows the Bible to a phlegmatic Peter, who lowers the key of the Catholic Church in submission to the Word of God. On the far right, a choleric Paul holds a book in one hand and a sword in the other, and a sanguine Mark gazes to the future. The passive temperaments are to the left, the active to the right.

growled – but how then could we measure our 'emotional temperament' more objectively? He consulted a thesaurus and identified 1,000 adjectives relating to character, many of which overlapped in meaning.[21] L. L. Thurstone of the University of Chicago took up the idea fifty years later when he compiled a list of sixty commonly used adjectives and asked people to think of someone they knew well and to underline the adjectives that best described them.[22] The judgements fell into distinct clusters: one described people as friendly, generous and cheerful; another as patient, calm and earnest; a third as persevering and hard-working; and a fourth as capable, frank, self-reliant and courageous. The fifth (and largest) cluster was composed entirely of derogatory epithets! Thurstone was impressed to find that the vast spectrum of personality could be lumped into so few categories.

It might seem bizarre to assess personality by listing adjectives, but this is how we do it. Psychologists now use a computerized dictionary to list them, and the quest has been extended to other languages in the attempt to bridge cultural differences. The same word clusters tend to emerge, and many agree with the empirically derived Big Five categories – extraversion, agreeableness, conscientiousness, emotional stability and openness to experience – although terminology varies.[23] All cultures rate extraversion and agreeableness highly, followed by conscientiousness; openness to experience is rated more highly in some cultures than in others. One group of researchers described a 'Chinese tradition' factor defined by a cluster of terms relating to inner and social harmony.[24]

There has been dispute as to whether 'personality disorders' are categorical variables (i.e. different in kind from normal) as against dimensional variables (different in degree), with more recent agreement that they fall within the same spectrum.[25] The more profitable game of selecting people for the armed services or business began when the Woodworth Personal Data Sheet was developed (although not in time to be used) to screen American servicemen for susceptibility to shell shock in the First World War. Personality testing by means of instruments such as the Myers-Briggs Type Indicator went on to become an intensely profitable business. Many have found Myers-Briggs a useful aid to introspection, but its claim to select the right person for the job has often been questioned.[26]

A MIRROR FOR THE MIND

How did our ancestors think? For the Victorians, with their concept of a perilous ascent from more debased versions of humanity, it seemed obvious that the so-called 'primitive' peoples they encountered thought and behaved like children, and that their thinking became more adult as their society ascended the ladder of technical development. Two famous twentieth-century works of social anthropology challenged this belief. Franz Boas argued in *The Mind of Primitive Man* (1911) that their thought processes were just as sophisticated as ours – equal but different. Claude Lévi-Strauss made the same point in *La Pensée sauvage* (1962), noting for instance that the botanical knowledge of traditional societies often outstripped a modern technical vocabulary. Oddly enough, neither Boas nor Lévi-Strauss commented upon the most fundamental difference between themselves and the people they studied: literacy.

Socrates could read, but he lived by the spoken word, and his voice comes to us through the writings of his disciple. In the *Phaedrus*, Plato imagines a dialogue between two Egyptian gods concerning the invention of writing: 'This discovery of yours', says the god Thamus,

> will create forgetfulness in the learners' souls, because they will not use their memories; they will trust to the external written characters and not remember of themselves. The specific which you have discovered is an aid not to memory, but to reminiscence, and you give your disciples not truth, but only the semblance of truth; they will be hearers of many things and will have learned nothing: they will appear to be omniscient and will generally know nothing; they will be tiresome company, having the show of wisdom without the reality.

Sound familiar? Isn't he talking about the internet?

Writing is so habitual that we forget how unnatural it is. 'Sound and sight, speech and print, ear and eye, have nothing in common,' says linguist Arthur Lloyd James in *Our Spoken Language*.

> The human brain has done nothing that compares in complexity with this fusion of ideas involved in linking up the two forms of language.

But the result of the fusion is that once it is achieved in our early years, we are for ever after unable to think clearly, independently and surely about any one aspect of the matter. We cannot think of sounds without thinking of letters; we believe letters have sounds. We think the printed page is a picture of what we say. We believe we ought to speak as we write, and that the mysterious thing called 'spelling' is sacred. [27]

Children pick up language by ear but must reinvent the process when they learn to read and write. Our brains are preconfigured for spoken language, but natural selection did not prepare us for the written word, which might explain why difficulties with reading and writing are more common and diverse than difficulties with spoken language.

Writing reduced reliance on memory, but the speeches of preachers and politicians held emotional sway over their listeners in ways that we can scarcely comprehend. Radio condensed the lengthy peroration into the fireside chats of Franklin D. Roosevelt or the rants of Adolf Hitler, and television then reduced the spoken word to sound bites. As a result, our ability to absorb spoken information in the absence of visual cues has been drastically reduced by comparison with previous generations. To judge by modern textbooks, the same applies to written information.

Writing established a new type of dialogue between the writer and the written, for it liberates thought from the thinker, launching it into an external and impersonal domain where it becomes a form of intellectual currency. The facility with which a modern reader navigates a book such as this was virtually unknown in former times. Manuscripts were intended to be read out loud, and lone readers would speak the words as they worked their way through a text.[28] Script was merely notation. William Shakespeare appears to have shown limited interest in the printed version of his works, or even in the spelling of his own name. Writing was merely a way of transporting the spoken word from one person to another, until Gutenberg invented the printing press. Only then did the written word become the 'literal' truth.

Many of us have vivid memories of the transformative effect of reading, but few had this opportunity in the past; UNESCO estimates that only 10 per cent of the world's population could read 200 years ago. Print was at first largely restricted to westerners and the Latin alphabet, although it soon spread to westernized elites elsewhere, who were often puzzled to note that Europeans did not practise the freedom and equality they preached. High-grade literacy was (in the words of UNESCO) initially 'limited to religious leaders, state servants, far-travelling traders, members of specialized guilds and certain nobility' and only filtered its way through to other levels of society over the past century or so. European-style literacy conveyed an alien thought pattern to non-westerners in an alien language and retained its distinctive mental style even in translation; it was a form of cultural imperialism. The reverse flow from East to West did less well in the new medium, and Orientalism – the backwash of learning and insight from the East – was initially overwhelmed by the tidal wave of structured information from the West.

The worldwide spread of literacy was complicated by the proliferation of languages and scripts. In 1971 there were thought to be 3,000 living languages, of which only seventy-eight had a written literature.[29] European languages came to be standardized within the borders of nation-states in the nineteenth century, and this process (with the bitterly resented exclusion of some languages and dialects) was extended at the Treaty of Versailles in 1919. Polyglot societies are more common in other parts of the world, obliging many to acquire literacy in a second language; language acquired after the age of eight is stored in a different part of the brain. The simplicity of the Latin alphabet and the emotional neutrality of its symbols greatly aided its spread. Arabic, for example, is orthographically more complex than written English and is therefore less easy to decipher at a glance. Fluent English readers use both sides of their brains when reading, but Arab readers show greater reliance upon the left hemisphere, possibly because of a greater need to process writing on a letter-by-letter basis.[30]

Around half of the global population was literate in 1950. This facility divided the generations, and older members of newly literate societies turned to the young for help, just as my children help me to cope with my computer. Literacy enabled readers to distinguish between the 'I' that observes and the self that is acted upon, thus introducing greater self-knowledge and making it easier for us to construct a connected narrative for our lives. Pre-literate people did not see themselves in this way. When asked 'What sort of person are you?' by an anthropologist, an African villager responded with indignation: 'What can I say about my own heart? How can I talk about my character? Ask others; they can tell you about me. I myself can't say anything.'[31]

The literature of early medieval Europe drew no clear distinction between a person's status and sense of honour and the person themselves: like the African villager, people saw themselves from the outside. In anthropologist Ruth Benedict's formulation, they were members of a 'shame' society. Literacy did not become a mirror for the self until sixteenth-century Reformation times, when people could read the Bible in the common tongue and confront the deity in private, and it was not far from there to the idea of an introspective and autonomous individual driven by guilt rather than shame.

Near-universal literacy is a recent phenomenon. When intelligence tests were applied to US servicemen in the First World War, one in four was unable to take the Alpha test, which required reading ability, and these went on to take the Beta test, which was based upon pictures and symbols.[32] The testing procedures are now seen as irredeemably flawed, not least because they did not allow for the concrete thought processes of poorly literate people. Literacy is a brain-changer. It requires the complex translation of sound into a visual medium and back again, detaches the thinker from the thought, requires a new form of internal narrative and promotes the development of a refined self-consciousness with (potentially) greater empathy for others. This new duality emphasized the uniqueness of the individual. The sixteenth-century essayist Michel de Montaigne spent much of his life in a tower room, engrossed in a personal exploration of the experience of being alive. His motto of 'que scais je?' ('what do I know?') marks an important new development in human consciousness. Increasing self-awareness fed on the rise of literacy, with its proliferation of diaries, memoirs, novels and so forth, and exposure to the intimate thoughts of others set the scene for the rise of empathy. Self-awareness and insight into other people went hand in hand.

THE GREENING OF THE HUMAN HEART

Three decades ago, an academic colleague was given a special treat by his hosts in Saudi Arabia. The 'treat' was to sit in a public square and watch someone being decapitated. This might not have seemed out of place in eighteenth-century Britain, when parents took their children to watch executions, but it arouses revulsion today. One reason is that we are insulated from the business of killing animals and are therefore more squeamish, whereas any eighteenth-century child would have seen animals being slaughtered. Previous generations were taught that killing is praiseworthy. A boy attending his first English fox hunt was smeared with blood from the mangled victim, a ritual known as 'blooding', and entry into manhood in warrior tribes was equated with killing your first enemy. Nazi death squads ordered new recruits to kill in the knowledge that this rite of passage made subsequent killing much easier. In *The Omnivore's Dilemma*, Michael Pollan describes how he learned to slaughter chickens. 'In a way', he comments, 'the most morally troubling thing about killing chickens is that after a while it is no longer morally troubling.'[33] The twentieth century has taught us that ordinary people can be converted into killers with appalling ease.

If squeamishness is one reason for our revulsion at the prospect of watching someone's head being cut off, shame is another. Two English people were present at the execution in Saudi Arabia, and they studiously avoided each other thereafter. The notorious Milgram experiments in Chicago showed that volunteers are fully prepared to torment other people if invited to do so by someone in authority, and more recent experiments in Stanford showed that students readily fall into a pattern of sadistic bullying when role playing as prison guards. Empathy, it seems, is a response to social norms: it must be learned, and can also be unlearned.

There is, of course, more to it than that. The father of a Danish friend was a farmer who trapped rats and nailed them – alive – to a beam in his barn. Their screams kept the other rats away. My grandmother, a town girl who moved to the country a century ago, was also obliged to trap rats. Her device tempted the rats onto a trapdoor which dropped them into a cage; they could then be drowned by lowering the cage into a bucket of water. My grandmother, bless her, always warmed the water to make the experience less unpleasant. She could imagine being drowned in cold water, but the farmer could not imagine being nailed to a beam. The contrast spans the phenotypic transition and is summed up in the word 'empathy'. This term did not enter the English language until the twentieth century, and its core meaning is to feel yourself into another person's place. By extension, this includes greater insight into the vulnerability of women, children, the poor, the enslaved, the imprisoned and the mentally ill, together with some fellow feeling for animals.

The psychologist Steven Pinker introduces his study of the decline in violence in society by saying that this 'may be the most important thing that has ever happened in human history', and comments that 'the growth of writing and literacy strikes me as the best candidate for an exogenous change' that triggered what he called the Humanitarian Revolution. He argues that 'across time and space, the more peaceable societies also tend to be richer, healthier, better educated, better governed, more respectful of their women, and more likely to engage in trade'.[34] Sadly, this does not necessarily stop them from dropping bombs on those who are less enlightened.

MYSELF ALONE

At the dawn of the phenotypic transition, the fading certainties of a stable social order and of a purposeful universe were replaced by a passionate appeal to the authenticity of personal experience. Some found this in the stormy passion of the Romantic movement, others in evangelical religion. Acute – often painful – self-analysis came with a marked increase in empathy towards the downtrodden. Literary critics write of something called sensibility, an elusive concept that describes the way in which novelists or writers of diaries experienced the world. Conventional piety and virtue were no longer sufficient to guarantee a smooth passage into eternal life, for the soul must also be subjected to the searing fires of introspection.

The social chronicler Peter Gay has written extensively about the changing sensibility of people in the nineteenth century, based upon the intimate memoirs of the bourgeoisie. 'The nineteenth century', as he points out, 'was intensely preoccupied with the self, to the point of neurosis.'[35] He confines his attentions to the middle class, brash in its attention to money and facts, increasingly aware of its social power, but insecure as to its place in the world. Appropriately enough, Gay finishes his potholing trip through the Victorian unconscious with Sigmund Freud, whose quest in life was directed inwards.

The self is an internalized set of social responses: a social homunculus. Freud viewed the mind as a microcosm of the nineteenth-century city: the id represented the turbulent masses, with their primal energy, undisciplined moods and impermissible desires; the bourgeoisie represented the ego, firmly holding the lid down on this seething tumult; and the super-ego was the way they formulated their reasons for doing so. Pinker characterized this as a 'hydraulic' view of the personality, and modern novels from Conrad's *Heart of Darkness* to Golding's *Lord of the Flies* have pictured innate savagery breaking through civilized restraint. Freud himself took the pessimistic view that civilization of the individual could only be achieved by ever-increasing repression of libidinous desire; the best that a therapist could aspire to was to 'transform neurotic misery into common unhappiness'.

By the middle of the twentieth century the pop ethologist Robert Ardrey offered a more mundane view of the individual's adjustment to society in the Theory of Central Position. According to this, the baby in its cradle sees itself as master of a universe whose only function is to minister to its needs. Slowly, and with the utmost reluctance, the child concedes limits to this omnipotence by sharing toys and accepting other people's agendas. In time, its sympathies and understanding spread outward to the community and from there to society at large. Pinker calls this the Expanding Circle. The self may expand into a mature and tolerant member of society but is also prone to stall along the way. If so, the expanding circle grinds to a halt, leaving other races, creeds or expressions of sexual identity on the outside.

ANOMIE

Rootlessness, whether social or religious, is a leading characteristic of modern life. The British anthropologist Alfred Haddon (1855–1940) came face to face with its ultimate expression when he made his first trip to the Torres Strait (which lies between Australia and New Guinea) in 1887. He went as a marine biologist with an interest in coral reefs, but one experience changed his life. It happened on the island of Yam:

> We found near the landing-stage a wind-screen or break-wind under which a few men were squatting. The total inhabitants of the island had dwindled down to 3 men and 2 boys only. All the women were dead or had migrated to neighbouring islands. The old men were sitting still, listlessly, doing nothing, caring for nothing, and waiting to join the majority. I felt quite sad about them.[36]

He realized that coral reefs could wait but that the people who lived on them could not, and he set out to record as much as he could of their lives before they were lost for ever.

The sense of utter annihilation that must accompany the loss of friends, family, tribe, culture and language is unimaginable, and our modern experience ranges from the extinction of whole groups to the isolation of old age. This sense of desolation has been called *anomie*, loss of identity – also known as 'the malady of the infinite'. The term was introduced by the sociologist Émile Durkheim (1858–1917) with particular reference to the sense of loss associated with the transition from an 'organic' to an industrial society. More generally, it has been used to mean the loss of identity that goes with social or cultural redundancy.

The newest addition to the experience of anomie is the anomie of old age, for the combination of a longer life with a rapidly changing environment has left many old people stranded in a world whose language and culture are increasingly incomprehensible. They feel obsolete, out of touch, deprived of meaning and purpose. If the anomie of the old is to be pitied, the anomie of the young is to be feared. Full employment was the expectation in western countries during the Golden Age of consumption – roughly from 1950 to 1980 – with its guarantee of a house, a car, a social role and something that could be passed on to your children. This changed when post-industrial society created an 'empirical vacuum' for which there was no precedent. Young people were cut adrift from meaningful participation in the life of their own society, obsolete before they began.

A new consciousness encountered a new source of heartbreak: loss of religious faith. The people of eighteenth-century Europe had a formal relationship with the deity which expressed the values of their society. The nineteenth century brought a more anguished sense of existential loneliness; individuals turned to their own hearts in search of God, and many found there a divine witness of their inmost thoughts and yearnings. Suffering cannot be shared, but it can be witnessed, and witnessing can somehow validate suffering. Others encountered a terrifying void.

Few westerners currently believe that their thoughts and actions are judged by a divine witness, or that our time on earth is a testing ground for admission to a higher form of existence. Others see these beliefs as the central meaning of their existence, and religious faith held a central position in the mental universe of previous generations. It is easy to forget what losing it meant. Let us try to revisit that world.

Reverend C. Maurice Davies (1828–1910) entered the Hall of Science in Old Street in London at quarter to seven, one Sunday evening in 1873. He had come to see Charles Bradlaugh, the apostle of infidelity, in action. Although Davies took care to arrive early, the hall was already crowded. Looking around, he noted that the audience was largely drawn from the tradesman and artisan class, but included 'men-of-war's men in their naval costume, and real labourers and navvies in their working clothes'. How was it, he wondered wryly, that people who would never dream of coming to church for free were willing to pay fourpence to hear that God did not exist?[37] The hall was packed by the time Bradlaugh himself forced his way through the throng, steering his daughters Alice and Hypatia towards the group of men seated around a table on the platform. Davies saw 'a tall, commanding figure, with a clean shaven face, and hair brushed back from his forehead; a quick, bright eye, and that massive appearance of the jaw which is so often seen in the habitual speaker'. Soon after, Bradlaugh rose to his feet in a hush of expectation and began to castigate God for failing to exist. The concept of Divine Providence was laughable. Tell that to the people of Torre del Greco, a village engulfed in lava by the recent eruption of Vesuvius. As for prayer, how ludicrous to imagine that 1.2 billion people should daily petition the Lord in the expectation that He would fulfil their wishes. There was no such thing as a religious instinct, for he himself ('here [his] brazen voice sank to tones of the very tenderest pathos') as a young man had tried to pray in agony of spirit, but no answering signal came.

Religion, he concluded, had blinkered freedom of thought for millennia, had burned its martyrs at the stake, but the voices of Bruno, of Shelley, of Voltaire and Paine could no longer be silenced. 'We have only been able to talk for the last two hundred years,' he said in conclusion; 'you have had thousands of years to deaden men's brains in.' The applause was thunderous. Two speakers followed: Mr Jenkins offered a lacklustre defence of Christianity against a background of voices telling him to shut up, but theistic Mr Williams gained a scatter of applause when he gamely maintained that atheism could no more be proved than its converse. Were there only such straw men, pondered the Reverend Davies, to step forward and defend religion? And would the audience have stayed to listen?

Maurice Davies knew about the pitfalls of doctrinal purity. Ordained in 1851, he repudiated his initial adherence to the Oxford Movement, poked fun at the High Church in a series of novels and turned to journalism as his faith declined. His quest through the spiritual labyrinths of London began when he was working as a jobbing London curate in the 1860s, forever nipping off on adventurous excursions between services. Like many other Victorian explorers, he soon discovered that the city was odder and more unexpected than readers of *The Times* might believe. Every possible shade of belief was represented in London, from the spiritual to the material, and from religion to politics. Edward Gibbon had described the fission of the early Church into innumerable sects, each with its own direct pipeline to God and instant readiness to pronounce anathema upon the rest; Davies found this to be true in the camp of the disbelievers. Unbelief, as he noted, was the doctrinal equivalent of the dance of the seven veils, each level defined by what had been discarded. The Unitarians – whose name belied their manifold variety of opinion – denied a triune God. The Deists (some Christian and some not) believed in a *Deus incognitus* whose resolute hands-off policy allowed Him neither to intervene nor to reveal Himself. Atheism – which to the nineteenth-century mind stood in opposition to Theism rather than to revealed religion – repudiated the very notion of a divinity and held Him very much to blame for His failure to exist.

One striking feature of these groups was that each, as a matter of course, organized itself on the model of a dissenting congregation, with its own meeting hall, its own preachers (many of whom, like the early Methodists, travelled tirelessly around the country) and its own newsletter or pamphlets. Each defined itself through these outlets, and each statement of disbelief, with equal inevitability, provoked others to oppose or undermine it. No matter which way you looked, whether at Theosophists, Spiritualists, Freethinkers, Socialists, those with revealed religion and those with none, you met the same organization, the same schismatics and the same studiously masked struggle for power. Free Thought drew its energy from religious orthodoxy and had its own saints and martyrs; it flourished as organized religion wavered on the brink of retreat and died once the rout was accomplished.

There were two great milestones in the life of the pious unbeliever. The first was the loss of faith, and the second was the encounter with death. William James provides a detailed description of religious conversion and its reverse in *The Varieties of Religious Experience*. Conversion, a recurring theme in Victorian autobiography, is typically preceded by a period of despair, a profound sense of one's own unworthiness, and many features of clinical depression. The conversion experience itself was accompanied by a flood of joyous relief and an overwhelming sense of acceptance. The corresponding experience in the atheist counter-culture came when the believer turned from belief to unbelief; James refers to this as counter-conversion. Many accounts testify to this slow and agonizing descent as the unbeliever progressively relinquished everything that had previously given hope and purpose to existence. The French philosopher Jouffroy described his own crisis of infidelity as follows:

Vainly I clung to these last beliefs as a shipwrecked sailor clings to the fragments of his vessel; vainly, frightened at the unknown void in which I was about to float, I turned with them towards my childhood, my family, my country, all that was dear and sacred to me ... I seemed to feel my earlier life, so smiling and so full, go out like a fire, and before me another life opened, sombre and unpeopled, where in future I must live alone, alone with my fatal thought which had exiled me thither, and which I was tempted to curse. The days which followed this discovery were the saddest of my life.[38]

Just as religious converts faced the fear of a lapse into disbelief, the acid test for an unbeliever was to deny salvation to the very end. The moribund atheist offered an irresistible lure to evangelicals seeking to snatch an unbeliever from the jaws of Hell. They were only too willing to interpret a squeeze of the hand as a sign of repentance and to announce this triumphantly to the world. The death-beds of atheists were jealously defended by their friends.

In April 1874, Maurice Davies chose to end his series of reports from heterodox London with the funeral of atheist Austin Holyoake, who worked by printing infidel literature, advocated birth control and republicanism, and co-authored the *Secularist's Manual of Songs and Ceremonies*. True to his faith, Holyoake dictated his testament of unrepentant disbelief to his wife until the power of speech failed. Davies attended the funeral on a fine spring day, noting the abounding buds and blossoms of nature's own resurrection as he did so. No such hope for Holyoake, whose memorial in the paper was headed simply 'Gone before'. Noting the omission of key words from the Christian equivalent ('*Not lost* but gone before'), Davies pondered that 'no such speaking symbol of the difference between the two systems could be instanced as [that] negative one'. The burial, in unconsecrated ground in Highgate Cemetery, had a finality that exceeded even that of the Christian ceremony. The service, composed by Holyoake himself, may be judged by the following extract:

in the last solemn moments of his life, when he was gazing as it were into his own grave, it [secularism] procured him the most perfect tranquillity of mind. There were no misgivings, no doubts, no tremblings lest he should have missed the right path; but he went undaunted into the land of the great departed, into the silent land ... The atoms of this earth once were living man, and in dying we do but return to our kindred who have existed through myriads of generations.

Charles Bradlaugh spoke the final words over the departed, struggling to control the 'quivering nerves of his rigid face'. Men, as Davies observed, are so vastly better than their creeds.

Lingering alone by the freshly turned earth, Davies reread a kindly letter to himself from the departed. As he did so 'the utter hopelessness of mere negation seemed to come so forcibly upon me as to carry its own assurance that it could not be true. God would be an austere man, and life the cruel infliction of a tyrant, if all ended in the grave yonder.' Holyoake would have agreed, but in the opposite sense. Davies turned back towards the great city whose infinite variety of belief he had catalogued, with poet Arthur Hugh Clough's lines on the resurrection ringing in his ears:

> Eat, drink, and die, for we are souls bereaved.
>   Of all the creatures under heaven's wide cope
>   We are most hopeless, who had once most hope,
> And most beliefless, that had most believed ...
> Yea, daughters of Jerusalem, depart;
> Build up as best ye may your own sad bleeding heart!

To conclude this brief excursion into the country of the past, it seems clear that we experience life, express ourselves and interact in ways that cannot be quantified yet seem irredeemably different from those of our predecessors. This chapter began with a question: are we still the same? That is a question for the reader. My own answer is that the eternal verities are unchanged; that we pass the same landmarks in life, but that we see them from a different perspective. We are variations on the same theme. But how does that affect our thinking?

17
New Minds for Old

It is challenging enough to have insight into our own thought processes, let alone those of people from different periods of history. Homer – if he was indeed a single poet – composed his two masterpieces in his head and recited them from memory; a mind capable of this was evidently very different from our own. The magical prism of poetry allows us privileged insight into his way of thinking, but our minds would be almost incomprehensible to him. The past really is a foreign country. There is, however, one yardstick, albeit controversial, against which to measure our minds against those of recent generations: intelligence tests. These are supposed to measure raw intellectual ability, unaffected by training or cultural background and independent of time, place or circumstance. We score much better now than in the past – but are we really more intelligent?

THE QUEST FOR INTELLIGENCE

The French psychologist Alfred Binet (1857–1911) began his quest to understand intelligence by measuring the skulls of schoolchildren and soon came to realize that there was little or no difference in size between those who were clever and those who were not; worse still, he realized that he himself was subject to unconscious bias when estimating the cranial capacity of the more able pupils. He concluded after many wearisome field trips that 'there was often not a millimetre of difference between the cephalic measures of intelligent and less intelligent students. The idea of measuring intelligence by measuring heads seemed ridiculous.'[1] He turned to mental function, but the classification system of the day was crude in the extreme. Children who could not learn to speak were referred to as 'idiots' and considered to have a mental age below three. Those who could not learn to write were referred to as 'imbeciles' (both terms were readily assimilated into the vocabulary of abuse), with a mental age ranging from three to seven. A further term was coined by the American psychologist H. H. Goddard to designate those whose mental age spanned the range from eight to eleven; these he called 'morons'.

France convened an expert group in 1904 to review mental subnormality in children but had no real way of measuring it. Binet was, however, able to use his long experience of working with children to devise simple tests of memory, comprehension, association and reasoning which could be used to relate a child's development to its age. If performance equalled expectation the score was 1, with lower or higher ratios according to mental age. Multiplied by 100, this later became the basis for the familiar IQ test.[2]

US servicemen underwent wholesale psychological testing in the First World War, and the findings were published in 1923 as *A Study of American Intelligence*. As noted above, 24.9 per cent of servicemen were considered functionally illiterate; i.e. incapable of reading a newspaper or writing a letter home. They were then offered a version of the test based on pictures and symbols.[3] The tests were used to assess mental age, with an average that ranged from fifteen years in white officers to eleven in black recruits. White Americans had an average score of 13.08, which implied that one in three could be classed as a moron. Needless to say, all this reflected – and reinforced – the widespread assumption that races, genders and social classes were separated by immutable barriers of intelligence.

At some risk of stating the obvious, intelligence tests score your ability to perform well in tests of intelligence, and definitions of intelligence based on test scores soon become circular. The justification for using them is that those with the mental agility to do well in one type of test generally score well on other tests and are more likely to do well in competition for jobs. There are, however, some striking exceptions in either direction, and many would agree with Stephen Hawking that people who boast of their IQ are losers. Test scores are useful as a marker of that elusive quality we recognize as intelligence, but they are no substitute for the thing itself.

Opinions vary on this, and those who believe that intelligence tests measure raw intelligence, unaffected by culture or schooling, will see no difference between 'intelligence' and IQ tests. Important conclusions flow from this assumption. If intelligence truly is innate, there will be little point in offering educational opportunity to children who are constitutionally incapable of taking advantage of it. Imagine a world in which each child has to take an IQ test at the age of eleven and will be trained as an artisan, a clerk or an administrator according to the results. This is not science fiction; it was my childhood.

I remember the 'eleven plus' exam vividly; it was the first serious test of my life, and I knew the result would be important. My mother found me pacing the landing at midnight and tried to assure me that the result didn't really matter, but I knew that it did. Next day, I was confronted by sheets of paper covered with numbers, weird shapes and tests of verbal manipulation. Luckily, I knew what to expect, but some of those around me had never seen anything like it before. We were then assigned to three levels of school to prepare for blue-collar jobs, white-collar jobs or university. I scraped into the upper echelon at around the 5th percentile. The intention was to replace the British class system with a hierarchy based on merit, but it had no such effect. The middle classes sent their children to private schools, which paid no heed to IQ, and they did so in the confident expectation that they would get the best jobs anyway. It was all very British. It is hard to believe that anyone took this selection procedure seriously, but they did. Michael Young wrote a satire about it called *The Rise of the Meritocracy*, but many readers failed to see the satirical intent. The inevitable reaction then set in, and it became politically incorrect to imply that children might differ in ability: all must sit in the same class for mathematics. A talented teacher of my acquaintance had a nervous breakdown when he attempted the task.

Intelligence testing is supposedly unaffected by external circumstances, training, social class system or chronological time. The first indication that this might be wrong came from Scotland. A sample of eleven-year-old children took a now obsolete intelligence test in 1932 and, when a later sample took the same test for purposes of comparison in 1947, they scored 6.3 per cent higher.[4] IQ scores take the form of a bell curve in any population, and the average for each sample is then adjusted to a score of 100. Your score is *relative* to the population average. Psychologist James Flynn noticed in the 1980s that IQ testing centres were in the habit of readjusting this average upwards from time to time, and his analysis showed that scores had been increasing at a rate of around 3 points per decade. This implies that an *average* teenager of today would have scored 118 in 1950 or 130 in 1910 – thus placing her in the top 2 per cent of the population! Conversely, Americans who scored 100 in 1917 would now score 72, just 2 points above the cut-off for mental subnormality.[5]

Why might the IQ of our population be rising so rapidly? It seems unlikely that we have actually become more intelligent. Two alternative lines of explanation suggest themselves. The first is that reasons for underperformance have been removed. Quite apart from the fact that the functionally illiterate are likely to struggle with any form of testing, poverty is far and away the most common reason for poor cognitive function. Learning difficulties affect three to five children per thousand in high-income countries, but up to twenty-four per thousand in developing nations. At a conservative estimate, 200 million children under the age of five today will fail to reach their cognitive potential because of 'poverty, poor health and nutrition, and deficient care'.[6] Many of these will also be stunted. WHO estimated in 1997 that cognitive function and work efficiency were affected by iron deficiency (usually due to parasites) in 1.5 billion people worldwide, and that losses of 10–13 IQ points could be attributed to unrecognized iodine deficiency in an equal number of people. Lack of zinc, folate and Vitamins A and B12 have also been implicated. Over and above this, childhood illness, more common in the poor, often takes the form of infective diarrhoea. Persistent or recurrent gut infection is estimated to affect one child in three in poorer nations, with consequences amounting to an 8 cm shortfall in growth and a 10 point loss of IQ by the time they are seven to nine years old.[7]

Poverty and illiteracy were common in western societies in the first half of the twentieth century, and better living conditions might therefore have contributed to a rising IQ at a population level. Even so, this cannot explain why intelligence scores have continued to increase. It might be imagined that these gains were due to better verbal skills or teaching of arithmetic, but the improvement is mainly in tests of abstract reasoning (X is to Y as A is to?), which are considered to measure general intelligence. Flynn believes that the improvement is due to exposure to a high-tech symbol-rich environment with many problem-solving challenges, plus the decline of pre-scientific (pre-literate) reasoning. Post-literate skills involve the ability to step back and conceptualize, and to think in abstract terms, the sort of difference that distinguished previous generations of town dwellers from their country cousins. It remains hard to explain why differences in IQ persist between socio-economic groups in wealthier societies. Some of this might be explained by social mobility (smarter individuals are more likely to move upwards, and the intellectually challenged to move downwards) but no society is friction-free in this respect. Social deprivation has widespread effects on our phenotype, some of which are poorly understood, and it seems possible that performance in intelligence tests may be among them.

PLASTICITY

The brain is our most plastic organ. An immune system can learn and remember, but only brains can think. Which brings us back to Alfred Russel Wallace's question: why did we evolve such big brains in the first place? The biological investment is huge. Seymour S. Kety, a founding father of neurobiology, showed that the energy consumption of brain cells increases as you move from the older to the newer evolutionary layers. One unhappy consequence of this is that a period without oxygen or glucose can wipe out your higher centres but leave the vegetative functions intact, the closest you will ever see to a body without a soul. I once visited a girl who had destroyed her higher centres in an attempt to kill herself with insulin. The silence, the thousand-mile stare and the eternity between each tick of the ward clock haunt me still. Nerves maintain their electrical charge by pumping ions across their membranes, an activity that requires endless consumption of high-energy ATP. The brain, about 2 per cent of the body by weight, thus consumes about 25 per cent of adult energy intake – and more than 60 per cent of the energy required by a new-born child. Handel is said to have composed the *Messiah* in two weeks, and his brain would have consumed its own weight in glucose (just under 1,500 grams) while doing so.

Bigger brains helped to provide our distant ancestors with increasing amounts of food energy, a spiral development which gave them simpler guts and larger brains. Wallace argued that the evolutionary ratchet should have ended when we reached the top of this food ladder, but his conclusion was based on competition with other species: he did not consider the role of rivalry between humans. The extent to which social position can influence the transfer of genes to the next gener-ation was shown in an analysis of the Yanomama Indians of South America, where masculine success gave privileged access to the birth canals of women. Thus it was that of 114 men with at least one adult grandchild, 84 produced 10 or fewer, with an average of 4.3. The remaining 30 averaged 23.7. One Yanomama headman had 62 adult grandchildren,[8] but his achievement is thrown into the shade by the 16 million male descendants attributed to Genghis Khan.[9] Given that social success is linked to sexual success, and that intelligence is an important factor in this – as few could doubt – our genetic heritage has long been skewed towards increasing brainpower.

Most authorities agree that social interaction was the impetus to our accumulation of expensive brain cells. The Dutch historian Johan Huizinga characterized us as *Homo ludens* – playful man. Play offers us a protected space in which we can explore imaginary situations and pretend to be someone else, and the story is its chosen vehicle. Those who live in complex societies must learn to predict the responses of their peers. This requires second-guessing, which, in its turn, depends upon sophisticated insight into the thought processes of other people. Empathy and the ability to manipulate others are opposite sides of the coin which separates a saint from a psychopath. The need to interpret, influence and deceive others is the likely explanation for our large and expensive brains, and this is known as a theory of mind.

The theory of mind is brilliantly exemplified in chapter 21 of Stend-hal's *Le Rouge et le Noir*. Monsieur de Rênal, mayor of a provincial town in France, has just received a shocking piece of intelligence. He hired Julien Sorel, a local youth of humble background, to tutor his children, mainly to enhance his prestige in local society. Madame de Rênal falls for the boy, and they start an affair. Elisa, a housemaid, spurned in her own love for Julien, reports this to a local notable, Monsieur de V, who has long had his own eye on Madame de Rênal; enraged, he sends an anonymous letter to the mayor denouncing his wife. Although nearly hysterical with rage, Monsieur de Rênal is restrained by two prudential considerations. The first is that he will for ever be a laughing stock in the local community if this becomes known, and the second is that his wife is due to receive a large inheritance on the death of an aunt, which will be lost if he divorces her. Alerted to the danger, Julien concocts an anonymous letter for Madame de Rênal to show to her husband, a letter which accuses her of having an affair. The second anonymous letter makes her husband doubt the first, for – as he reasons – she would scarcely have shown it to him if she had been guilty. Blushingly, she tells her husband of Elisa's frustrated passion for Julien and mentions in passing that Monsieur de V himself – the likely originator of the first anonymous letter – has written amorous notes to herself. Her husband demands to see them; she modestly refuses. He stamps his authority on the situation by smashing his way into her locked desk and emerges clutching the letters, which prove her point. His wrath now safely diverted, husband and wife put their heads together to plot the next move.

This tightly woven narrative pits the wits of five characters against one another. Each has their own agenda and each is busily second- or triple-guessing the others. Our brains revel in such mind-play, and combining this with advanced language skills and cultural transmission of knowledge might well have driven our brains forwards.

Happily asleep before we are born, our plastic brain enters the world equipped with a set of preprogrammed responses and a ravenous appetite for learning. Its size increases from 400 grams at birth to 1,000 grams at twelve months. A decade of training will be needed before the child can play a full role in its social environment, and yet more years before it can navigate that environment with adult competence. How is this done? Like other complex traits, intelligence is conferred by multiple genes which work together to organize the sequence of rule-based processes by which a brain is assembled.

These processes are vulnerable to external influence at certain critical periods of development – as when the mother takes too much alcohol – but the play of chance largely determines the astonishing diversity that parents witness in their children. The aptitudes or avocations they develop are often self-fulfilling. Athletes develop specialized skills by training, as the rest of us do when we learn to ride a bicycle, play the piano or repair a watch. Our brains do not upload a learning programme, they *create* it – and reconfigure themselves until the learned skill becomes automatic.

When our ancestors left Africa, they carried an undiscovered world within themselves. Our minds – the brain's phenotype – were constructed step by step in response to cultural evolution. We are no smarter than our ancestors, but we have learned to process much more information. Not for nothing do we commit decades of life to internalizing our cultural and technical heritage, and those who lack such training are sadly disadvantaged in any society.

THE SILENT CONTINENT

The higher you go in the nervous system, the more complex it becomes. The spinal cord that feeds into the brain is like an old-fashioned telephone network. Cut the wire to your house, and the line goes dead. You have more connections when you ascend into the hindbrain, where the operator may have the option to re-route your call via Hamburg. Higher still, you enter the cerebral cortex and find that everything connects to everything else: it is like jumping from landlines to the internet. The cerebral cortex has a vast amount of spare capacity, which made it hard for early neurologists to discover what it actually did. Like early geographers, they populated the map of this silent continent with imaginary beasts. It took a long time for them to appreciate that the whole is greater than the parts, and that the cortex can function in remarkably plastic ways.

The most famous brain injury of all time demonstrated that our cortex functions like the internet. At twenty-five years of age Phineas Gage was the fit, handsome and well-respected foreman of a railroad construction gang in Vermont. On Wednesday, 13 September 1848, his team was blasting through rock. This was done by drilling a deep hole, packing it with gunpowder, tamping it with sand and retreating to detonate it. The tamping iron was a metre long, 3 cm in diameter and 6 kg in weight, and tapered towards a point at the upper end. Gage was busy tamping in the sand when a spark detonated the charge and drove the bar clean through his head, entering below the cheekbone and bursting out through the top of his skull; it landed 20 metres away. Although blinded in the left eye, Gage remained conscious. This is less extraordinary than it might seem, for soldiers with penetrating brain injuries could sometimes make their own way to a dressing station in the Vietnam War. An ox-cart took Gage back to his lodging, where he was able to converse normally with young Dr John Harlow when he arrived. A coffin was prepared, but against all odds he survived.

Tantalizingly little is known about the rest of his career, except that the story everyone knows appears to be wrong. Legend relates that his personality changed after the injury, that he became shiftless and unreliable, that 'Gage was no longer Gage', to the point that he became unemployable. More recent research has revealed that Gage was an exhibit in a travelling circus for a while before working for eighteen months at a livery stable. He was then recruited to establish a stagecoach service in (of all places) Chile. He arrived there in 1852 or 1854, and this one-eyed man then drove stagecoaches on a thirteen-hour journey along appallingly bad roads. His health had deteriorated by the time he rejoined his family in San Francisco in 1859, but he was able to do farm work until the first of a series of epileptic fits occurred in February 1860; he died three months later.[10] The Phineas Gage of the stagecoach seems more like the respected foreman of 1848 than the degenerate wastrel described to generations of medical students, and so indeed does his photograph (figure 59). He certainly did well for a man with a big hole in his head.

As this and other nineteenth century anecdotes testified, large areas of the cerebral cortex can be lost with little apparent consequence, whereas damage to specific regions results in catastrophic loss of motor or sensory function. Small regions in the left hemisphere of right-handed people, known as Broca's and Wernicke's areas, proved to have very specific roles in speech and language. Damage to the corresponding region of the non-dominant hemisphere had no such

Figure 59: Phineas Gage holding the metal bar that went through his head.

effect, showing that the two halves of the brain perform specialized functions. Imaging studies later showed that some general functions are delegated to separate regions of the brain; non-verbal skills such as empathy and spatial awareness are concentrated in the non-dominant hemisphere, for example. Such boundaries are fluid, however, and many regions of the cortex interact when we perform complex tasks. This fluidity allows the brain to find a way around some remarkable disabilities.

While I was busy with this book, our local electrician (known in this part of Wales as 'Tom the Grid') became a father. An alert ultrasound technician noted before birth that the two halves of the baby's brain were not joined in the usual way. The two arms which form the two cerebral hemispheres separate like the arms of a 'Y' above the midbrain, after which they press together in the midline like the two halves of a walnut. The two segments are joined by a bridge formed by the trunks of some 200 million nerves and known as the corpus callosum. One baby in 4,000 is born with a partial or complete absence of this structure, Tom the Grid's son among them. What, he asked me, did I think this would mean?

I had a vague recollection of the famous split-brain experiments. In the 1950s, neurosurgeons dared to cut through the corpus callosum in a last-ditch attempt to treat people disabled by epilepsy. Much to their relief they found, in the words of Roger Sperry, who shared a Nobel Prize for this work, that 'speech, verbal intelligence, calculation, motor co-ordination, verbal reasoning and recall, personality and temperament are all preserved to a surprising degree'. Not that the victims were unaffected, merely that the effects were far less devastating than might have been feared. Residual problems affected complex reasoning, interpersonal relationships and expression of the emotions.

Sperry figured that experimenters should be able to communicate separately with each half of a surgically divided brain. This is possible because the right side of the brain processes the left field of vision and vice versa. If your brain is divided, something shown on the left field is 'seen' in the right hemisphere but cannot be communicated to the left. Since only one side of the brain processes language, an apple will be named correctly if shown to the verbal side of the brain. If displayed to the other side, your volunteer will deny seeing anything but will nonetheless select an apple by touch from a range of objects on a tray. Your non-dominant hemisphere knows what is going on, but lacks words to communicate the experience. A split-brain person experiences an emotion which cannot be expressed in words, a sensation not unknown to those whose brains are still intact.

So where does this leave Tom the Grid's baby? People who are born with a split brain are far less affected than surgical patients, presumably because their developing brains have adjusted to its absence; they also make greater use of a much smaller bridge known as the anterior commissure. Inborn lack of a corpus callosum 'has a surprisingly limited impact on general cognitive ability', and more people go through life with an undiagnosed split brain than anyone previously imagined. Behavioural problems are not uncommon, however, and those affected struggle with complex mental tasks which require intimate cooperation between the two sides of the brain and may lack insight into complex social situations or interpersonal relationships.[11]

As shown by examples like this, plasticity is a leading feature of the cerebral cortex. Its operations are free-floating, relatively fluid and interactive. This means that some areas can be destroyed with apparent impunity, and that the two halves of the brain can function almost autonomously. One of its best characterized functions relates to speech and language. This is located in the dominant hemisphere in 95 per cent of right-handed people but in only 72 per cent of left-handers and can in rare instances be present on either side. The most celebrated example was Kim Peek, the man on whom the film *Rain Man* was based. Peek had several neurological abnormalities, including absence of the corpus callosum, and he could process language on both sides of his brain. An avid reader, he read 12,000 books and could recall them with reasonable accuracy. His habit was to use the left eye for the left page and the right eye for the other side. How he put them together is a mystery.

THE BRAIN THAT TRANSLATES EVERYTHING

When you watch television, something remarkable is happening. A camera was pointed at an object, and its image was converted into pixels which were stored, transmitted to a satellite, bounced to a television receiver and reassembled into a visual image. This image is captured by your retina and chemical transmitters are transduced into neuronal signals. These reach a region of grey matter at the back of your head which converts them into a visual image which is then inverted by the brain and presented for your appreciation. All this happens in synchrony with an auditory message that has been processed in the same complex way. Pity it's just a commercial.

Our current bandwidth of experience is limited by our sensory receptors: insects can 'see' thermal images, and bats can convert sound into sight. People blind from birth can use parts of their visual cortex for hearing, and redundant bits of cortex can learn a new function or lose the possibility of performing the original one. A classic and cruel physiological experiment was to blindfold one eye of a kitten during the crucial first few weeks of visual experience. The cat will be blind in that eye thereafter. Surgeons learned from this that it is vital to operate early upon children born with potentially reversible visual loss. It has sometimes been possible to restore vision to people who became blind in childhood, and you might imagine no greater boon than the gift of sight. Not so, for the few people in whom this has been accomplished have been made confused and unhappy by the experience. Their brains simply don't know how to handle the sensory input.

In 'William and Mary', one of Roald Dahl's short stories, a bullying husband terrorizes his apparently compliant wife. He arranges for his brain to be kept alive after his death, still connected to a single eye. His wife claims the right to keep his brain at home and amuses herself by blowing smoke in the eye of her fanatically non-smoking husband. Imagine that you are a totally isolated brain – the ultimate sensory deprivation. How could you restore sensation to such a brain? In theory, this should be possible, for the nervous system converts incoming sensory information into impulses which are relayed to the sensory cortex for conversion into the smell of an onion or the opening bars of Beethoven's Fifth Symphony. You might imagine that the cells in your sensory cortex that perform this miracle would be highly specialized, but the same six layers of nerve cells seem able to handle anything. If it were truly possible to isolate brains and to keep them alive in perpetuity, it should also be possible to convince them that they still had a body. They could then engage in endless thrilling adventures or acid trips, much better than having smoke blown in your eye or spending eternity watching reruns of old movies. The brain is our most plastic organ.

THE USES OF METAPHOR

Many believe that *Homo sapiens* began to use its brain differently some 50,000 years ago, a development referred to as behavioural modernity. Since we have no anatomical or genetic explanation for this, the change was presumably functional. One standard explanation is that social competition gave us more complex brains, and that unexpected possibilities began to emerge when critical mass was reached. If so, astonishing latent abilities awaited discovery. Great mathematicians and musicians spent their lives flaking stones long before society could offer them a means of expression. Only then could new concepts come into being, or new thoughts be conceived and passed on to future generations.

In Athens airport, much to his delight, palaeontologist Stephen Jay Gould discovered that *metaphoros* is the Greek name for a baggage trolley. Metaphors transport a familiar concept from one sphere of experience to another, and we could scarcely begin to understand the world around us without them. The problem is to find the right metaphor. When René Descartes compared the body to a machine, the machines he knew operated by means of pipes and levers. Two centuries later, scientific metaphors could draw upon electricity, combustion and steam engines; later still we had telephone exchanges and computers.

The idea of progress – self-sustaining intellectual and technical growth – was virtually unknown before the eighteenth century. Edward Gibbon saw Rome under the Antonine emperors as the pinnacle of civilization. When science – the only reasonably reliable way in which our species has ever managed to learn from its mistakes – was coupled with technology, previous metaphors soon went out of date. Future scientists will have access to metaphors that are, quite literally, beyond our imagination, and – should our civilization endure – our descendants will understand things that we cannot even begin to think about. Who knows what latent abilities might then emerge?

In summary, there seems little doubt that the ways in which we think, feel, interact and experience the world have been changing. With the exception of performance in intelligence tests these differences are hard to measure, yet they are far-reaching in their consequences. We are creatures of the environment we made for ourselves. If we fail to understand this, we are condemned to sleepwalk into the future.

PART 5

Living Together

18

The Domestication of the Human Species

I toured an industrial farm recently and watched the milking. Cows with distended udders moved of their own accord towards an electronic gateway which scanned a chip on their neck and let them through when ready. Once inside the pen they were milked by a robot, and their output was recorded before they were shunted back into the enclosure in which they passed their days. Next day I watched the shoppers in a supermarket moving into pens, presenting their electronic tags and being milked into a cash register. A high level of compliance is a condition of life in modern society, and of a domesticated species. Blumenbach saw so many points of resemblance to our tame animals that he wondered if we too might be domesticated. The outlines of a possible answer are beginning to emerge.

Darwin's cousin Francis Galton wondered why so few large mammals had been domesticated: fourteen of 148 herbivores according to a more recent estimate. Since people often try to raise young animals in captivity, he concluded that those capable of domestication had already been domesticated – which suggested that evolution had equipped them with characteristics particularly suited to life in captivity.[1]

Darwin drew a distinction between the natural selection that operates in nature and the artificial selection practised by breeders. Artificial or 'methodical' selection (as he would later call it) was a relatively modern innovation, and could be contrasted with the 'unconscious' selection that would have operated in the early days of domestication. Unconscious selection implied that individual members of a species which were unusually hardy, docile and able to breed in captivity would soon come to outnumber the rest, and millennia of unconscious selection preceded the more recent introduction of breeding towards a predetermined goal.[2] We do indeed share a remarkable number of anatomical and behavioural characteristics with our domestic animals. Could these have evolved, over thousands of generations, by a process of unconscious selection?

THE ROAD TO DOMESTICATION

Three main routes led to the domestication of animals. The first was commensality. A commensal 'feeds from the same table', and scavengers were no doubt attracted to early settlements for this reason. Captured puppies would show their value as guard dogs (tame dogs bark; their ancestors didn't) and for hunting and herding. Cats would be attracted by the proliferation of vermin, and tolerated for keeping them down. Dogs readily accept hierarchy, and their combination of pack behaviour and sensitivity to non-verbal signals allows them to bond to us closely. The cat, meanwhile, is a solitary animal that has accepted domestication upon its own terms – you might say that it has domesticated us – and could still survive in the wild if obliged to do so.

A second route to domestication came via the cooking pot, and sheep, goats, cows and pigs reached us that way. Herd animals generally follow a single dominant individual, making them easy to control. The first food animals were probably corralled and guarded at night but allowed to roam more freely by day, and the age-old division into herders and cultivators arose from the fact that some herd animals are more mobile than others.

A third and more heterogeneous category includes animals domesticated for reasons other than meat or milk. Oxen were used for haulage, for example, and horses and camels for transport. Sheep were hairy when first domesticated, and fleece evolved from their woolly underparts; from around 3000 BC they came to be prized for their wool.

The earliest domestic animals were small, which is why the Greeks and the Trojans – referred to by Homer as 'breakers of horses' – fought from chariots rather than horseback. A slow increase in size can be traced through bony remains from medieval settlements, but our farm animals were minuscule when targeted breeding began at

Figure 60: Farm animals were smaller in the Middle Ages.

the start of the eighteenth century.[3] Sheep were bred for wool rather than meat and were 'small in frame, active, hardy, able to pick up a living on the scantiest food, patient of hunger ... breeds formed by centuries of far travelling, close feeding on scanty pasturage, and a starvation allowance of hay in winter'. We saw earlier that those sold in Smithfield Market averaged around 13 kg in 1710, as against 36 kg nearly a century later.[4] Modern ewes weigh 45–100 kg.

Tame animals are remarkably plastic in terms of physique and behaviour, whereas the size and shape of wild animals is remarkably stable, suggesting that natural selection has converged upon the one best way of surviving in a particular environment. This mould must be broken before a species can be diverted into a plastic developmental pathway. The history of domestication suggests that breaking the mould generally happened only once, and that it was easier to work with a species that had already been 'broken in' than to start again from scratch. Some classic twentieth-century experiments suggest how this first step towards domestication came about.

GREY RATS AND SILVER FOXES

In 1919, Dr Helen King of the US Wistar Institute set out to compare laboratory-bred with wild rats. The dominant wild species in northern latitudes is the grey or Norway rat, which (despite its name) originated somewhere in Asia and invaded Europe in the first half of the eighteenth century, displacing the black rat (*Rattus rattus*) from many of its habitats as it did so. 'The wild Norway are more excitable and much more savage,' she reported. 'They gnaw their cages.' Within twenty-five generations her feral rats had become 20 per cent heavier, were more fertile – 10.2 litters as against 3.5 – and could be handled safely. Their brains, adrenals and thyroid glands became smaller.[5] Had unconscious genetic selection taken place? Researchers in Siberia set out to answer this question by breeding wild rats in captivity and sampling from the most and the least aggressive specimens as they went along. The investigators avoided handling the rats and based their selection purely upon docile behaviour. A domesticated species eventually emerged and made it seem likely that a similar procedure, unconsciously followed, was involved in the early domestication of animals. Furthermore, and since no training was involved, this experiment showed that the capacity for domestication is a genetic trait.

The Siberians were engaged in a more famous experiment with fox cubs. The silver fox is a colour variant of the red fox, and the two can interbreed. Silver foxes are widely distributed in northern regions of Russia and North America and generally come in stripes of black and grey. One fox in four is pure silver, however, and a single pelt was valued at 40 beaver skins in the Canadian fur trade. Inbreeding produces a uniform silver coat, and animals were farmed for this in North America. They were exported to Estonia in 1924 and spread from there into Soviet Russia. The foxes were notoriously vicious, and no one would have been prepared to bet upon the possibility of domesticating them.

Dmitry Belyaev, a geneticist in Novosibirsk, Siberia, set out to do just this with the assistance of Lyudmila Trut in 1959. Their selection was based purely upon behaviour: young foxes were screened for aggression by extending a prudently gloved hand into their cages. Few showed any hint of friendly interest, but extensive search found 130 who did – mostly female – and these were selected for further experiment. Human contact was restricted to the glove test, and those who passed it were selected for onward breeding. Six generations later, four of 213 cubs responded to human contact in a distinctly dog-like way by wagging their tails, whining, whimpering, sniffing and licking. By thirty generations, 49 per cent had become ultra-friendly, and by forty generations they were a domesticated species.[6] The transformation did not just affect their behaviour for (among other things) their snouts became shorter, their coats became more variegated, their ears became floppy and they learned to bark.

Figure 61: Dmitry Belyaev with silver foxes.

Belyaev's experiment showed that the propensity to domestication is genetic, and his initial attempts to explain it focused upon a single feature: loss of fear. Newborn animals are initially fearless, but develop a flight or fright response as they mature. This is triggered by a developmental surge of stress hormones from the adrenal gland, and most animals are impossible to approach once this has happened. A farm cat becomes irreversibly wild unless handled early in life, for example, but her kittens are easily tamed. Wild fox cubs develop a fear response at six weeks of age, ushered in by a massive surge of adrenal hormones, whereas domesticated cubs have a later and less intense response. Helen King's rats and Belyaev's foxes both had smaller adrenal glands, suggesting that subdued adrenal responses might be the genetic basis of domestication.

The answer was not to be so simple, for the research stimulated by Belyaev's work clearly demonstrated that the initial step towards domestication is associated with a whole cascade of anatomical, physiological and behavioural changes. More remarkable still, quite unrelated species have independently converged upon surprisingly similar developmental pathways. This convergence would become known as the *domestication syndrome*.

THE DOMESTICATION SYNDROME

Domestic animals differ from their wild progenitors in a number of characteristic respects. Anatomically speaking, they tend to smaller brains, lighter bones, flatter snouts, lighter jaws, smaller teeth that are crowded together and loss of defensive features such as horns. Their coat colour becomes more variable, their ears become floppy (Darwin pointed out that the elephant is the only animal with naturally floppy ears), they reach sexual maturity earlier and they breed in and out of season.[7] How might all of these things be connected?

Physical differences apart, behavioural change is the key feature of domestication. The placid temperament associated with the syndrome is associated with lower levels of stress hormones and is accompanied by changes in brain chemistry, including increased levels of serotonin, a neurotransmitter associated with a sense of well-being. Another key feature of domestic animals, particularly those we prefer as pets, is that, like Peter Pan, they never quite grow up; they remain trusting, playful and affectionate, and juvenile features affecting both behaviour and appearance persist into adult life.

The persistence of infantile features is a key feature of domestication, and Stephen Jay Gould explored the theme in a delightful foray into the evolution of Mickey Mouse.[8] Mickey looked distinctly like a rodent when he made his first appearance in 1928, but his snout regressed over the years, his head got rounder, his eyes got bigger and eyebrows appeared. The effect was to transform Mickey into a child-like creature designed to arouse our indulgent good-will or to trigger the innate releasing mechanisms described by Konrad Lorenz. Persistence of child-like traits into adult life is known as *neoteny*, and Gould went on to discuss the possibility that humans are retarded apes. On this argument, our big brains need to keep growing after birth, and this requirement slowed the pace of our early development while allowing us greater functional flexibility.

The idea that a general developmental slowdown underlies domestication is appealing, but should not be pushed too far. A more accurate term might be *heterochrony*, defined as 'morphological changes resulting from shifts in the rate and timing of ancestral patterns of development'.[9]

It has been suggested that the domestication syndrome arose by modification of a single family of cells early in the course of development. Our bodies contain more than 200 specialized cells, each of which originated in an ancestral cell which gave rise to descendants with related properties, and one such family traces its descent from a part of the embryo known as the neural crest. Despite their common

Figure 62: The development of Mickey Mouse.

origin, these cells perform a wide variety of functions: some make chemical messengers, which range from adrenaline to neurotransmitters, others produce pigments such as melanin, and others affect the development of the face and skull. These features may be associated with persistence of a child-like appearance, docility and other behavioural changes. In sum, the suggestion is that selection for toned-down responses to fear and aggression effectively uncovered a whole developmental package.[10]

To what extent does the domestication syndrome affect our own species? Developmentally speaking, we are highly plastic. We tolerate crowding and breed freely. Anatomically, we resemble domesticated animals in our light skeleton, defencelessness and small jaws and teeth. Male faces are craggier than female ones, with more prominent brow ridges, cheeks and jaws, a development that coincides with the surge in pubertal hormones. Analysis of skulls over the past 80,000 years shows progressive feminization of the male face, with diminishing brow ridges and flattening of the midfacial region. The authors interpret this as reduced androgen reactivity and, by inference, lower androgen production, driven by sexual selection for less aggressive and more socialized males.[11] Unconscious selection may thus have favoured elements of the domestication syndrome in our own make-up.

LIVING TOGETHER

Since a developmental package must exist before it can be uncovered, it might be expected to have some evolutionary utility. This notion was supported by a comparison of free-living dogs and wolves. Both live in packs, but with a difference. The wolf pack is a family with a well-defined hierarchy and a sophisticated ability to communicate. Dogs roam in single-sex packs, are aggressive within the group and raise their offspring in isolation. A wolf pack shares its food when fed in captivity, whereas dogs engage in snarling and displays of dominance and submission. Wolf hierarchy is implicit, in other words, whereas dog hierarchy is explicit and constantly challenged.[12]

An Austrian study compared dog and wolf packs reared in captivity and tested the effects of training upon individual pack members.

Dogs and wolves that had been handled early in life soon learned to obey cues from a trainer in one-to-one sessions, especially when hungry. The degree of stress involved in this interaction was measured by testing the animal's saliva for cortisol, and it soon emerged that some trainers had a more calming influence than others.[13] The study showed that wolves work together efficiently with minimal stress whereas dogs spend more time squabbling over status. The fact that wolves were only marginally less responsive to humans than dogs suggests that pack life has given them advanced communication skills – skills which enabled them to become the dog's ancestor.

Social animals must be able to handle aggression. Male aggression plays a useful role in animals when it comes to defending the group or establishing a dominance hierarchy, but it can also be highly disruptive. Primatologist Richard Wrangham distinguishes between proactive and reactive varieties of aggression.[14] Proactive aggression is premeditated and purposeful, as when one group attacks another or a personal rival is bullied or murdered. Reactive aggression is an unpremeditated and purposeless reaction to a threatening situation. Wrangham argues that the two patterns are activated by distinct neural pathways, and that they have been subject to natural selection. Our legal system makes a similar distinction between reactive and proactive aggression. A nineteenth-century Australian returned from the outback to find his wife in bed with another man. He raced to the local store, bought a pistol and returned to kill his rival. Unfortunately for him, he was a notorious skinflint and haggled over the price of the weapon. This detail convinced the jury that the crime was premeditated – proactive rather than reactive – and sent him to the gallows.

Aggression is characteristic of some primate societies. Chimpanzees fight lethal skirmishes with other groups and frequently engage in within-group battle for status and mating opportunities. Males are bigger than females, and male violence towards females is frequent. Wrangham contrasts chimpanzees with bonobos, a species so closely related that it was not recognized as distinct until 1933. Bonobos are far more socialized and are notable for lower rates of aggression, greater equality between the sexes in size and behaviour, and ready resort to promiscuous sex as an outlet for social tension.[15]

Human behaviour, needless to say, is far more complex. The distinction between proactive and reactive aggression is frequently blurred, and even the most blatantly proactive aggressors justify themselves by blaming their victims. Proactive, goal-directed aggression may succeed in its objective, but reactive aggression is almost always counter-productive. Wrangham argues that we combine high levels of proactive violence with a bonobo-like inhibition of reactive aggression. This might explain our remarkable capacity to combine murderous hostility towards groups defined as alien with kindness and tolerance towards those with whom we identify.

THE DOMESTICATION OF THE HUMAN SPECIES

The World Happiness Report for 2018 scored nations according to well-being, income, healthy life expectancy, social support, freedom, trust and generosity. The top ten were the Scandinavian states and Iceland, the Netherlands, Switzerland, Canada, New Zealand and Australia. All are social democracies with high levels of tax and low scores for corruption and inequality. They are civilized, humane, tolerant, kind and free; their politicians are mercifully unknown; they are strangers to violence, economic brutality and exploitation; you would wish for them as neighbours; they are among the tallest and longest-lived people in the world, and you would be right to envy them. But for all this, and I say it reluctantly, a high degree of personal liberty also requires a high level of compliance. In sum, our behaviour has features of the domestication syndrome which include docility (a reduction in reactive but not in proactive aggression) and acceptance of hierarchy.

We differ from other social animals, however, in that we vary so widely at an individual level. Every parent knows that children grow up differently, and individual diversity underpins our collective strength. We evolved to live in small groups, and a group of cloned individuals would have limited survival value: we need the thinkers and doers, the story-tellers and planners, the chancers and the cautious, the wily trackers and the strongmen – provided these can pull together.

A diverse group whose members act as one, fully prepared to risk everything for one another, will generally prevail over other groups. There has been much debate as to the evolutionary advantages of altruism, but the advantages of social cohesion could scarcely be doubted. It has been argued that the genes of altruistic individuals will be lost to the community, whereas those of selfish individuals will persist. This is true in outbred societies, but the genes of a mother who sacrifices herself for her children will live on, and the same will apply within small groups which share the same genes.[16] For them, the group comes first. We heap praise and reward upon individual success, but hunter-gatherer communities do not. A !Kung hunter who kills a large animal feeds a whole community but is required to be rigorously self-deprecatory about his success. As one account phrased it 'when he gets back to the village he walks in silently, sits down by the fire, and, after greeting people, waits. Slowly others elicit the information about the kill, but if he shows any sign of boasting or arrogance "pointed jokes and derision may be used to pressure him back into line".'[17] This describes what has been called a reverse dominance society in which the group counterbalances the pretensions of the individual, and intra-group violence is virtually unknown. Reactive aggression is a destructive trait in such an environment and might well have been bred out of our species (incompletely, alas!) in the course of endless generations.

Our evolution as a social animal has set a high premium upon the ability to live in harmony with one another and to act together when confronted with a common threat. This imperative might well have resulted in unconscious selection for the ability to function effectively within society, with sociability at a premium. To this extent, it seems reasonable to believe that we are evolving towards a more domesticated variant. Conversely, however, we are all predisposed to game our social situation to our own advantage, whether to bask in the approval of others, to rise in the social hierarchy or to acquire the sexual partner of our choice. To this extent we are all social predators, and the overarching pressure towards conformity and cooperation provides us with the fields over which we hunt.

Genetic diversity predisposes us to this complex and conflicted behaviour. Gene variants pointing in one direction – aggression, for example – predominate in some members of a community, but would self-destruct if they became too widespread. Overall, therefore, a balance exists between characteristics predisposing to intolerance or submission within a population, thus creating the dynamic equilibrium known as a balanced polymorphism. Since multiple genes are involved, a similar tension will be created within each one of us. The constraints of social life are such that we readily accept hierarchy, yet social life flourishes on diversity. The optimal society, therefore, is one in which diversity is fostered yet everyone pulls together. This rarely works well, which is why Plato lamented that Prometheus failed to teach us the art of politics when he instructed us in the practical sciences. Our society is one in which tensions simmer beneath a surface of outward conformity.

And so – are we domesticated? Yes, if considered in terms of behaviour and anatomy. We may not have been subject to breeding, but unconscious selection for social traits might well have achieved the same result over many generations. Our acceptance of hierarchy, compliance with social pressure and distaste for reactive aggression are consistent with this. Even so, tension persists beneath the surface of our society, and within each of its members. Covertly or overtly we exist in a state of dynamic equilibrium; a balance between assertiveness and submission, collective and personal advantage, love and hate. We value diversity, provided it does not threaten us. We compete among ourselves, but close ranks against external threats. We seek to control our impulses but defer (however unwillingly) to the threat of proactive violence. We build and we destroy. Domesticated? Not yet.

19

Changing Phenotype, Changing Society

As we approach the end of our journey, we should pause to consider two distinctively modern developments. The first is the way in which changes in individual life have transformed the society in which we live, and the second is the extent to which our society has taken on responsibility for shaping the phenotype of its members.

THE SOCIAL IMPACT OF THE PHENOTYPIC TRANSITION

Manners – the way people treat one another – have changed in recent centuries, and the change began with the privileged classes. Married women were the closest thing to slaves in seventeenth-century western society, according to social historian Lawrence Stone. Wife and children were seen as vassals of the husband and very much at his mercy. John Bunyan's Pilgrim, an exemplar of the religious life, did not hesitate to abandon them in his pursuit of everlasting life. The philosopher Jean-Jacques Rousseau set a trend in sentimental adulation of childhood in his writings but had no compunction about handing his own children over to a foundling hospital.

Stone argues that child-rearing beliefs and practices in England were transformed between 1660 and 1800. This resulted in a new mode of behaviour which he characterizes as 'maternal, child-orientated, affectionate and permissive'.[1] The companionate marriage – easier for those blessed with servants – brought a new focus upon children and domestic life, thus introducing patterns of thought and behaviour that we now take for granted. Class came into it, however, as always in Britain, and there was a world of difference between the poignant depiction of a rich man's daughter grieving for a dead bird and the mother who lined up for work at the factory after burying yet another baby. In time, however, sentiment percolated down the social gradient, even as the kindness and realism of working people worked their way upwards.

Women and children emerged as self-directed entities in the upper echelons of eighteenth-century society. Privileged women began to breastfeed their babies instead of handing them over to wet nurses, a habit variously explained as preventing the mother from forming too close an attachment to a child she was quite likely to lose or (more realistically) to avoid the taboo against men having sex with a lactating woman. Mothers bonded with their children, to mutual benefit, and fathers got more involved. Compare, for example, the childhood experience of two statesmen. Robert Walpole (1676–1745), a future prime minister, spent no more than a few weeks at home between the ages of six (when he was sent to school) and twenty-two, when he was summoned home from Cambridge because his older brother and heir to the estate had died. In contrast, Charles James Fox (1749–1806), another famous politician, found an astonishingly indulgent father in Lord Holland. On one occasion, an enormous bowl of cream was displayed on the table in the midst of a stately banquet, and the infant expressed a desire to climb into it. Lord Holland had the bowl placed on the floor to oblige the boy.[2]

The poor had little room for sentiment. Endless toil and recurrent childbirth were their lot, and children were needed to keep the family afloat, even if this meant sending them down a mine at the age of seven. The gulf between the rich and the poor in Victorian times is vividly portrayed in The Water-Babies by Charles Kingsley. In this fantasy Tom, a young chimney sweep, climbs down the wrong chimney and enters a luxurious chamber where an angelic little girl lies asleep on her pillow. Turning away from this vision, he recoils in horror from an ugly black figure with bleared eyes and grinning white teeth – his first encounter with a mirror. Childhood scarcely existed for the poor, but later came to be pictured from a zone of middle-class comfort, a depiction which reached its apotheosis in the early twentieth-century celebration of the safely prepubescent world of Peter Pan, Toad of

Figure 63: A scene from *The Water-Babies*.

Toad Hall and Winnie the Pooh. Childhood was seen as a second Eden from which expulsion was inevitable.

Children went on to become the icons of consumer culture: they were what the good life was for. Childhood also became shorter. The prepubescent idyll of Victorian girlhood contracted as puberty came one to two weeks earlier for each calendar year of birth. The combination of earlier physical maturity with extended educational requirements then created adolescence, a new transitional stage on the road to maturity. The growing child, no longer locked into the family by the need to provide its labour, was physically mature yet disengaged from the rest of society. The resulting adolescent peer group created its own model for behaviour, even more so when the contraceptive pill opened the door to freelance sex, postponed child-rearing responsibilities and created a disengaged yet spendthrift youth culture. The affluent adolescent was a short-lived phenomenon, however, for a declining industrial base produced a free-floating population of underemployed young people in western countries. Adolescence threatens to become a long-term parking lot for lives which are going nowhere in more affluent parts of the world; elsewhere, it has generated an explosive surplus of frustrated young people.

Meanwhile, older people accumulated at the other end of the age spectrum. In premodern times the over-sixties formed around 5 per cent of the population, a relatively light burden, and property – with its accompanying social responsibilities – circulated rapidly from one generation to the next. In 1891, 35 per cent of people in Britain were under the age of fifteen, and 7 per cent were over the age of sixty. By 1991, the proportions were 19 per cent and 21 per cent. The shift is a western one, for the age pyramid in present-day Egypt – 40 per cent under fifteen and 6 per cent over sixty – looks much like 1891 Britain. Increasing age delays the transfer of wealth, property and responsibility from one generation to the next, even as increasing dependency adds to the burden on those of working age. High-tech medical interventions prolong the business of dying and make it more expensive; intergenerational transfer of wealth is reduced by the cost of caring for the elderly, and the gulf between the rich and the rest grows wider. Even prosperous nations now stagger under these burdens.

In short, we have far higher expectations concerning personal security, happiness and fulfilment, and we feel cheated when these are denied. Ours is indeed a brave new world, inhabited by brave new people.

THE RISE OF RESPONSIBLE SOCIETY

Societies have rules: some people make them, others obey. This all-important difference was once justified by divine decree, for kings were seen as divinely appointed stewards whose subjects owed them obedience. The idea that kings too must abide by the rules took root, however, and progressed from a sense of mutual obligation towards a legal contract. The law (no stranger to fictional entities) then established the novel principle that people have *rights*. It was on this basis – retrospectively justified by a hasty Act of Parliament – that the English executed their own king in 1649 for setting his personal interest 'against the public interest, common right, liberty, justice and peace of the people of this nation'.

Abstract notions such as human rights are like paper money: they can only circulate while all concerned accept their validity. The social contract evolved into the great principle of democracy – government of the people by the people, for the people. We may feel about this as Mahatma Gandhi did about western civilization – that 'it would be a very good idea' – but the problem is in the application rather than in the theory. The great principle of equality in the eyes of the law, so often challenged, has prevailed because it is merely a reformulation of the Golden Rule, the best moral compass we happen to have.

Politicians must pay lip-service to the wishes of their voters. Slowly but surely, those wishes changed. Charles Dickens played upon the sentiments of an increasingly literate public in his descriptions of childhood and poverty, and Benjamin Disraeli explained in a novel called *Sybil: or The Two Nations* (1845) that class divided Britain down the middle (his readers are assumed not to have considered this possibility). Ideas such as these fed into the main stream of public opinion, which now began to flow in the direction of tolerance, inclusiveness and compassion.

Liberated from serial childbirth, women now began to play a much greater role in public life, and male-dominated societies adjusted – or failed to adjust – to the new biological reality. Before long, nineteenth-century feminists drew attention to the previously unmentionable topic of venereal disease. Members of the British Parliament were inclined to blame the problem on women, and the height of their achievement was the compulsory medical inspection of prostitutes in garrison towns. The need was nonetheless urgent: 400,000 British soldiers were treated for venereal disease in the First World War as against 188,000 for gas poisoning. Salvarsan, the most effective treatment for syphilis, had been a German monopoly; patriotic manufacturers raced to fill the gap. Physicians were unwilling to record the diagnosis, thus encouraging its spread. Little has changed: I ran a search for 'syphilis' in the *Oxford Dictionary of National Biography* some years ago and was gratified to learn that prominent

Britons appear to have been virtually exempt. The Suffragettes were less convinced. Christabel Pankhurst claimed in *The Great Scourge and How to End It* (1913) that 20 per cent of men had syphilis and 70–80 per cent had gonorrhoea, startling figures that found some support in the contemporary medical literature: even conservative estimates put the figures at 10 per cent and 20 per cent respectively.[3] The way to end the scourge, in Pankhurst's view, was for men to rein in their bestial appetites. It is no coincidence that the campaign to give women the vote followed close on the heels of the demographic transition, or that Women's Lib coincided with the contraceptive pill.

MANAGING THE PHENOTYPE

Two centuries ago, people lived by the immemorial rhythm of the seasons, sunlight defined the working day, soil and season defined the activity, and the exchange of money formed a small though essential part of the week's activity. Few could read. People lived within 15 kilometres of their place of birth and were launched into oblivion from unmarked graves; the parish register was the only record of their existence. They deferred to a legal system administered by local landowners who doubled up as magistrates, they steered clear of the recruiting sergeant and they paid taxes if they had to. This apart, they had nothing to do with the state, and the state had nothing to do with them.

This changed when the countries of Europe began to transform themselves into modern nation-states, for states are hungry for information. They need to know how many people they have, what languages they speak, what religions they acknowledge and what roles they play in the economy. State information – 'statistics' – became a central element of policy. Although caricatured in Charles Dickens's Mr Gradgrind, who denied the imagination and insisted upon fact, statistics were also liberating. They overcame the tyranny of unchallenged prejudice, and – despite many pitfalls – established a new standard of truth. Patterns emerged where none had been seen before, among them incontrovertible evidence of the effect of poverty upon life and health. Observations such as these, although stubbornly resisted, were effective weapons for the social reformer and would in time be converted into interventions whose outcome could be judged – by statistics.

The most insistent outcome was money. It was said of an eighteenth-century British finance minister who gained his position by graft that a restaurant bill would have challenged his intellectual capacity. Some of his successors might not inspire greater confidence, but the central task of a modern government is to balance the books. Britain, the wealthiest country in the world, spent an estimated £425.5 million over and above its income in the Napoleonic Wars and had accumulated £816 million of public debt by January 1816. In that year, interest alone accounted for £32.9 million of a national income of £62.8 million. In 1912, the editor of *The Economist* suggested that the country could finish paying for the Napoleonic Wars by the year 2160 if it steered clear of future conflicts.[4] By 1849, taxes accounted for £9.7 million of public revenue, as against £34.6 million from Customs and Excise. The moral was clear: a country's fortunes depended upon its ability to raise credit in time of need, and its creditworthiness rested upon trade and industry. The first duty of a politician was to the economy.

The labouring masses were feared, but they could not be ignored. Their labour supported the economy, they manned the police force and the army, and their newly acquired voting power began to influence the behaviour of their masters. The principles of social insurance took root in the nineteenth century, initially in Bismarck's Germany. Profoundly reactionary himself, he was smart enough to undercut the socialists by delivering the reforms they had been agitating for. Voluntary mutual aid schemes had already shown their value, but Bismarck made them compulsory and required contributions from the employer. Sickness insurance came in 1883 and was followed by state-subsidized old age insurance in 1889. Politicians elsewhere resented the compulsory element in Bismarck's 'state socialism', but the basics of social security were in place across much of Western Europe by the outbreak of the First World War.

One principle of insurance is that it is cheaper to prevent misfortune than to pay for the consequences. It is more cost-effective to insure a healthy population than a sick one. Healthy workers are more productive, healthy mothers make healthier babies, and healthier babies make better soldiers. The logic of social insurance impelled modern states towards ever-increasing responsibility for the phenotype of their citizens, and political parties defined themselves by their readiness to accept this responsibility.

Regardless of its politicians, the state is now involved in almost every aspect of the life of its members, from antenatal care to death duties, from vaccination to education, from health to disease, and from employment to indigence. This requires a high level of surveillance by those doing the monitoring and a high level of compliance on the part of those being monitored. The impersonal and witless authority of computers has replaced armies of clerical administrators, and information technology has shifted the invisible contract between a state and its citizens into cyberspace. Totalitarian states were once limited in their ability to keep tabs on their Winston Smiths (the protagonist in George Orwell's *1984*), but their rulers never dreamed of the facilities for routine surveillance which free societies now have at their disposal.

The happiest people in the world, according to the World Happiness Report, live in social democracies. The task of politicians in these rare but fortunate societies is to promote the well-being of their citizens. In Britain, public sentiment and political realities came together in the welfare state legislation of the post-war period. This inspiring vision of social support from cradle to grave was based upon the assumptions of full employment, a thriving economy, a limited lifespan and the inability of wealth to evade taxation, but ran into difficulties when these conditions no longer applied. Sadly, the idea that a state might exist for the benefit of its citizens only works in countries with a healthy economy which do not pursue an active foreign policy. Few qualify, and Britain has not been among them. National welfare soon began to take second place to national income, based on the dubious premise that individual wealth benefits everyone. The facts argue otherwise, and the widening gap between the wealthy and the rest may well come to be mirrored by corresponding changes in our biology. If declining longevity is anything to go by, the process has already begun.

Epilogue

People who lived 20–30,000 years ago were leaner, fitter and capable of surviving in conditions we could scarcely endure. Some hunted the great herds that roamed post-glacial Europe and grew nearly as tall as we do. They too knew love, loyalty, the warmth of kinship and the mystery of death. Consider the haunting story of Ishi, a Native American Yahi who made the transition to modern society in a single lifetime. His people were hunter-gatherers who had been hunted to the point of extinction by white settlers. Five survivors lived on in the Californian wilderness for two decades until he alone remained. He walked into a farm in 1911, expecting to be killed on sight. Instead, he became a janitor in an ethnological museum in San Francisco. This fifty-year-old man, the loneliest on the planet, found himself with friends who included the anthropologist Alfred Kroeber and the linguist Edward Sapir. He acclimatized astonishingly well to trolley cars and restaurants and bonded with a doctor who shared his passion for archery. Ishi died of rampant TB, against which he had no protection, in 1916. 'He was my best friend,' lamented the physician.[1]

Something similar happened in reverse. In 1978, a helicopter spotted signs of cultivation in a remote Siberian wilderness. A party of geologists reached it by overland trek and found a Russian family that had lived in total isolation for forty-two years. The parents were Old Believers, members of a much-persecuted sect who had moved to Siberia in the 1930s to avoid the Bolsheviks. When Karp Lykov's brother was shot in 1936, he fled into the wilderness with his wife and two small children, taking few possessions other than seeds and potatoes. Two more children had been added to the family by the time they were contacted in 1978, but the mother had died. The

Figure 64: Ishi, the last Yahi.

geologists found five people in a filthy wooden hovel heated by a rudimentary stove. They wove their own clothes, had no guns or bows, no metal container for boiling water, and the two youngest had never seen bread. Dmitry, born in 1940, hunted barefoot in the Siberian winter and could run a deer to exhaustion.[2] We are only a generation away from our Palaeolithic ancestors.

Our ancestors had the same genes as we do (with minor variations), but their bodies and minds were not the same. We differ from them because our genes have adjusted our growth and development to the world we live in, a world transformed by our own efforts. The dice of genetic variation are thrown each time a new person is made, but natural selection has programmed us to respond to similar circumstances in broadly similar ways. This is most evident in extreme circumstances, such as the 'survival phenotype' which a challenged foetus resorts to under stress, or in the standard ways in which we respond to starvation. 'Off-the-peg' responses such as these appear to have been built into us, and they resemble the species-wide patterns of variation which Richard Woltereck called norms of reaction. Certain of these norms – the Palaeolithic, agrarian, privileged and consumer phenotypes included – have characterized the human journey.

The music merges with the dancer in the dance, and so do genes and environment. It is pointless to try to separate them. The music changes, but we dance on. The biology of this interaction is complex, controversial and unresolved, which is why I have opted to focus upon description. My point is that we have changed, that we are still changing, and that this is telling us something important about what it means to be human.

RIDERS OF THE APOCALYPSE

We are a highly adaptable species, and it is taken for granted that our adaptability resides in our brains, the work we do and our cultural traditions. We forget that changing conditions are also reflected in our biology, which might explain why the phenotypic transition seems to have taken everyone by surprise. No leading thinker or biologist in the first half of the twentieth century ever predicted that we would live so long, grow so tall or encounter epidemic obesity. This book has argued that our changing bodies and minds represent an integrated phenotypic response to the conditions in which we live. Our attempt to treat each manifestation as an isolated phenomenon has been correspondingly ineffective, irrational and uncomprehending. Obesity and extreme old age are characterized as medical problems, for instance – thus distancing those concerned from the rest of the population – and expensive and ineffective medical remedies are offered, often too late, in place of policies directed towards lifelong health.

The greater part of our evolutionary journey was played out on the plains of Africa. It was governed by the pursuit of food and it was transformed by the invention of cooking. A further quantum leap came with the domestication of crops and animals, and this created the conditions for the interplay between cultivation and cities that we call civilization. Farming methods improved slowly over the millennia, and famine and plague regulated our numbers. In recent centuries, however, science, industry and access to cheap energy allowed us to get the jump on these agents of natural selection and to set the scene for our escape from Rabbit Island.

The concept of developmental plasticity emerged in the second half of the twentieth century, and its medium was the female body; the invisible sexism of science had largely ignored the role of the mother until then. Only then was it appreciated that mother and child form part of the same functional unit, and that the first thousand days of life have an abiding imprint upon the life of the child. We are forged within a mother, and recent changes in our phenotype are largely due to women who are well-nourished, healthy and able to plan their pregnancies. Their children grow faster, reach sexual maturity earlier, and the composition and proportions of their bodies have changed. A more startling realization was that early conditions affect not only the rate at which we grow, but also the rate at which we age. Some 90 per cent of people in affluent countries now survive past the age of sixty. Biological markers suggest that we really do age at different rates, and that this rate is influenced by our experience of life. The trajectory of our phenotype is flexible: we live much longer than before, and we die from degenerative disorders which relate to an ageing phenotype. This phenotype can be modified, and offers us the potential to live longer still.

Our immune systems have undergone their own version of the phenotypic transition. In Palaeolithic times our immune phenotype developed in response to a long-term co-evolutionary dialogue with parasites and infections which had adapted to small mobile groups. Agriculture allowed new infections to batten onto densely settled communities and to travel along the trade routes linking them together. Changes in our living conditions invited epidemic diseases into the human population, and simple changes to our way of life were generally sufficient to expel them. Our long-term co-evolutionary partners were less easily dislodged, however, and rank among the leading causes of death in the world today. The loss of other immemorial partners may underlie our increased susceptibility to dysfunctional patterns of allergy or autoimmunity.

We are social animals, and our journey through time is remarkably sensitive to social conditions. Listen to the anonymous head teacher of a primary school in the north of England, speaking in 2018:

> My children, who have gone from me up to the local secondary school, have grey skin, poor teeth, poor hair, poor nails. They are smaller, they are thinner . . . at sporting events, you see your children in the age

group compared to other children in an affluent area and you think:
our kids are really small. You don't notice it because you're with them
all the time, but when you see them with children of the same age who
are from an affluent area, they just look tiny.

Her children are not just smaller, they are configured differently.
Not just *socially* disadvantaged: *biologically* disadvantaged. They
will age more rapidly, they will die earlier, and this is already obvious
in primary school. Doors have already closed in front of them. Socio-
economic differences in height have proved hard to eliminate, but
excess weight has taken over from short stature as a marker of social
disadvantage, and the gap is getting wider.[3] The impact of social inequality is underlined by the massive discrepancies in life expectancy
that exist within countries such as the UK and USA.

Society impacts upon the biology of its members, but it also bears
the imprint of our changing biology. Womanhood has been transformed by the ability to regulate fertility, childhood has been
transformed by accelerated growth and earlier sexual maturity,
adolescence is a new phenomenon, the composition of our bodies has
been transformed by overabundance of food and the decline of physical labour, the longevity of US Supreme Court Justices has become a
matter of considerable political significance, and we are haunted by
Jonathan Swift's Struldbruggs, people who grew old but could not die.
The full extent of our developmental plasticity has only been fully
recognized within the past generation or so, and the message it sends,
although far from new, is compelling. Should we invest in technologies that help rich people to outlive their brains, or should we give a
billion people the chance to live longer and more fulfilling lives?

A changing physique has been matched by changes in many other
dimensions. Our tenure on life is more secure, and this has produced
far-reaching changes in our experience of life and death, in our social
relations, and in our search for the consolations of religion. We are
(on the whole) more capable of empathy, and the bandwidth of our
sympathies has been expanded by near-universal literacy and exposure to drama. We perform better in tests of intelligence – although
the significance of this is open to debate – and there seems little doubt
that our minds work differently.

Blumenbach's suggestion that we are a domesticated species has been given a new lease of life by the identification of the domestication syndrome, features of which we share with many domesticated animals. This raises the possibility that a common genetic pathway might underlie our remarkable facility for mutual tolerance and cooperation under the most crowded of conditions; combined – alas – with an unsurpassed propensity for proactive aggression.

ARE WE THE SAME?

Thanks to a rich literary heritage, we can imagine what it might have been like to hurl a heavy bronze spear on the plains of Troy, or to sit in one of Jane Austen's drawing rooms dreaming of eligible young men. We have some insight into our ancestors, but we would appear very alien to them. Archery formed a bond between Ishi and a twentieth-century physician, but there are no self-reflective statements in his biography. We do not think as he did.

And so, to answer the question, have we changed? Much has been written about something called 'human nature', generally concluding that 'you can't change it'. To my mind, the only certainty is that you can't define it. Human nature encompasses anything and everything that people have ever thought or done, and good luck to you if you can draw any useful conclusion from this. In its way, the age-old quest to understand human nature is a search for a metaphorical Garden of Eden against which to judge our current way of life. A recent version of this age-old narrative tells us that we were designed for life on the African savannah, and that the genes that evolved there are mismatched to life in the twenty-first century, and thus responsible for many of our contemporary malaise.

This book reaches a very different conclusion, which is that we have adapted remarkably well to a life for which natural selection could not possibly have prepared us. We live twice as long and enjoy better health than ever before. The coronary epidemic, long portrayed as nature's revenge for modern life, is receding from our population. Cancer looms large because we are failing to die for other reasons. The obesity epidemic has many undesirable consequences, but the predicted apocalypse never happened. Chronic overnutrition has become the new norm, and we are learning to adjust to it. If atavistic genes are indeed seeking to punish us for bad behaviour, they have a very odd way of doing so. Even so, our escape from natural selection has confronted us with challenges for which nothing in the past could have prepared us, chronic overnutrition and extreme old age among them.

THE MALADY OF THE INFINITE

We have entered a fantasy world of luxury and ease, but our future is insecure. Political leaders once offered the vision of a better future, but have now fallen remarkably silent on the subject; they prefer to harp on a glorified past. Jerome Carcopino, a historian of ancient Rome, once noted that 'to struggle with success against the evils of their day, societies have need to believe in their own future',[4] and a similar void confronts us in the twenty-first century.

Sociologist Émile Durkheim called anomie the 'malady of the infinite' because it stimulates a desire that can never be satisfied. In more general use, the word refers to a sense of meaninglessness or lack of purpose produced by changes in the social order. It is a pervasive malady. Older people find that their values and experience are downrated in a world of rapid technical progress, and that their brand of literacy means little to young people for whom connectivity is everything. The young, meanwhile, find that hard-won skills and training have a limited shelf life, that their job prospects are at the mercy of computerization, that older people with different habits of thought have the power and the money, and that traditional aspirations about working your way up the job ladder and owning your own home have little hope of realization. They feel sidelined by the society to which they belong.

So, what of the future? Those who make money by writing about it offer a starkly polarized vision. Ecological meltdown is one such alternative, and some form of environmental crisis seems likely. In contrast, a new generation of meliorists offer the prospect of unlimited economic growth and a future of genetic engineering and electronic brain implants. Like all utopians, they imagine worlds in which no sane person would wish to live. Genetic engineering can correct single-gene defects, but we are light years away from remodelling complex traits coordinated by multiple genes. Information technology could potentially extend the range of our senses (its main role at present is to narrow them), but the ability to perform computations faster is unlikely to extend the range of human understanding.

More realistically, we have the opportunity to engineer the phenotype. The best and most effective way of doing so would be to optimize growth, education and opportunity for everyone. Failing this, more people will resort to phenotypic engineering by pharmacological means. The ultimate in phenotypic engineering is pharmacological manipulation of the embryo, and an unsuccessful attempt to remodel the fat composition of unborn babies was the first step in this direction.

Since plasticity reflects the man-made environment, those who control the environment will, intentionally or otherwise, direct the phenotype of future generations. Who will control the controllers? The nation-state was once seen as the universal parent of its citizens but has been irrevocably weakened by the flight of capital. Wealth was once tangible; it could be located in bank vaults and landed estates, equally vulnerable to revolutionary mobs or to the demands of central government. Money has now migrated into cyberspace and exists only in the minds and computers of those who trade in it. Would it vanish like a dream if the internet went down and world trade fell apart? Survivalists may fantasize about starting afresh, but there could be no second start. If the networks upon which our lives depend really do collapse, our successors would soon discover that all accessible mineral deposits and fossil fuels have been exhausted – and that what remains cannot be reached without advanced technologies. They would live in a pre-industrial world for ever.

The final point to emphasize is that we are not a natural species. We are artefacts of our own culture, adapting to the world we made and struggling to come to terms with an uncertain future. There is no 'natural' mode of existence for us to pursue. On past performance, we will continue to sleepwalk into a future that we will consistently fail to predict. And yet, to conclude on a personal note, let me add that I have sat with many dying people and have learned from this last extremity that we are a species to be proud of, a species worth fighting for.

Notes

PROLOGUE

1. Isaiah 65:20, New International Version translation.
2. Hinrichs (1955).
3. Pleij (2001).
4. Johannsen (1911).
5. Schwekendiek (2009); NCD Risk Factor Collaboration (2016).
6. Shapiro (1939).
7. Clark (2007).
8. Broadberry et al. (2010).
9. Stone (1977).
10. UNESCO Fact Sheet #45, September 2017.
11. Flynn (2012).

CHAPTER 1: THE PROMETHEAN MOMENT

1. Plato (1958), p. 53.
2. Boas (1911), p. 83.
3. Wrangham (2009).
4. Wallis (2018); Tyson (2018).
5. Milton (2003).
6. Lee (1968), p. 33.
7. Organ et al. (2011).
8. Ponzer et al. (2016).
9. Klein (1999), pp. 512ff.
10. Gould (1983a), p. 49.
11. Eaton and Eaton (1999), p. 450.
12. Holt and Formicola (2008).
13. Formicola and Giannecchini (1999).
14. Childe (1942), p. 22.

15. Green (1981).
16. Cannon (1932), p. 69.
17. Mithen (2003).
18. Hodder (2004).
19. Cohen (1977).
20. Lobell and Patel (2010).
21. Tacitus (1948), p. 122.
22. Khaldun (1969), p. 94.
23. Koepke and Baten (2005).
24. James (1979).
25. Mays (1999).
26. Scott (2017), p. 83.
27. Macintosh et al. (2017).

CHAPTER 2: CHARLEMAGNE'S ELEPHANT

1. Einhard and Notker the Stammerer (1969).
2. Pirenne (2006), Introduction.
3. Pomeranz (2000).
4. Hoskins (1955), p. 56.
5. Cited in McKeown (1979).
6. Read (1934).
7. Linklater (2014).
8. Trevelyan (1942), p. 165.
9. Ernle (1936), p. 177.
10. Braudel (1981), p. 196.
11. Schwartz (1986), pp. 41–2.
12. Ernle (1936), pp. 188–9,
13. Broadberry et al. (2010).

CHAPTER 3: THE ROAD TO RABBIT ISLAND

1. Gurven and Kaplan (2007).
2. Finch (1990), p. 150.
3. James (1979).
4. James (1979).
5. Smith (1991).
6. Stone (1977), p. 476.
7. Malthus (1985).

8. Darwin (1958), p. 120.
9. Wrigley (1969).
10. Harris (1993), p. 44.
11. Carr-Saunders (1936), p. 30.
12. Wrigley (1969), p. 197.
13. Thompson (1929).
14. Davis (1945).

CHAPTER 4: THE INVENTION
THAT FED THE WORLD

1. Giffen (1904), vol. 2, pp. 274, 275.
2. Crookes (1917), p. 11.
3. Leigh (2004), p. 69.
4. Cushman (2013).
5. Sohlman (1983).
6. Tuchman (1994).
7. Grey (1925), vol. 2, p. 289.
8. Smil (2001), p. 103.
9. Prescott (n.d.), p. 296.
10. Stern (1977), p. 469.
11. Smil (2001).
12. Jones (1920).
13. Collingham (2013), p. 416.
14. Consett (1923).
15. Offer (1989).
16. Charles (2005).
17. Borkin (1979).
18. Smil (2001).
19. Nystrom (1929).
20. Boyd-Orr (1966).
21. Smil (2001), p. 113.
22. Rehm (2018).
23. McNeill and Engelke (2014).
24. Smil (2004), p. 102.
25. Food and Agriculture Organization of the United Nations (1975), paras 77–82.
26. Walpole et al. (2012); Thornton (2010).
27. Van Ittersum et al. (2016).
28. Thomas (2003).

CHAPTER 5: THE DISCOVERY OF HUMAN PLASTICITY

1. Blumenbach (1865).
2. Cited in Poliakov (1971), p. 173.
3. Ripley (1899), p. 453.
4. Keynes (1936).
5. Lamarck (1963), p. 108.
6. Wallace (1880).
7. Darwin (1922).
8. Boas (1909).
9. Jordan (1993), p. 171.
10. Anon. (1904).
11. Cited in Himmelfarb (1984), p. 350.
12. Barnardo and Marchant (1907).
13. MacMillan (2001), pp. 318–21.
14. Ripley (1899), p. 52.
15. Boas (1912).
16. Hulse (1981).
17. Bateson et al. (2004).
18. Planck (1949).
19. American Anthropological Association (1998).

CHAPTER 6: MATRIX

1. Steinach and Loebel (1940).
2. Vogel and Motulsky (1997), p. 377.
3. Potts and Short (1999).
4. Eaton and Mayer (1953).
5. Frisch (1978).
6. Eaton and Mayer (1953).
7. Smith et al. (2012).
8. Ellison (2001), pp. 145–60.
9. Women's Co-operative Guild (1915).
10. Chamberlain (2006).
11. Chamberlain (2006).
12. Molina et al. (2015).
13. Kaunitz et al. (1984).
14. Mitteroecker et al. (2016).
15. Walton and Hammond (1938).
16. Cited in Cameron (1979).

17. Lawlor (2013).
18. Brudevoll et al. (1979).
19. Tanner (1981), pp. 106–12.
20. Moller (1985).
21. Barbier (1996), p. 91.
22. Zanatta et al. (2016).
23. Hochberg et al. (2011).
24. Potts and Short (1999), p. 162.
25. Short (1976).
26. Belva et al. (2016).
27. Barclay and Myrskylä (2016).
28. Kong et al. (2012).
29. Aviv and Susser (2013).
30. Bordson and Leonardo (1991).
31. Eisenberg and Kuzawa (2018).
32. Barclay and Myrskylä (2016).
33. Dratva et al. (2009).

CHAPTER 7: LIFE BEFORE BIRTH

1. George (1925), p. 34.
2. Sullivan (2011).
3. Ballantyne (1904).
4. Gale (2008).
5. Smith (1947).
6. Stein et al. (1975).
7. Lenz (1988).
8. Forsdahl (1978).
9. Barker (2003).
10. Gluckman and Hanson (2005).
11. Hayward and Lummaa (2013).
12. Roseboom et al. (2006).
13. Schlichting and Pigliucci (1998).
14. Waddington (1957).

CHAPTER 8: GROWING TALL

1. Stanhope (1889).
2. Tanner (1981), p. 114.
3. Komlos (2005).

4. Julia and Valleron (2011).
5. Tanner (1981), p. 162.
6. Tanner (1981), p. 163.
7. Tanner (1981), p. 122.
8. Quetelet (1835).
9. NCD Risk Factor Collaboration (2016).
10. Jantz and Jantz (1999).
11. Bakewell (2011).
12. Leitch (2001).
13. Pawlowski et al. (2000).
14. Ives and Humphrey (2017).
15. Amherst data from UNCG digital collections, http://libcdm1.uncg. edu/cdm/compoundobject/collection/PEPamp/id/3067/rec/2.
16. Bowles (1932).
17. Morton (2016).
18. O'Brien and Shelton (1941), p. 28.
19. Shapiro (1945).
20. Rose (2016).
21. Jantz and Jantz (2016).
22. http://www.scientificamerican.com/article/the-power-of-the-human-jaw/.
23. Keith (1925), vol. 2, p. 671.
24. Katz et al. (2017).
25. Lieberman (2013), p. 306.
26. Zeuner (1963), p. 68.
27. Weiland et al. (1997).
28. Sun et al. (2015).

CHAPTER 9: PERFORMANCE

1. Sargent (1887).
2. Morris (2001), pp. 84 and 129.
3. Norton and Olds (2001).
4. Day (2016).
5. Tanner (1964), p. 108.
6. http://www.bbc.co.uk/news/magazine-34290980.
7. Sedeaud et al. (2014).
8. Syed (2012).
9. Bejan et al. (2010).
10. Charles and Bejan (2009).

CHAPTER 10: DESIGNER PHENOTYPES

1. http://www.lostateminor.com/2013/04/26/infographic-of-barbie-doll-vs-human-woman/.
2. Norton and Olds (2001).
3. Sharp (2009).
4. Saner (2018).
5. Cochrane (2016).
6. Finch (1990), p. 90.
7. *Early Eighteenth-Century Newspaper Reports: A Sourcebook*, rictor norton.co.uk/grubstreet/gelder.htm.
8. Holt and Sönksen (2008).
9. http://www.businessinsider.com/nfl-players-arrested-2013-super-bowl-2013-6.
10. Perkins (1919).
11. Olshansky and Perls (2008).
12. Levine et al. (2017).
13. Cooper et al. (2010).
14. Skakkebaek et al. (2016).
15. Colborn and Clement (1992).
16. Gore et al. (2015).

CHAPTER 11: THE FAT OF THE LAND

1. Brink (1995).
2. Komlos and Brabec (2011).
3. West (1978), p. 275.
4. Association of Life Insurance Medical Directors and the Actuarial Society of America (1912).
5. Schwartz (1986).
6. Sun et al. (2012).
7. Collingham (2013).
8. Hawkes (2005).
9. De Vogli et al. (2014).
10. Monteiro et al. (2004).
11. Howel et al. (2013).
12. Strøm and Jensen (1951).
13. Trowell (1974).
14. Franco et al. (2008).
15. Komlos and Brabec (2011).

16. USDA: What we eat in America: NHANES 2007–2010.
17. Neel (1962).
18. Neel (1994).
19. Ó Gráda (2009), p. 99.
20. Loos and Yeo (2014).
21. Hales and Barker (2001).
22. Chiswick et al. (2015).
23. Kuczmarski et al. (1994).
24. Flegal (2006).
25. German (2006).
26. Prentice and Jebb (2001).
27. Kuczmarski and Flegal (2000).
28. Blüher (2014).
29. Flegal (2006).
30. Kuulasmaa et al. (2000).
31. Gregg et al. (2005).

CHAPTER 12: AT HOME IN THE MULTIVERSE

1. Brock (1961), p. 11.
2. Rosebury (1969), p. 10.
3. Dubos (1965).
4. Rook (2013).
5. Omran (2005).
6. Brooks and McLennan (1993), p. 5.
7. Roberts and Janovy (2000).
8. Nunn et al. (2003).
9. Dounias and Froment (2006).
10. Stoll (1947).
11. Chan (1997).
12. Cited in Brooks and McLennan (1993), p. 405.
13. Cowman et al. (2016); Loy et al. (2017).
14. Zinsser (1935), p. 185.
15. Maunder (1983).
16. Stedman (1796), p. 5.
17. Maunder (1983).
18. Van Emden and Piuk (2008), p. 196.
19. Bonilla et al. (2009).
20. Donoghue (2011).
21. Dubos and Dubos (1952), p. 185.

CHAPTER 13: THE RETREAT OF INFECTIOUS DISEASE

1. Dowling (1977), p. 40.
2. Dubos (1976), p. 23.
3. Charlton and Murphy (eds.) (1997).
4. McKeown (1988).
5. Cited in Lancaster (1990), p. 90.
6. Dubos and Dubos (1952).
7. Dormandy (1999), p. 387.
8. Marshall (ed.) (2002).
9. Barlow (2000).
10. Grytten et al. (2015).

CHAPTER 14: THE FINAL FRONTIER

1. Wallace, cited in Beeton and Pearson (1899).
2. Fisher (1909).
3. Pearl (1920), pp. 161–5.
4. Haldane (1923).
5. Dublin (1928).
6. Fries (1980).
7. GOV.UK Health profile for England, 13 July 2017, https//www.gov.uk/government/publications/health-profile-for-england.
8. Oeppen and Vaupel (2002).
9. Olshansky and Carnes (2001), p. 86.
10. Levine and Crimmins (2018).
11. Jones (1956).
12. Sebastiani et al. (2017).
13. Belsky et al. (2015).
14. Levine and Crimmins (2018).
15. Levine and Crimmins (2014).
16. Field et al. (2018).
17. Goto et al. (2013).
18. Hardman (2001).
19. Gavrilov et al. (2002).
20. Gemmell et al. (2004).
21. McCurry (2018).
22. Evert et al. (2003); Ailshire et al. (2015).
23. Powell (1994).

24. Festinger et al. (1956).
25. Fraser and Shavlik (2001).
26. Geronimus et al. (2006).
27. Kulkarni et al. (2011).
28. Stiglitz (2001).
29. Lenfant (2003).
30. Finch (1990), p. 161.

CHAPTER 15: FASTENED TO A DYING ANIMAL

1. Greene (2007).
2. Kole et al. (2013).
3. Bliss (1999), pp. 274, 372.
4. Dalen et al. (2014).
5. Lawlor et al. (2002).
6. Townsend et al. (2016).
7. Hansson (2005).
8. Gaziano et al. (2010).
9. Centers for Disease Control (1999).
10. Tryggvadottir et al. (2006).
11. Moore et al. (2017).
12. DECODE Study Group (2003).
13. Godlee (2018).

CHAPTER 16: THE MILK OF HUMAN KINDNESS

1. Rule et al. (2013).
2. Nichols (2003), p. 120.
3. Todorov et al. (2005).
4. Godwin (1834).
5. Lavater (n.d.), p. 11.
6. Buffon (1797), vol. 4, pp. 94–5.
7. Bell (1885), p. 54.
8. Green (1990), p. 578.
9. Bell (1885), p. 58.
10. Rhodes (2006).
11. McNeill (1998).
12. Bjornsdottir and Rule (2017).
13. Burrows et al. (2014).

14. Darwin (1965), p. 359.
15. James (1890), vol. 2, p. 451.
16. Dixon (2015).
17. Jones (2014).
18. Ginosar et al. (2015).
19. Sacks (2010).
20. Stewart (1892).
21. Galton (1884).
22. Thurstone (1934).
23. Goldberg (1993).
24. Nisbett (2003), p. 122.
25. Trull and Widiger (2013).
26. Emre (2018).
27. James (1938).
28. Chaytor (1945).
29. Edmonson (1971).
30. Ibrahim and Eviatar (2009).
31. Ong (1982).
32. Brigham (1923).
33. Pollan (2006), p. 233.
34. Pinker (2011), p. xxii.
35. Gay (1998).
36. Quiggin (1942).
37. Davies (1969).
38. James (1902).

CHAPTER 17: NEW MINDS FOR OLD

1. Gould (1984).
2. Gould (1984).
3. Brigham (1923).
4. Scottish Council for Research in Education (1949).
5. Flynn (2012).
6. Bergen (2008).
7. Guerrant et al. (2013).
8. Neel (1970).
9. Zerjal et al. (2003).
10. Macmillan (2008).
11. Anderson et al. (2017).

CHAPTER 18: THE DOMESTICATION
OF THE HUMAN SPECIES

1. Galton (1865).
2. Darwin (1905), vol. 2, pp. 231–3, 332.
3. Thomas et al. (2013).
4. Ernle (1936), p. 177.
5. Castle (1947).
6. Dugatkin and Trut (2017).
7. Leach (2003).
8. Gould (1983b).
9. Shea (1992), p. 104.
10. Wilkins et al. (2014).
11. Cieri et al. (2014).
12. Range et al. (2015).
13. Vasconcellos et al. (2016).
14. Wrangham (2018).
15. Wrangham (2018).
16. Hare (2017).
17. Wilson (1988), p. 38.

CHAPTER 19: CHANGING PHENOTYPE,
CHANGING SOCIETY

1. Stone (1977).
2. Trevelyan (1928).
3. Pankhurst (1913).
4. Porter (1912), pp. 617, 622.

EPILOGUE

1. Kroeber (1961).
2. Peshkov (1994).
3. Bann et al. (2018).
4. Carcopino (1941), p. 88.

List of References

Ailshire, J. A. et al. (2015). Becoming centenarians: disease and functioning trajectories of older US adults as they survive to 100. *The Journals of Gerontology Series A: Biological Sciences and Medical Sciences* 70(2): 193–201.

American Anthropological Association (1998). *Statement on Race*. www. americananthro.org/ConnectWithAAA/Content.aspx?ItemNumber=2583.

Anderson, L. B. et al. (2017). Emotional intelligence in agenesis of the corpus callosum. *Archives of Clinical Neuropsychology* 32(3): 267–79.

Anon. (1904). The report of the Privy Council upon physical deterioration. *Lancet*, 6 August 1904, 390–92.

Anon. (1949). *The Trend of Scottish Intelligence: A Comparison of the 1947 and 1932 Surveys of the Intelligence of Eleven-year-old Pupils*. University of London Press.

Association of Life Insurance Medical Directors and the Actuarial Society of America (1912). *Medico-Actuarial Mortality Investigation*. New York.

Aviv, A. and Susser, E. (2013). Leukocyte telomere length and the father's age enigma: implications for population health and for life course. *International Journal of Epidemiology* 42: 457–62.

Bakewell, S. (2011). *How to Live: A Life of Montaigne in One Question and Twenty Attempts at an Answer*. Vintage Books.

Ballantyne, J. W. (1904). *Manual of Antenatal Pathology and Hygiene: The Embryo*. William Green and Sons.

Bann, D. et al. (2018). Socioeconomic inequalities in childhood and adolescent body-mass index, weight and height from 1953 to 2015: an analysis of four longitudinal, observational, British birth cohort studies. *Lancet Public Health* 3: e194–e203.

Barbier, P. (1996). *The World of the Castrati: The History of an Extraordinary Operatic Phenomenon*. Souvenir Press.

Barclay, K. and Myrskylä, M. (2016). Advanced maternal age and offspring outcomes: reproductive aging and counterbalancing period trends. *Population and Development Review* 42(1): 69–94.

Barker, D. (2003). The midwife, the coincidence, and the hypothesis. *BMJ* 327: 1428–30.

Barlow, C. (2000). *The Ghosts of Evolution: Nonsensical Fruit, Missing Partners and Other Ecological Anachronisms*. Basic Books.

Barnardo, Mrs and Marchant, J. (1907). *Memoirs of the Late Dr Barnardo*. Hodder and Stoughton.

Bateson, P. et al. (2004). Developmental plasticity and human health. *Nature* 430: 419–21.

Beeton, M. and Pearson, K. (1899). Data for the problem of evolution in man. II. A first study of the inheritance of longevity and the selective death-rate in man. *Proceedings of the Royal Society of London* 65: 290–305.

Bejan, A. et al. (2010). The evolution of speed in athletics: why the fastest runners are black and swimmers white. *International Journal of Design and Nature* 5: 199–211.

Bell, C. (1885). *The Anatomy and Philosophy of Expression: As Connected with the Fine Arts*. 7th edn, George Bell.

Belsky, D. W. et al. (2015). Quantification of biological aging in young adults. *PNAS* 112(30): E4104–10.

Belva, F. et al. (2016). Semen quality of young adult ICSI offspring: the first results. *Human Reproduction* 31(12): 2811–20.

Bergen, D. C. (2008). Effects of poverty on cognitive function. *Neurology* 71: 447–51.

Bjornsdottir, R. T. and Rule, N. O. (2017). The visibility of social class from facial cues. *Journal of Personality and Social Psychology* 113(4): 530–46.

Bliss, M. (1999). *William Osler: A Life in Medicine*. Oxford University Press.

Blüher, M. (2014). Are metabolically healthy obese individuals really healthy? *European Journal of Endocrinology* 171(6): R209–19.

Blumenbach, J. F. (1865). *The Anthropological Treatises*. Trans. Thomas Bendyshe. Longman, Green, Longman, Roberts & Green.

Boas, F. (1909). Race problems in America. *Science*, New Series, 29: 839–49.

Boas, F. (1911). *The Mind of Primitive Man*. Macmillan Co.

Boas, F. (1912). *Changes in Bodily Form of Descendants of Immigrants*. Columbia University Press.

Bonilla, D. L. et al. (2009). *Bartonella quintana* in body lice and head lice from homeless persons, San Francisco, California, USA. *Emerging Infectious Diseases* 15(6): 912–15.

Bordson, B. L. and Leonardo, V. S. (1991). The appropriate upper age limit for semen donors: a review of the genetic effects of paternal age. *Fertility and Sterility* 56(3): 397–401.

Borkin, J. (1979). *The Crime and Punishment of I.G. Farben: The Birth, Growth and Corruption of a Giant Corporation.* André Deutsch.

Bowles, G. T. (1932). *New Types of Old Americans at Harvard.* Harvard University Press.

Boyd-Orr, Lord (1966). *As I Recall.* MacGibbon and Kee.

Braudel, F. (1981). *Civilization and Capitalism 15th–18th Century*, vol. 1: *The Structures of Everyday Life.* Collins.

Brigham, C. C. (1923). *A Study of American Intelligence.* Princeton University Press.

Brink, P. J. (1995). Fertility and fat: the Annang fattening room. In de Garine, I. and Pollock, N. J. (eds.), *Social Aspects of Obesity*, Gordon and Breach, 71–86.

Broadberry, S. et al. (2010). British economic growth, 1270–1870. https://warwick.ac.uk/fac/soc/economics/staff/broadberry/wp/britishgdplongrun8a.pdf.

Brock, T. (1961). *Milestones in Microbiology.* Prentice Hall.

Brooks, D. R. and McLennan, D. A. (1993). *Parascript: Parasites and the Language of Evolution.* Smithsonian Institution Press.

Brudevoll, J. et al. (1979). Menarcheal age in Oslo during the last 140 years. *Annals of Human Biology* 6: 407–16.

Buffon, G.-L. (1797). *Natural History.* Translated from the French in 10 volumes. Vol. 4. H. D. Symonds, Paternoster Row.

Burrows, A. M. et al. (2014). Human faces are slower than chimpanzee faces. *PLOS One* 9(10): e110523.

Cameron, N. (1979). The growth of London schoolchildren 1904–1966: an analysis of secular trend and intra-county variation. *Annals of Human Biology* 6: 505–25.

Cannon, W. B. (1932). *The Wisdom of the Body.* W. W. Norton.

Carcopino, J. (1941). *Daily Life in Ancient Rome.* Peregrine Books.

Carr-Saunders, A. M. (1936). *World Population: Past Growth and Present Trends.* 2nd impression. Frank Cass and Co.

Castle, W. E. (1947). The domestication of the rat. *PNAS* 33: 109–17.

Centers for Disease Control (1999). Tobacco use – United States, 1900–1999. *Morbidity and Mortality Weekly Report*, 5 November, 48(43): 986–93.

Chamberlain, G. (2006). British maternal mortality in the 19th and early 20th centuries. *Journal of the Royal Society of Medicine* 99: 559–63.

Chan, M.-S. (1997). The global burden of intestinal nematode infections – fifty years on. *Parasitology Today* 13(11): 438–43.

Charles, D. (2005). *Between Genius and Genocide: The Tragedy of Fritz Haber, Father of Chemical Warfare.* Jonathan Cape.

Charles, J. D. and Bejan, A. (2009). The evolution of speed, size and shape in modern athletics. *Journal of Experimental Biology* 212: 2419–25.

Charlton, J. and Murphy, M. (eds.) (1997). *The Health of Adult Britain 1841–1994.* Office for National Statistics, London.

Chaytor, H. J. (1945). *From Script to Print: An Introduction to Medieval Literature.* Cambridge University Press.

Childe, V. G. (1942). *What Happened in History.* Pelican Books.

Chiswick, C. et al. (2015). Effect of metformin on maternal and fetal outcomes in obese pregnant women (EMPOWaR): a randomised, double-blind, placebo-controlled trial. *Lancet Diabetes and Endocrinology* 3(10): 778–86.

Cieri, R. L. et al. (2014). Craniofacial feminization, social tolerance, and the origins of behavioral modernity. *Current Anthropology* 55: 419–43.

Clark, G. (2007). *A Farewell to Alms: A Brief Economic History of the World.* Princeton University Press.

Clarke, E. M. et al. (2014). Is atherosclerosis fundamental to human aging? Lessons from ancient mummies. *Journal of Cardiology* 63(5): 329–34.

Cochrane, J. (2016). Indonesia approves castration for sex offenders who prey on children. *New York Times*, 25 May 2016.

Cohen, M. N. (1977). *The Food Crisis in Prehistory: Overpopulation and the Origins of Agriculture.* Yale University Press.

Cohen, S. and Cosgrove, C. (2009). *Normal at Any Cost: Tall Girls, Short Boys, and the Medical Industry's Quest to Manipulate Height.* Jeremy P. Tarcher/Penguin.

Colborn, T. and Clement, C. (1992). *Chemically-Induced Alterations in Sexual and Functional Development: The Wildlife/Human Connection.* Princeton Scientific Publishing Company.

Collingham, L. (2013). *The Taste of War: World War II and the Battle for Food.* Penguin.

Consett, M. W. W. P. (1923). *The Triumph of Unarmed Forces (1914–1918): An Account of the Transactions by Which Germany during the Great War Was Able to Obtain Supplies Prior to Her Collapse Under the Pressure of Economic Forces.* Williams and Norgate.

Cooper, T. G. et al. (2010). WHO reference values for human semen characteristics. *Human Reproduction Update* 16: 231–45.

Corner, G. W. (1964). *A History of the Rockefeller Institute 1901–1953: Origins and Growth*. Rockefeller Institute Press.

Cowman, A. F. et al. (2016). Malaria: biology and disease. *Cell* 167(3): 610–24.

Crookes, W. (1917). *The Wheat Problem: Based on Remarks Made in the Presidential Address to the British Association at Bristol in 1898*. 3rd edn. Longmans, Green and Co.

Cushman, G. T. (2013). *Guano and the Opening of the Pacific World: A Global Ecological History*. Cambridge University Press.

Dalen, J. E. et al. (2014). The epidemic of the 20th century: coronary heart disease. *American Journal of Medicine* 127: 807–12.

Damon, A. (1968). Secular trend in height and weight within Old American families at Harvard, 1870–1965. *American Journal of Physical Anthropology* 29: 45–50.

Darwin, C. (1905). *The Variation of Animals and Plants Under Domestication*. 2 vols. John Murray (first published 1868).

Darwin, C. (1922). *The Descent of Man and Selection in Relation to Sex*. John Murray (first published 1871).

Darwin, C. (1958). *The Autobiography of Charles Darwin 1809–1882*. Ed. Nora Barlow. Reprinted Collins (first published 1887).

Darwin, C. (1965). *The Expression of the Emotions in Man and Animals*. Phoenix Books (first published 1872).

Davies, C. M. (1969). Mr Bradlaugh *versus* God. In *Heterodox London, or Phases of Free Thought in the Metropolis*. Augustus M. Kelley (first published 1874).

Davis, K. (1945). The world demographic transition. *Annals of the American Academy of Political and Social Science* 237: 1–11.

Day, J. (2016). Hang up your running shoes. *London Review of Books*, October, 23–4.

De Vogli, R. et al. (2014). Economic globalization, inequality, and body mass index: a cross-national analysis of 127 countries. *Critical Public Health* 24(1): 7–21.

Deaton, A. (2013). *The Great Escape: Health, Wealth and the Origins of Inequality*. Princeton University Press.

DECODE Study Group (2003). Age- and sex-specific prevalences of diabetes and impaired glucose regulation in 13 European cohorts. *Diabetes Care* 26(1): 61–9.

Din-Dzietham, R. et al. (2007). High blood pressure trends in children and adolescents in national surveys, 1963–2002. *Circulation* 116(13): 1488–96.

Dixon, T. (2015). *Weeping Britannia: Portrait of a Nation in Tears*. Oxford University Press.

Donoghue, H. D. (2011). Insights gained from palaeomicrobiology into ancient and modern tuberculosis. *Clinical Microbiology and Infection* 17: 821–9.

Dormandy, T. (1999). *The White Death: A History of Tuberculosis*. Hambledon Press.

Dounias, E. and Froment, A. (2006). When forest-based hunter-gatherers become sedentary: consequences for diet and health. *Unasylva* 57: 26–33.

Dowling, H. F. (1977). *Fighting Infection: Conquests of the Twentieth Century*. Harvard University Press.

Dratva, J. et al. (2009). Is age at menopause increasing across Europe? Results on age at menopause and determinants from two population-based studies. *Menopause* 16(2): 385–94.

Dublin, L. I. (1928). *Health and Wealth*. Harper.

DuBois, T. D. and Gao, A. (2017). Big meat: the rise and impact of mega-farming in China's beef, sheep and dairy industries. *Asia-Pacific Journal* 15(17/1): 1–20.

Dubos, R. (1965). *Man Adapting*. Yale University Press.

Dubos, R. (1976). *The Professor, the Institute and DNA: Oswald T. Avery, His Life and Scientific Achievements*. Paul and Co.

Dubos, R. and Dubos, J. (1952). *The White Plague: Tuberculosis, Man and Society*. Victor Gollancz.

Dugatkin, L. A. and Trut, L. (2017). *How to Tame a Fox (and Build a Dog)*. University of Chicago Press.

Eaton, J. W. and Mayer, A. J. (1953). The social biology of very high fertility among the Hutterites: the demography of a unique population. *Human Biology* 25: 206–64.

Eaton, S. B. and Eaton, S. B., III (1999). Hunter-gatherers and human health. In Lee, R. B. and Daly, R. (eds.), *The Cambridge Encyclopedia of Hunters and Gatherers*, Cambridge University Press.

Edmonds, T. R. (1835). On the mortality of the people of England. *Lancet* 24: 310–16.

Edmonson, M. S. (1971). *Lore: An Introduction to the Science of Folklore and Literature*. Holt, Rinehart and Winston.

Einhard and Notker the Stammerer (1969). *Two Lives of Charlemagne*. Trans. Lewis Thorpe. Penguin.

Eisenberg, D. T. A. and Kuzawa, C. W. (2018). The paternal age at conception effect on offspring telomere length: mechanistic, comparative and adaptive perspectives. *Proceedings of the Royal Society B* 373: 20160442.

EFERENCES

Ellison, P. T. (2001). *On Fertile Ground: A Natural History of Human Reproduction.* Harvard University Press.

Emre, M. (2018). *What's Your Type? The Strange History of Myers-Briggs and the Birth of Personality Testing.* William Collins.

Ernle, Lord (1936). *English Farming: Past and Present.* 5th edn. Longmans, Green.

Evert, J. et al. (2003). Morbidity profiles of centenarians: survivors, delayers and escapers. *The Journals of Gerontology Series A: Biological Sciences and Medical Sciences* 58: 232–7.

Festinger, L. et al. (1956). *When Prophecy Fails: A Social and Psychological Study of a Modern Group that Predicted the Destruction of the World.* University of Minnesota Press.

Field, A. E. et al. (2018). DNA methylation clocks in aging: categories, causes and consequences. *Molecular Cell* 71(6): 882–95.

Finch, C. E. (1990). *Longevity, Senescence and the Genome.* University of Chicago Press.

Fisher, I. (1909). Economic aspect of lengthening human life. Address delivered before the Association of Life Insurance Presidents, February 5, 1909, New York. Available via www.Forgotten.Books.com.

Flegal, K. M. (2006). Commentary: the epidemic of obesity – what's in a name? *International Journal of Epidemiology* 35: 72–4.

Floud, R., Fogel, R. W., Harris, B. and Hong, Sol Chul (2011). *The Changing Body: Health, Nutrition and Human Development in the Western World since 1700.* Cambridge University Press.

Flynn, J. R. (2012). *Are We Getting Smarter? Rising IQ in the Twenty-First Century.* Cambridge University Press.

Food and Agriculture Organization of the United Nations (1975). The state of food and agriculture 1974. FAO Library AN:129636.

Formicola, V. and Giannecchini, M. (1999). Evolutionary trends of stature in Upper Palaeolithic and Mesolithic Europe. *Journal of Human Evolution* 36(3): 319–33.

Forsdahl, A. (1978). Living conditions in childhood and subsequent development of risk factors for arteriosclerotic heart disease: the cardiovascular survey in Finnmark 1974–75. *Journal of Epidemiology and Community Health* 32: 34–7.

Franco, M. et al. (2008). Obesity reduction and its possible consequences: what can we learn from Cuba's special period? *CMAJ* 178(8): 1032–4.

Fraser, G. E. and Shavlik, D. J. (2001). Ten years of life: is it a matter of choice? *Archives of Internal Medicine* 161(13): 1645–52.

Fries, J. F. (1980). Aging, natural death, and the compression of morbidity. *New England Journal of Medicine* 303(3): 130–35.

Frisch, R. E. (1978). Population, food intake and fertility. *Science* 199: 22–30.

Frisch, R. E. (1987). Body fat, menarche, fitness and fertility. *Human Reproduction* 2(6): 521–33.

Gale, E. A. M. (2008). Congenital rubella: citation virus or viral cause of type 1 diabetes? *Diabetologia* 51(9): 1559–66.

Galton, F. (1865). The first steps towards the domestication of animals. *Transactions of the Ethnological Society of London* 3: 122–38.

Galton, F. (1884). Measurement of character. *Fortnightly Review* 36: 179–85.

Gavrilov, L. A. et al. (2002). Genealogical data and the biodemography of human longevity. *Social Biology* 49(3–4): 160–73.

Gay, P. (1998). *Pleasure Wars: The Bourgeois Experience, Victoria to Freud.* HarperCollins.

Gaziano, T. A. et al. (2010). Growing epidemic of coronary heart disease in low- and middle-income countries. *Current Problems in Cardiology* 35(2): 72–115.

Gemmell, N. J. et al. (2004). Mother's curse: the effect of mtDNA on individual fitness and population viability. *Trends in Ecology and Evolution* 19(5): 238–44.

George, M. D. (1925). *London Life in the XVIIIth Century.* Kegan Paul, Trench, Trübner.

German, A. J. (2006). The growing problem of obesity in dogs and cats. *Journal of Nutrition* 136: 1940S–1946S.

Geronimus, A. T. et al. (2006). 'Weathering' and age patterns of allostatic load scores among blacks and whites in the United States. *American Journal of Public Health* 96(5): 826–33.

Giffen, R. (1904). *Economic Inquiries and Studies.* 2 vols. George Bell and Sons.

Ginosar, S. et al. (2015). A century of portraits. A visual historical record of American High School Yearbooks: people.eecs.berkeley.edu/~shiry/projects/yearbooks/yearbooks.html.

Gluckman, P. and Hanson, M. (2005). *The Fetal Matrix: Evolution, Development and Disease.* Cambridge University Press.

Godlee, F. (2018). Pills are not the answer to unhealthy lifestyles. *BMJ* 362: doi: 10.1136/bmj.k3046.

Godwin, W. (1834). *Lives of the Necromancers.* F. J. Mason.

Gold, E. B. (2011). The timing of the age at which natural menopause occurs. *Obstetrics and Gynecology Clinics of North America* 38(3): 425–40.

Goldberg, L. R. (1993). The structure of phenotypic personality traits. *American Psychologist* 48(1): 26–34.

Gore, A. C. et al. (2015). Executive summary to EDC-2: the Endocrine Society's second scientific statement on endocrine-disrupting chemicals. *Endocrine Reviews* 36(6): 593–602.

Goto, M. et al. (2013). Werner syndrome: a changing pattern of clinical manifestations in Japan (1917–2008). *Bioscience Trends* 7(1): 13–22.

Gould, S. J. (1983a). Natural selection and the human brain: Darwin vs Wallace. In *idem, The Panda's Thumb*. Pelican (first published 1980).

Gould, S. J. (1983b). A biological homage to Mickey Mouse. In *idem, The Panda's Thumb*. Pelican (first published 1980).

Gould, S. J. (1984). *The Mismeasure of Man*. Pelican.

Grant, M. (1916). *The Passing of the Great Race*. Charles Scribner's Sons.

Green, P. (1990). *Alexander to Actium: The Hellenistic Age*. Thames and Hudson.

Green, S. (1981). *Prehistorian: A Biography of V. Gordon Childe*. Moonraker Press.

Greene, J. A. (2007). *Prescribing by Numbers: Drugs and the Definition of Disease*. Johns Hopkins University Press.

Gregg, E. W. et al. (2005). Secular trends in cardiovascular disease risk factors according to body mass index in US adults. *JAMA* 293: 1868–74.

Grey, E. (1925). *Twenty-Five Years 1892–1916*. 3 vols. Hodder and Stoughton.

Grytten, N. et al. (2015). Time trends in the incidence and prevalence of multiple sclerosis in Norway during eight decades. *Acta Neurologica Scandinavica* 132 (Suppl. 199): 29–36.

Guerrant, R. L. et al. (2013). The impoverished gut – a triple burden of diarrhoea, stunting and chronic disease. *Nature Reviews Gastroenterology and Hepatology* 10(4): 220–29.

Gurven, M. and Kaplan, H. (2007). Longevity among hunter-gatherers: a cross-cultural examination. *Population and Development Review* 33(2): 321–65.

Haldane, J. B. S. (1923). *Daedalus, or Science and the Future*. Kegan Paul, Trench, Trübner.

Hales, C. N. and Barker, D. J. (2001). The thrifty phenotype hypothesis. *British Medical Bulletin* 60: 5–20.

Hansson, G. K. (2005). Inflammation, atherosclerosis and coronary artery disease. *New England Journal of Medicine* 352: 1685–95.

Hardman, R. (2001). Family almanac will unmask the noble pretenders. *Daily Telegraph*, 19 June.

Hare, B. (2017). Survival of the friendliest: *Homo sapiens* evolved via selection for prosociality. *Annual Review of Psychology* 68:155–86.

Harris, J. (1993). *Private Lives, Public Spirit: Britain 1870–1914*. Penguin.

Hawkes, C. (2005). The role of foreign direct investment in the nutrition transition. *Public Health Nutrition* 8(4): 357–65.

Hayward, A. D. and Lummaa, V. (2013). Testing the evolutionary basis of the predictive adaptive response in a preindustrial human population. *Evolution, Medicine and Public Health* 2013(1): 106–17: doi: 10.1093/emph/eot007.

Himmelfarb, G. (1984). *The Idea of Poverty: England in the Early Industrial Age*. Faber and Faber.

Hinrichs, H. (1955). *The Glutton's Paradise: Being a Pleasant Dissertation on Hans Sachs's 'Schlaraffenland' and Some Similar Utopias*. Peter Pauper Press.

Hochberg, Z. et al. (2011). Evolutionary fitness as a function of pubertal age in 22 subsistence-based traditional societies. *International Journal of Pediatric Endocrinology* 2: http:/www.ijpeonline.com/content/2011/1/2.

Hodder, I. (2004). Women and men at Çatalhöyük. *Scientific American*, January: 77–83.

Holt, B. M. and Formicola, V. (2008). Hunters of the Ice Age: the biology of Upper Palaeolithic people. *Yearbook of Physical Anthropology* 51: 70–99.

Holt, R. I. G. and Sönksen, P. H. (2008). Growth hormone, IGF-I and insulin and their abuse in sport. *British Journal of Pharmacology* 154(3): 542–56.

Hoskins, W. G. (1955). *The Making of the English Landscape*. Penguin.

Howel, D. et al. (2013). Are social inequalities widening in generalised and abdominal obesity and overweight among English adults? *PLOS One*, 8 November, https://doi.org/10.1371/journal.pone.0079027.

Howells, W. (1959). *Mankind in the Making: The Story of Human Evolution*. Pelican.

Hulse, F. S. (1981). Habits, habitats, and heredity: a brief history of studies in human plasticity. *American Journal of Physical Anthropology* 56: 495–501.

Ibn Khaldun (1969). *The Muqaddimah: An Introduction to History*. Trans. F. Rosenthal, edited and abridged by N. J. Dawood. Bollingen Series, Princeton University Press.

Ibrahim, R. and Eviatar, Z. (2009). Language status and hemispheric involvement in reading: evidence from trilingual Arabic speakers tested in Arabic, Hebrew and English. *Neuropsychology* 23(2): 240–54.

Ives, R. and Humphrey, L. (2017). Patterns of long bone growth in a mid-19th century documented sample of the urban poor from Bethnal Green, London, UK. *American Journal of Physical Anthropology* 163: 173–86.

James, P. (1979). *Population Malthus: His Life and Times*. Routledge and Kegan Paul.

James, W. (1890). *The Principles of Psychology*. 2 vols. Macmillan and Co.

James, W. (1902). *The Varieties of Religious Experience*. Longmans, Green & Co.

Jantz, L. M. and Jantz, R. L. (1999). Secular changes in long bone length and proportion in the United States, 1800–1970. *American Journal of Physical Anthropology* 110: 57–67.

Jantz, R. L. et al. (2016). Secular changes in the postcranial skeleton of American whites. *Human Biology* 88(1): 65–75.

Jantz, R. L. and Jantz, L. M. (2016). The remarkable change in Euro-American cranial shape and size. *Human Biology* 88(1): 56–64.

Johannsen, W. (1911). The genotype conception of heredity. *American Naturalist* 45: 129–59.

Johnson, W. et al. (2012). Eighty-year trends in infant weight and length growth: the Fels Longitudinal Study. *Journal of Pediatrics* 160(5): 762–8.

Jones, C. (2014). *The Smile Revolution in Eighteenth Century Paris*. Oxford University Press.

Jones, G. (1920). Nitrogen: its fixation, its uses in peace and war. *Quarterly Journal of Economics* 34(3): 391–41.

Jones, H. B. (1956). A special consideration of the aging process, disease, and life expectancy. *Advances in Biological and Medical Physics* 4: 281–337.

Jordan, T. E. (1993). *The Degeneracy Crisis and Victorian Youth*. State University of New York Press.

Julia, C. and Valleron, A. J. (2011). Louis-René Villermé (1782–1863), a pioneer in social epidemiology: re-analysis of his data on comparative mortality in Paris in the early 19th century. *Journal of Epidemiology and Community Health* 65(8): 666–70.

Katz, D. C. et al. (2017). Changes in human skull morphology across the agricultural transition are consistent with softer diets in preindustrial farming groups. *PNAS* 114(34): 9050–55.

Kaunitz, A. M. et al. (1984). Perinatal and maternal mortality in a religious group avoiding obstetric care. *American Journal of Obstetrics and Gynecology* 150: 826–31.

Keith, A. (1925). *The Antiquity of Man*. 2nd edn. 2 vols. J. B. Lippincott Co.

Keynes, J. M. (1936). *The General Theory of Employment, Interest and Money*. Macmillan & Co.

Klein, R. G. (1999). *The Human Career: Human Biological and Cultural Origins.* 2nd edn. University of Chicago Press.

Koepke, N. and Baten, J. (2005). The biological standard of living in Europe during the last two millennia. *European Review of Economic History* 9(1): 61–95.

Kole, A. J. et al. (2013). Mature neurons: equipped for survival. *Cell Death and Disease* 4: e689.

Komlos, J. (2005). On English pygmies and giants: the physical stature of English youth in the late 18th and early 19th centuries. Discussion papers in economics, University of Munich.

Komlos, J. et al. (2009). The transition to post-industrial BMI values among US children. *American Journal of Human Biology* 21: 151–60.

Komlos, J. and Brabec, M. (2011). The trend of BMI values of US adults by deciles, birth cohorts 1882–1986 stratified by gender and ethnicity. *Economics and Human Biology* 9(3): 234–50.

Kong, A. et al. (2012). Rate of *de novo* mutations and the importance of father's age to disease risk. *Nature* 488: 471–75.

Kroeber, T. (1961). *Ishi in Two Worlds: A Biography of the Last Wild Indian in North America.* University of California Press.

Kuczmarski, R. J. et al. (1994). Increasing prevalence of overweight among US adults: the National Health and Nutrition Examination Surveys, 1960 to 1991. *JAMA* 272(3): 205–11.

Kuczmarski, R. J. and Flegal, K. M. (2000). Criteria for definition of overweight in transition: background and recommendations for the United States. *American Journal of Clinical Nutrition* 72: 1074–81.

Kulkarni, S. C. et al. (2011). Falling behind: life expectancy in US counties from 2000 to 2007 in an international context. *Population Health Metrics* 9(1): 16: doi: 101186/1478-7954-9-16.

Kuulasmaa, K. et al. (2000). Estimation of contribution of changes in classic risk factors to trends in coronary-event rates across the WHO MONICA Project populations. *Lancet* 355(9205): 675–87.

Lamarck, J.-B. (1963). *Zoological Philosophy: An Exposition with Regard to the Natural History of Animals.* Trans. Hugh Elliot. University of Chicago Press (first published 1809).

Lancaster, H. O. (1990). *Expectations of Life: A Study in the Demography, Statistics, and History of World Mortality.* Springer-Verlag.

Lavater, J. C. (n.d.). *Essays on Physiognomy.* Trans. Thomas Holcroft. 18th edn. Ward Lock and Co.

Lawlor, D. A. (2013). Developmental overnutrition – an old hypothesis with new importance? *International Journal of Epidemiology* 42(1): 7–29.

Lawlor, D. A. et al. (2002). Secular trends in mortality by stroke subtype in the 20th century: a retrospective analysis. *Lancet* 360: 1818–23.

Leach, H. M. (2003). Human domestication reconsidered. *Current Anthropology* 44(3): 349–68.

Lee, R. B. (1968). What hunters do for a living, or, how to make out on scarce resources. In Lee, R. B. and DeVore, I. (eds.), *Man the Hunter*, Aldine Publishing Company, 33.

Leigh, G. J. (2004). *The World's Greatest Fix: A History of Nitrogen and Agriculture*. Oxford University Press.

Leitch, I. (2001). Growth and health. Reprinted in *International Journal of Epidemiology* 30: 212–16 (first published 1951).

Lenfant, C. (2003). Shattuck Lecture. Clinical research to clinical practice – lost in translation? *New England Journal of Medicine* 349(9): 868–74.

Lenz, W. (1988). A short history of thalidomide embryopathy. *Teratology* 38: 203–15.

Levine, H. et al. (2017). Temporal trends in sperm count: a systematic review and meta-regression analysis. *Human Reproduction Update* 23: 646–59.

Levine, M. E. and Crimmins, E. M. (2014). Evidence of accelerated aging among African Americans and its implications for mortality. *Social Science and Medicine* 118: 27–32.

Levine, M. E. and Crimmins, E. M. (2018). Is 60 the new 50? Examining changes in biological age over the past two decades. *Demography* 55(2): 387–402.

Lieberman, D. E. (2013). *The Story of the Human Body: Evolution, Health and Disease*. Vintage Books.

Linklater, A. (2014). *Owning the Earth: The Transforming History of Land Ownership*. Bloomsbury.

Lloyd James, A. (1938). *Our Spoken Language*. Thomas Nelson and Sons.

Lobell, J. A. and Patel, S. S. (2010). Bog bodies rediscovered. *Archaeology* 63(3): archive.archaeology.org/1005/bogbodies/.

Loos, R. J. and Yeo, G. S. (2014). The bigger picture of FTO: the first GWAS-identified obesity gene. *Nature Reviews Endocrinology* 10(1): 51–61.

Loy, D. E. et al. (2017). Out of Africa: origins and evolution of the human malaria parasites *Plasmodium falciparum* and *Plasmodium vivax*. *International Journal for Parasitology* 47: 87–97.

Macintosh, A. A. et al. (2017). Prehistoric women's manual labor exceeded that of athletes through the first 5500 years of farming in central Europe. *Science Advances* 3: eaao3893.

MacMillan, M. (2001). *Paris 1919: Six Months that Changed the World*. Random House.

Macmillan, M. (2008). Phineas Gage – unravelling the myth. *The Psychologist* 21: 828–31.

Maixner, F. et al. (2018). The Iceman's last meal consisted of fat, wild meat and cereals. *Current Biology* 28: 2348–55.

Malthus, T. R. (1985). *An Essay on the Principle of Population.* 1st edn. Penguin (first published 1798).

Marshall, B. (ed.) (2002). *Helicobacter Pioneers: Firsthand Accounts from the Scientists Who Discovered Helicobacters, 1892–1982.* Blackwell.

Maunder, J. W. (1983). The appreciation of lice. *Proceedings of the Royal Institution of Great Britain* 55: 1–31.

Maurice, F. (1903). National health: a soldier's study. *Contemporary Review* 83: 41–56.

Mays, S. A. (1999). Linear and appositional long bone growth in earlier human populations: a case study from mediaeval England. In Hoppa, R. D. and FitzGerald, C. M. (eds.), *Human Growth in the Past: Studies from Bones and Teeth.* Cambridge University Press.

McCurry, J. (2018). Japanese centenarian population edges towards 70,000, *Guardian*, 14 September.

McKeown, T. (1979). *The Role of Medicine: Dream, Mirage or Nemesis?* Princeton University Press.

McKeown, T. (1988). *The Origins of Human Disease.* Blackwell.

McNeill, D. (1998). *The Face: A Guided Tour.* Hamish Hamilton.

McNeill, J. R. and Engelke, P. (2014). *The Great Acceleration: An Environmental History of the Anthropocene since 1945.* Belknap Press.

Milton, K. (2003). The critical role played by animal source foods in human (Homo) evolution. *Journal of Nutrition* 133(11 Suppl. 2): 3886S–3892S.

Mithen, S. (2003). *After the Ice: A Global Human History, 20,000–5000 BC.* Phoenix.

Mitteroecker, P. et al. (2016). Cliff-edge model of obstetric selection in humans. *PNAS* 113(51): 14680–85.

Molarius, A. et al. (2000). Educational level, relative body weight, and changes in their association over 10 years: an international perspective from the WHO MONICA project. *American Journal of Public Health* 90(8): 1260–68.

Molina, G. et al. (2015). Relationship between Caesarean delivery rate and maternal and neonatal mortality. *JAMA* 314(21): 2263–70.

Moller, H. (1985). Voice change in human biological development. *Journal of Interdisciplinary History* 16(2): 239–53.

Monteiro, C. A. et al. (2004). Socioeconomic status and obesity in adult populations of developing countries: a review. *Bulletin of the WHO* 82(12): 940–46.

Moore, J. X. et al. (2017). Metabolic syndrome prevalence by race/ethnicity and sex in the United States, National Health and Nutrition Survey, 1988–2012. *Preventing Chronic Disease* 14.

Morris, E. (2001). *Theodore Rex*. HarperCollins.

Morton, E. (2016). 100 years ago, American women competed in intense Venus de Milo lookalike contests: https://www.atlasobscura.com/articles/100-years-ago-american-women-competed-in-serious-venus-de-milo-look alike-contests.

NCD Risk Factor Collaboration (2016). A century of trends in adult human height. *eLife* 5: e13410.

Neel, J. V. (1962). Diabetes mellitus: a 'thrifty' genotype rendered detrimental by 'progress'? *American Journal of Human Genetics* 14(4): 353–62.

Neel, J. V. (1970). Lessons from a 'primitive' people. *Science*, 170: 815–22.

Neel, J. V. (1994). *Physician to the Gene Pool: Genetic Lessons and Other Stories*. John Wiley and Sons.

Nichols, P. (2003). *Evolution's Captain*. Perennial.

Nisbett, R. E. (2003). *The Geography of Thought: How Asians and Westerners Think Differently . . . and Why*. Free Press.

Norton, K. and Olds, T. (2001). Morphological evolution of athletes over the 20th century. *Sports Medicine* 31: 763–83.

Nunn, C. L. et al. (2003). Comparative tests of parasite species richness in primates. *American Naturalist* 162(5): 597–614.

Nystrom, P. H. (1929). *Economic Principles of Consumption*. Ronald Press Co.

Ó Gráda, C. (2009). *Famine: A Short History*. Princeton University Press.

O'Brien, R. and Shelton, W. C. (1941). *Women's Measurements for Garment and Pattern Construction*. US Department of Agriculture Miscellaneous Publication No. 454. US Government Printing Office.

Oeppen, J. and Vaupel, J. W. (2002). Broken limits to life expectancy. *Science* 296: 1029–31.

Offer, A. (1989). *The First World War: An Agrarian Interpretation*. Clarendon Press, Oxford.

Olshansky, S. J. and Carnes, B. A. (2001). *The Quest for Immortality: Science at the Frontiers of Aging*. W. W. Norton and Co.

Olshansky, S. J. and Perls, T. T. (2008). New developments in the illegal provision of growth hormone for 'anti-aging' and bodybuilding. *JAMA* 299(23): 2792–4.

Omran, A. R. (2005). The epidemiologic transition: a theory of the epidemiology of population change. *Milbank Quarterly* 83(4): 731–57.

Ong, W. J. (1982). *Orality and Literacy: The Technologizing of the Word*. Methuen.

Organ, C. et al. (2011). Phylogenetic rate shifts in feeding time during the evolution of *Homo*. *PNAS* 108: 14555–9.

Pankhurst, C. (1913). *The Great Scourge and How to End It*. E. Pankhurst.

Pawlowski, B. et al. (2000). Tall men have more reproductive success. *Nature* 403: 156.

Pearl, R. (1920). *The Biology of Death*. J. B. Lippincott.

Perkin, H. (1989). *The Rise of Professional Society: England since 1880*. Routledge.

Perkins, R. G. (1919). A study of the munitions intoxications in France. *Public Health Reports* 34(43): 2335–74.

Perry, G. H. (2014). Parasites and human evolution. *Evolutionary Anthropology* 23: 218–28.

Peshkov, Y. (1994). *Lost in the Taiga: One Russian Family's Fifty-Year Struggle for Survival and Religious Freedom in the Siberian Wilderness*. Doubleday.

Pinker, S. (2011). *The Better Angels of Our Nature: Why Violence Has Declined*. Viking.

Pirenne, H. (2006). *An Economic and Social History of Medieval Europe*. Routledge (first published 1936).

Planck, M. (1949). *Scientific Autobiography and Other Papers*. Philosophical Library.

Plato (1958). *Protagoras and Meno*. Penguin.

Pleij, H. (2001). *Dreaming of Cockaigne: Medieval Fantasies of the Perfect Life*. Trans. Diane Webb. Columbia University Press.

Poliakov, L. (1971). *The Aryan Myth: A History of Racist and Nationalist Ideas in Europe*. Barnes and Noble.

Pollan, M. (2006). *The Omnivore's Dilemma: A Natural History of Four Meals*. Penguin.

Pomeranz, K. (2000). *The Great Divergence: China, Europe, and the Making of the Modern World Economy*. Princeton University Press.

Ponzer, H. et al. (2016). Metabolic acceleration and the evolution of human brain size and life history. *Nature* 533: 390–92.

Porter, G. R. (1912). *The Progress of the Nation in Its Various Social and Economic Relations from the Beginning of the Nineteenth Century*. F. W. Hirst (ed.). New edn. Methuen and Co.

Potts, M. and Short, R. (1999). *Ever since Adam and Eve: The Evolution of Human Sexuality*. Cambridge University Press.

Powell, A. L. (1994). Senile dementia of extreme aging: a common disorder of centenarians. *Dementia* 5(2): 106–9.

Prentice, A. M. and Jebb, S. A. (1995). Obesity in Britain: gluttony or sloth? *BMJ* 311: 437–9.

Prentice, A. M. and Jebb, S. A. (2001). Beyond body mass index. *Obesity Reviews*, 2: 141–7.

Prescott, F. (n.d.). *Modern Chemistry: The Romance of Modern Chemical Discoveries*. Sampson Low, Marston and Co.

Quetelet, A. (1835). *Sur l'homme et le développement de ses facultés, ou Essai de physique sociale*. Bachelier, reprinted in Elibron Classics.

Quiggin A. H. (1942). *Haddon the Head Hunter: A Short Sketch of the Life of A. C. Haddon*. Cambridge University Press.

Range, F. et al. (2015). Testing the myth: tolerant dogs and aggressive wolves. *Proceedings of the Royal Society B* 282: 2015.0220.

Read, A. W. (1934). The history of Dr Johnson's definition of 'oats'. *Agricultural History* 8: 81–94.

Rehm, J. (2018). 'Green revolution' crops bred to slash fertilizer use, *Nature News*, 15 August.

Rhodes, G. (2006). The evolutionary psychology of facial beauty. *Annual Review of Psychology* 57: 199–226.

Ripley, W. Z. (1899). *The Races of Europe*. Kegan Paul, Trench, Trübner.

Roberts, L. S. and Janovy, J., Jr (2000). *Foundations of Parasitology*. 6th edn. McGraw-Hill.

Rook, G. A. (2012). Hygiene hypothesis and autoimmune diseases. *Clinical Reviews in Allergy and Immunology* 42: 5–15.

Rook, G. A. (2013). Regulation of the immune system by biodiversity from the natural environment: an ecosystem service essential to health. *PNAS* 110(46), 18360–67.

Rose, T. (2016). *The End of Average: How to Succeed in a World that Values Sameness*. Allen Lane.

Roseboom, T. et al. (2006). The Dutch famine and its long-term consequences for adult health. *Early Human Development* 82: 485–91.

Rosebury, T. (1969). *Life on Man*. Secker and Warburg.

Rule, N. O. et al. (2013). Accuracy and consensus in judgments of trustworthiness from faces: behavioral and neural correlates. *Journal of Personality and Social Psychology* 104(3): 409–26.

Sacks, O. (2010). Face-blind: why are some of us terrible at recognizing faces? *New Yorker*, 30 August.

Saner, E. (2018). Why there are more gym supplements in a London fatberg than cocaine and MDMA. *Guardian*, 24 April.

Sargent, D. A. (1887). The physical proportions of the typical man. *Scribner's Magazine* 2(1): 3–17.

Schlichting, C. D. and Pigliucci, M. (1998). *Phenotypic Evolution: A Reaction Norm Perspective*. Sinauer.

Schwartz, H. (1986). *Never Satisfied: A Cultural History of Diets, Fantasies and Fat*. Free Press.

Schwekendiek, D. (2009). Height and weight differences between North and South Korea. *Journal of Biosocial Science* 41: 51–5.

Scott, J. C. (2017). *Against the Grain: A Deep History of the Earliest States*. Yale University Press.

Scottish Council for Research in Education (1949). *The Trend of Scottish Intelligence: A Comparison of the 1947 and 1932 Surveys of the Intelligence of Eleven-year-old Pupils*. University of London Press.

Sebastiani, P. et al. (2017). Biomarker signatures of aging. *Aging Cell* 16: 329–38.

Sedeaud, A. et al. (2014). BMI, a performance parameter for speed improvement. *PLOS One*, 25 February: e90183.

Shapiro, H. L. (1939). *Migration and Environment: A Study of the Physical Characteristics of the Japanese Immigrants to Hawaii and the Effects of Environment on their Descendants*. Oxford University Press.

Shapiro, H. L. (1945). Americans yesterday, today, tomorrow. *Natural History* (publication of the American Museum of Natural History), June 1945.

Sharp, R. J. (2009). Land of the giants. *Growth Hormone and IGF Research* 19: 291–3.

Shea, B. T. (1992). Neoteny. In Jones, S. et al. (eds.), *Cambridge Encyclopedia of Human Evolution*, 104.

Short, R. V. (1976). The evolution of human reproduction. *Proceedings of the Royal Society B* 195: 3–24.

Shryock, R. H. (1948). *The Development of Modern Medicine: An Interpretation of the Social and Scientific Factors Involved*. Victor Gollancz.

Sims, E. A. H. and Horton, E. S. (1968). Endocrine and metabolic adaptation to obesity and starvation. *American Journal of Clinical Nutrition* 21(12): 1455–70.

Skakkebaek, N. E. et al. (2016). Male reproductive disorders and fertility trends: influences of environment and genetic susceptibility. *Physiological Reviews* 96(1): 55–97.

Smil, V. (2001). *Enriching the Earth: Fritz Haber, Carl Bosch, and the Transformation of World Food Production*. MIT Press.

Smil, V. (2004). *China's Past, China's Future: Energy, Food, Environment*. Routledge.

Smith, A. (1991). *The Wealth of Nations*. Everyman's Library (first published 1776).

Smith, C. A. (1947). The effect of wartime starvation in Holland upon pregnancy and its product. *American Journal of Obstetrics and Gynecology* 53: 599–608.

Smith, K. R. et al. (2012). Effects of *BRCA1* and *BRCA2* mutations on female fertility. *Proceedings of the Royal Society B* 279: 1389–95.

Sohlman, R. (1983). *The Legacy of Alfred Nobel*. Bodley Head.

Stamatakis, E. et al. (2010). Time trends in childhood and adolescent obesity in England from 1995 to 2007 and projections of prevalence to 2015. *Journal of Epidemiology and Community Health* 64: 167–74.

Stanhope, P. (1889). *Notes of Conversations with the Duke of Wellington (1831–51)*. Longmans.

Stedman, J. (1796). *Expedition to Surinam*. Folio Society.

Stein, Z. et al. (1975). *Famine and Human Development: The Dutch Hunger Winter of 1944–1945*. Oxford University Press.

Steinach, E. and Loebel, J. (1940). *Sex and Life: Forty Years of Biological and Medical Experiments*. Faber and Faber.

Stern, F. (1977). *Gold and Iron: Bismarck, Bleichröder and the Building of the German Empire*. Alfred A. Knopf.

Stewart, A. (1892). *Our Temperaments: Their Study and Their Teaching: A Popular Outline*. 2nd edn. Crosby Lockwood and Son.

Stiglitz, J. E. (2001). Foreword to Polanyi, K., *The Great Transformation*. Beacon Press.

Stoll, N. R. (1947). This wormy world. *Journal of Parasitology* 33: 1–18.

Stone, L. (1977). *The Family, Sex and Marriage in Engand 1500–1800*. Weidenfeld and Nicolson.

Strøm, A. and Jensen, R. A. (1951). Mortality from circulatory diseases in Norway 1940–1945. *Lancet* 257(6647): 126–9.

Sullivan, W. C. (2011). A note on the influence of maternal inebriety on the offspring. *International Journal of Epidemiology* 40: 278–82. First published 1899.

Sun, H. P. et al. (2015). Secular trends of reduced visual acuity from 1985 to 2010 and disease burden projection for 2020 and 2030 among primary and secondary school students in China. *JAMA Ophthalmology* 133(3): 262–8.

Sun, S. S. et al. (2012). Secular trends in body composition for children and young adults: the Fels Longitudinal Study. *American Journal of Human Biology* 24(4): 506–14.

Syed, M. (2012). Genetic advantage? It's not that black and white in sport. *The Times*, 9 August.

Tacitus (1948). *On Britain and Germany*. Penguin.

Tallis, R. (ed.) (1998). *Increasing Longevity: Medical, Social and Political Implications*. Royal College of Physicians of London.

Tanner, J. M. (1964). *The Physique of the Olympic Athlete*. George Allen and Unwin.

Tanner, J. M. (1981). *A History of the Study of Human Growth*. Cambridge University Press.

Thomas, D. E. (2003). A study on the mineral depletion of the foods available to us as a nation over the period 1940 to 1991. *Nutrition and Health* 17: 85–115.

Thomas, R. et al. (2013). 'So bigge as bigge may be': tracking size and shape change in domestic livestock in London (AD 1220–1900). *Journal of Archaeological Science* 40(8): 3309–25.

Thompson, W. S. (1929). Population. *American Journal of Sociology* 34: 959–75.

Thornton, P. K. (2010). Livestock production: recent trends, future prospects. *Philosophical Transactions of the Royal Society B* 365(1554): 2853–67.

Thurstone, L. L. (1934). The vectors of mind. *Psychological Review* 41(1): 1–32.

Todorov, A. et al. (2005). Inferences of competence from faces predict election outcomes. *Science* 308: 1623–6.

Townsend, N. et al. (2016). Cardiovascular disease in Europe: epidemiological update 2016. *European Heart Journal* 37: 3232–45.

Trevelyan, G. M. (1942). *English Social History*. Longmans.

Trevelyan, G. O. (1928). *The Early History of Charles James Fox*. Longmans, Green and Co.

Trowell, H. (1974). Diabetes mellitus death-rates in England and Wales 1920–70 and food supplies. *Lancet* 304(7887): 998–1002.

Trull, T. J. and Widiger, T. A. (2013). Dimensional models of personality: the five-factor model and the *DSM-5*. *Dialogues in Clinical Neuroscience* 15(2): 135–46.

Tryggvadottir, L. et al. (2006). Population-based study of changing breast cancer risk in Icelandic BRCA2 mutation carriers, 1920–2000. *Journal of the National Cancer Institute* 98(2): 116–22.

Tuchman, B. W. (1994). *The Guns of August*. Ballantine.

Tyson, E. (2018). The answer of Dr Tyson to the foregoing letter of Dr Wallis, concerning man's feeding on flesh. *Philosophical Transactions (1683–1775)* 22: 774–83. First published 1700.

Van Emden, R. and Piuk, V. (2008). *Famous 1914–18*. Pen and Sword Military.

Van Ittersum, M. K. et al. (2016). Can sub-Saharan Africa feed itself? *PNAS* 113(52): 14964–9.

Vasconcellos, A. da Silva et al. (2016). Training reduces stress in human-socialised wolves to the same degree as in dogs. *PLOS One*, 9 September: doi: 10.1371/journal.pone.0162389.

Vogel, F. and Motulsky, A. G. (1997). *Human Genetics: Problems and Approaches*. 3rd edn. Springer.

Waddington, C. H. (1957). *The Strategy of the Genes: A Discussion of Some Aspects of Theoretical Biology*. George Allen and Unwin.

Wallace, A. R. (1880). Degeneration. *Science* 1: 63.

Wallis, J. (2018). A letter of Dr Wallis to Dr Tyson, concerning mens feeding on flesh. *Philosophical Transactions (1683–1775)* 22: 769–73. First published 1700.

Walpole, S. C. et al. (2012). The weight of nations: an estimation of adult human biomass. *BMC Public Health* 12: 439.

Walton, A. and Hammond, J. (1938). The maternal effects on growth and conformation in Shire horse-Shetland pony crosses. *Proceedings of the Royal Society B* 125(840): 311–35.

Weiland, F. J. et al. (1997). Secular trends in malocclusion in Austrian men. *European Journal of Orthodontics* 19(4): 355–9.

Wells, J. C. K. (2015). Between Scylla and Charybdis: renegotiating resolution of the 'obstetric dilemma' in response to ecological change. *Philosophical Transactions of the Royal Society B Biological Sciences* 370: 20140067.

West, K. M. (1978). *Epidemiology of Diabetes and its Vascular Lesions*. Elsevier.

White, T. H. (1993). *The Age of Scandal*. Folio Books (first published 1950).

Wilkins, A. S. et al. (2014). The 'domestication syndrome' in mammals: a unified explanation based on neural crest cell behavior and genetics. *Genetics* 197: 795–808.

Wilson, P. J. (1988). *The Domestication of the Human Species*. Yale University Press.

Women's Co-operative Guild (1915). *Maternity: Letters from Working-Women*. Reissued as Llewelyn Davies, M. (ed.), *Maternity: Letters from Working Women*, Virago, 1978.

Wrangham, R. (2009). *Catching Fire: How Cooking Made Us Human*. Profile Books.

Wrangham, R. W. (2018). Two types of aggression in human evolution. *PNAS* 115: 245–53.

Wrigley, E. A. (1969). *Population and History*. Weidenfeld and Nicolson.

Zanatta, A. et al. (2016). Occupational markers and pathology of the castrato singer Gaspare Pacchierotti (1740–1821). *Scientific Reports* 6, article no. 28463.

Zerjal, T. el al. (2003). The genetic legacy of the Mongols. *American Journal of Human Genetics* 72: 717–21.

Zeuner, F. E. (1963). *A History of Domesticated Animals*. Hutchinson.

Zhou X. et al. (2009). The factor structure of Chinese personality terms. *Journal of Personality* 77(2): 363–400.

Zinsser, H. (1935). *Rats, Lice and History*. Little, Brown and Co.

Index

Page numbers in *italics* refer to illustrations.

ALLEN LANE
an imprint of
PENGUIN BOOKS

Also Published

Lisa Miller, *The Awakened Brain: The Psychology of Spirituality and Our Search for Meaning*

Michael Pye, *Antwerp: The Glory Years*

Christopher Clark, *Prisoners of Time: Prussians, Germans and Other Humans*

Rupa Marya and Raj Patel, *Inflamed: Deep Medicine and the Anatomy of Injustice*

Richard Zenith, *Pessoa: An Experimental Life*

Michael Pollan, *This Is Your Mind On Plants: Opium—Caffeine—Mescaline*

Amartya Sen, *Home in the World: A Memoir*

Jan-Werner Müller, *Democracy Rules*

Robin DiAngelo, *Nice Racism: How Progressive White People Perpetuate Racial Harm*

Rosemary Hill, *Time's Witness: History in the Age of Romanticism*

Lawrence Wright, *The Plague Year: America in the Time of Covid*

Adrian Wooldridge, *The Aristocracy of Talent: How Meritocracy Made the Modern World*

Julian Hoppit, *The Dreadful Monster and its Poor Relations: Taxing, Spending and the United Kingdom, 1707-2021*

Jordan Ellenberg, *Shape: The Hidden Geometry of Absolutely Everything*

Duncan Campbell-Smith, *Crossing Continents: A History of Standard Chartered Bank*

Jemma Wadham, *Ice Rivers*

Niall Ferguson, *Doom: The Politics of Catastrophe*

Michael Lewis, *The Premonition: A Pandemic Story*

Chiara Marletto, *The Science of Can and Can't: A Physicist's Journey Through the Land of Counterfactuals*

Suzanne Simard, *Finding the Mother Tree: Uncovering the Wisdom and Intelligence of the Forest*

Giles Fraser, *Chosen: Lost and Found between Christianity and Judaism*

Malcolm Gladwell, *The Bomber Mafia: A Story Set in War*

Kate Darling, *The New Breed: How to Think About Robots*

Serhii Plokhy, *Nuclear Folly: A New History of the Cuban Missile Crisis*

Sean McMeekin, *Stalin's War*

Michio Kaku, *The God Equation: The Quest for a Theory of Everything*

Michael Barber, *Accomplishment: How to Achieve Ambitious and Challenging Things*

Charles Townshend, *The Partition: Ireland Divided, 1885-1925*

Hanif Abdurraqib, *A Little Devil in America: In Priase of Black Performance*

Carlo Rovelli, *Helgoland*

Herman Pontzer, *Burn: The Misunderstood Science of Metabolism*

Jordan B. Peterson, *Beyond Order: 12 More Rules for Life*

Bill Gates, *How to Avoid a Climate Disaster: The Solutions We Have and the Breakthroughs We Need*

Kehinde Andrews, *The New Age of Empire: How Racism and Colonialism Still Rule the World*

Veronica O'Keane, *The Rag and Bone Shop: How We Make Memories and Memories Make Us*

Robert Tombs, *This Sovereign Isle: Britain In and Out of Europe*

Mariana Mazzucato, *Mission Economy: A Moonshot Guide to Changing Capitalism*

Frank Wilczek, *Fundamentals: Ten Keys to Reality*

Milo Beckman, *Math Without Numbers*

John Sellars, *The Fourfold Remedy: Epicurus and the Art of Happiness*

T. G. Otte, *Statesman of Europe: A Life of Sir Edward Grey*

Alex Kerr, *Finding the Heart Sutra: Guided by a Magician, an Art Collector and Buddhist Sages from Tibet to Japan*

Edwin Gale, *The Species That Changed Itself: How Prosperity Reshaped Humanity*

Simon Baron-Cohen, *The Pattern Seekers: A New Theory of Human Invention*

Christopher Harding, *The Japanese: A History of Twenty Lives*

Carlo Rovelli, *There Are Places in the World Where Rules Are Less Important Than Kindness*

Ritchie Robertson, *The Enlightenment: The Pursuit of Happiness 1680-1790*

Ivan Krastev, *Is It Tomorrow Yet?: Paradoxes of the Pandemic*

Tim Harper, *Underground Asia: Global Revolutionaries and the Assault on Empire*

John Gray, *Feline Philosophy: Cats and the Meaning of Life*

Priya Satia, *Time's Monster: History, Conscience and Britain's Empire*

Fareed Zakaria, *Ten Lessons for a Post-Pandemic World*

David Sumpter, *The Ten Equations that Rule the World: And How You Can Use Them Too*

Richard J. Evans, *The Hitler Conspiracies: The Third Reich and the Paranoid Imagination*

Fernando Cervantes, *Conquistadores*

John Darwin, *Unlocking the World: Port Cities and Globalization in the Age of Steam, 1830-1930*

Michael Strevens, *The Knowledge Machine: How an Unreasonable Idea Created Modern Science*

Owen Jones, *This Land: The Story of a Movement*

Seb Falk, *The Light Ages: A Medieval Journey of Discovery*

Daniel Yergin, *The New Map: Energy, Climate, and the Clash of Nations*

Michael J. Sandel, *The Tyranny of Merit: What's Become of the Common Good?*

Joseph Henrich, *The Weirdest People in the World: How the West Became Psychologically Peculiar and Particularly Prosperous*

Leonard Mlodinow, *Stephen Hawking: A Memoir of Friendship and Physics*

David Goodhart, *Head Hand Heart: The Struggle for Dignity and Status in the 21st Century*

Claudia Rankine, *Just Us: An American Conversation*

James Rebanks, *English Pastoral: An Inheritance*

Robin Lane Fox, *The Invention of Medicine: From Homer to Hippocrates*

Daniel Lieberman, *Exercised: The Science of Physical Activity, Rest and Health*

Sudhir Hazareesingh, *Black Spartacus: The Epic Life of Touissaint Louverture*

Judith Herrin, *Ravenna: Capital of Empire, Crucible of Europe*

Samantha Cristoforetti, *Diary of an Apprentice Astronaut*

Neil Price, *The Children of Ash and Elm: A History of the Vikings*

George Dyson, *Analogia: The Entangled Destinies of Nature, Human Beings and Machines*

Wolfram Eilenberger, *Time of the Magicians: The Invention of Modern Thought, 1919-1929*

Kate Manne, *Entitled: How Male Privilege Hurts Women*

Christopher de Hamel, *The Book in the Cathedral: The Last Relic of Thomas Becket*

Isabel Wilkerson, *Caste: The International Bestseller*

Bradley Garrett, *Bunker: Building for the End Times*

Katie Mack, *The End of Everything: (Astrophysically Speaking)*

Jonathan C. Slaght, *Owls of the Eastern Ice: The Quest to Find and Save the World's Largest Owl*

Carl T. Bergstrom and Jevin D. West, *Calling Bullshit: The Art of Scepticism in a Data-Driven World*

Paul Collier and John Kay, *Greed Is Dead: Politics After Individualism*

Anne Applebaum, *Twilight of Democracy: The Failure of Politics and the Parting of Friends*

Sarah Stewart Johnson, *The Sirens of Mars: Searching for Life on Another World*

Martyn Rady, *The Habsburgs: The Rise and Fall of a World Power*

John Gooch, *Mussolini's War: Fascist Italy from Triumph to Collapse, 1935-1943*

Roger Scruton, *Wagner's Parsifal: The Music of Redemption*

Roberto Calasso, *The Celestial Hunter*

Benjamin R. Teitelbaum, *War for Eternity: The Return of Traditionalism and the Rise of the Populist Right*

Laurence C. Smith, *Rivers of Power: How a Natural Force Raised Kingdoms, Destroyed Civilizations, and Shapes Our World*

Sharon Moalem, *The Better Half: On the Genetic Superiority of Women*

Augustine Sedgwick, *Coffeeland: A History*

Daniel Todman, *Britain's War: A New World, 1942-1947*

Anatol Lieven, *Climate Change and the Nation State: The Realist Case*

Blake Gopnik, *Warhol: A Life as Art*

Malena and Beata Ernman, Svante and Greta Thunberg, *Our House is on Fire: Scenes of a Family and a Planet in Crisis*

Paolo Zellini, *The Mathematics of the Gods and the Algorithms of Men: A Cultural History*

Bari Weiss, *How to Fight Anti-Semitism*

Lucy Jones, *Losing Eden: Why Our Minds Need the Wild*

Brian Greene, *Until the End of Time: Mind, Matter, and Our Search for Meaning in an Evolving Universe*

Anastasia Nesvetailova and Ronen Palan, *Sabotage: The Business of Finance*

Albert Costa, *The Bilingual Brain: And What It Tells Us about the Science of Language*

Stanislas Dehaene, *How We Learn: The New Science of Education and the Brain*

Daniel Susskind, *A World Without Work: Technology, Automation and How We Should Respond*

John Tierney and Roy F. Baumeister, *The Power of Bad: And How to Overcome It*

Greta Thunberg, *No One Is Too Small to Make a Difference: Illustrated Edition*

Glenn Simpson and Peter Fritsch, *Crime in Progress: The Secret History of the Trump-Russia Investigation*

Abhijit V. Banerjee and Esther Duflo, *Good Economics for Hard Times: Better Answers to Our Biggest Problems*

Gaia Vince, *Transcendence: How Humans Evolved through Fire, Language, Beauty and Time*

Roderick Floud, *An Economic History of the English Garden*

Rana Foroohar, *Don't Be Evil: The Case Against Big Tech*

Ivan Krastev and Stephen Holmes, *The Light that Failed: A Reckoning*

Andrew Roberts, *Leadership in War: Lessons from Those Who Made History*

Alexander Watson, *The Fortress: The Great Siege of Przemysl*

Stuart Russell, *Human Compatible: AI and the Problem of Control*

Serhii Plokhy, *Forgotten Bastards of the Eastern Front: An Untold Story of World War II*

Dominic Sandbrook, *Who Dares Wins: Britain, 1979-1982*

Charles Moore, *Margaret Thatcher: The Authorized Biography, Volume Three: Herself Alone*

Thomas Penn, *The Brothers York: An English Tragedy*

David Abulafia, *The Boundless Sea: A Human History of the Oceans*

Anthony Aguirre, *Cosmological Koans: A Journey to the Heart of Physics*

Orlando Figes, *The Europeans: Three Lives and the Making of a Cosmopolitan Culture*

Naomi Klein, *On Fire: The Burning Case for a Green New Deal*

Anne Boyer, *The Undying: A Meditation on Modern Illness*

Benjamin Moser, *Sontag: Her Life*

Daniel Markovits, *The Meritocracy Trap*

Malcolm Gladwell, *Talking to Strangers: What We Should Know about the People We Don't Know*

Peter Hennessy, *Winds of Change: Britain in the Early Sixties*

John Sellars, *Lessons in Stoicism: What Ancient Philosophers Teach Us about How to Live*

Brendan Simms, *Hitler: Only the World Was Enough*

Hassan Damluji, *The Responsible Globalist: What Citizens of the World Can Learn from Nationalism*

Peter Gatrell, *The Unsettling of Europe: The Great Migration, 1945 to the Present*

Justin Marozzi, *Islamic Empires: Fifteen Cities that Define a Civilization*

Bruce Hood, *Possessed: Why We Want More Than We Need*

Susan Neiman, *Learning from the Germans: Confronting Race and the Memory of Evil*

Donald D. Hoffman, *The Case Against Reality: How Evolution Hid the Truth from Our Eyes*

Frank Close, *Trinity: The Treachery and Pursuit of the Most Dangerous Spy in History*

Richard M. Eaton, *India in the Persianate Age: 1000-1765*

Janet L. Nelson, *King and Emperor: A New Life of Charlemagne*

Philip Mansel, *King of the World: The Life of Louis XIV*

Donald Sassoon, *The Anxious Triumph: A Global History of Capitalism, 1860-1914*

Elliot Ackerman, *Places and Names: On War, Revolution and Returning*

Jonathan Aldred, *Licence to be Bad: How Economics Corrupted Us*

Johny Pitts, *Afropean: Notes from Black Europe*

Walt Odets, *Out of the Shadows: Reimagining Gay Men's Lives*

James Lovelock, *Novacene: The Coming Age of Hyperintelligence*

Mark B. Smith, *The Russia Anxiety: And How History Can Resolve It*

Stella Tillyard, *George IV: King in Waiting*

Jonathan Rée, *Witcraft: The Invention of Philosophy in English*

Jared Diamond, *Upheaval: How Nations Cope with Crisis and Change*

Emma Dabiri, *Don't Touch My Hair*

Srecko Horvat, *Poetry from the Future: Why a Global Liberation Movement Is Our Civilisation's Last Chance*

Paul Mason, *Clear Bright Future: A Radical Defence of the Human Being*

Remo H. Largo, *The Right Life: Human Individuality and its role in our development, health and happiness*

Joseph Stiglitz, *People, Power and Profits: Progressive Capitalism for an Age of Discontent*

David Brooks, *The Second Mountain*

Roberto Calasso, *The Unnamable Present*

Lee Smolin, *Einstein's Unfinished Revolution: The Search for What Lies Beyond the Quantum*

Clare Carlisle, *Philosopher of the Heart: The Restless Life of Søren Kierkegaard*

Nicci Gerrard, *What Dementia Teaches Us About Love*

Edward O. Wilson, *Genesis: On the Deep Origin of Societies*

John Barton, *A History of the Bible: The Book and its Faiths*

Carolyn Forché, *What You Have Heard is True: A Memoir of Witness and Resistance*

Elizabeth-Jane Burnett, *The Grassling*

Kate Brown, *Manual for Survival: A Chernobyl Guide to the Future*

Roderick Beaton, *Greece: Biography of a Modern Nation*

Matt Parker, *Humble Pi: A Comedy of Maths Errors*

Ruchir Sharma, *Democracy on the Road*

David Wallace-Wells, *The Uninhabitable Earth: A Story of the Future*

Randolph M. Nesse, *Good Reasons for Bad Feelings: Insights from the Frontier of Evolutionary Psychiatry*

Anand Giridharadas, *Winners Take All: The Elite Charade of Changing the World*

Richard Bassett, *Last Days in Old Europe: Triste '79, Vienna '85, Prague '89*

Paul Davies, *The Demon in the Machine: How Hidden Webs of Information Are Finally Solving the Mystery of Life*

Toby Green, *A Fistful of Shells: West Africa from the Rise of the Slave Trade to the Age of Revolution*

Paul Dolan, *Happy Ever After: Escaping the Myth of The Perfect Life*

Sunil Amrith, *Unruly Waters: How Mountain Rivers and Monsoons Have Shaped South Asia's History*

Christopher Harding, *Japan Story: In Search of a Nation, 1850 to the Present*

Timothy Day, *I Saw Eternity the Other Night: King's College, Cambridge, and an English Singing Style*

Richard Abels, *Aethelred the Unready: The Failed King*

Eric Kaufmann, *Whiteshift: Populism, Immigration and the Future of White Majorities*

Alan Greenspan and Adrian Wooldridge, *Capitalism in America: A History*

Philip Hensher, *The Penguin Book of the Contemporary British Short Story*

Paul Collier, *The Future of Capitalism: Facing the New Anxieties*

Andrew Roberts, *Churchill: Walking With Destiny*

Tim Flannery, *Europe: A Natural History*

T. M. Devine, *The Scottish Clearances: A History of the Dispossessed, 1600-1900*

Robert Plomin, *Blueprint: How DNA Makes Us Who We Are*

Michael Lewis, *The Fifth Risk: Undoing Democracy*

Diarmaid MacCulloch, *Thomas Cromwell: A Life*

Ramachandra Guha, *Gandhi: 1914-1948*

Slavoj Žižek, *Like a Thief in Broad Daylight: Power in the Era of Post-Humanity*

Neil MacGregor, *Living with the Gods: On Beliefs and Peoples*

Peter Biskind, *The Sky is Falling: How Vampires, Zombies, Androids and Superheroes Made America Great for Extremism*

Robert Skidelsky, *Money and Government: A Challenge to Mainstream Economics*

Helen Parr, *Our Boys: The Story of a Paratrooper*

David Gilmour, *The British in India: Three Centuries of Ambition and Experience*

Jonathan Haidt and Greg Lukianoff, *The Coddling of the American Mind: How Good Intentions and Bad Ideas are Setting up a Generation for Failure*

Ian Kershaw, *Roller-Coaster: Europe, 1950-2017*

Adam Tooze, *Crashed: How a Decade of Financial Crises Changed the World*

Edmund King, *Henry I: The Father of His People*

Lilia M. Schwarcz and Heloisa M. Starling, *Brazil: A Biography*

Jesse Norman, *Adam Smith: What He Thought, and Why it Matters*

Philip Augur, *The Bank that Lived a Little: Barclays in the Age of the Very Free Market*

Christopher Andrew, *The Secret World: A History of Intelligence*

David Edgerton, *The Rise and Fall of the British Nation: A Twentieth-Century History*

Julian Jackson, *A Certain Idea of France: The Life of Charles de Gaulle*

Owen Hatherley, *Trans-Europe Express*

Richard Wilkinson and Kate Pickett, *The Inner Level: How More Equal Societies Reduce Stress, Restore Sanity and Improve Everyone's Wellbeing*

Paul Kildea, *Chopin's Piano: A Journey Through Romanticism*

Seymour M. Hersh, *Reporter: A Memoir*

Michael Pollan, *How to Change Your Mind: The New Science of Psychedelics*

David Christian, *Origin Story: A Big History of Everything*

Judea Pearl and Dana Mackenzie, *The Book of Why: The New Science of Cause and Effect*

David Graeber, *Bullshit Jobs: A Theory*

Serhii Plokhy, *Chernobyl: History of a Tragedy*

Michael McFaul, *From Cold War to Hot Peace: The Inside Story of Russia and America*